Engd by W. G. Jackman New York.

Very faithfully yours,
Winthrop M. Praed

WILLIAM J. WIDDLETON, NEW YORK

THE

POEMS

OF

WINTHROP MACKWORTH PRAED.

REVISED AND ENLARGED EDITION.

WITH A MEMOIR

BY THE REV. DERWENT COLERIDGE.

IN TWO VOLUMES:

VOL. I.

NEW YORK:

W. J. WIDDLETON, PUBLISHER.

M DCCC LXV.

M'CREA AND MILLER, STEREOTYPERS.

TO

THE MEMORY OF

HELEN PRAED,

THIS COLLECTION

OF HER LAMENTED HUSBAND'S POEMS,

PUBLISHED

IN FULFILMENT OF HER LONG-CHERISHED WISH AND INTENTION,

IS AFFECTIONATELY INSCRIBED

BY

HER DAUGHTERS.

AMERICAN PUBLISHER'S ADVERTISEMENT.

Inasmuch as several editions of these poems have already appeared in this country, it seems proper to explain the circumstances under which they were published. In 1844, Mr. Rufus W. Griswold made a collection of such of Praed's Poems as he could obtain, which was published by Henry G. Langley, of New York, in a volume of 287 pages.

In 1852, he edited a second edition of 290 pages, published by J. S. Redfield. The chief additions were "The Legend of the Teufel-Haus," the prize poems of "Australasia" and "Athens," and four Charades, making nine in all. In 1857, a third edition was issued by Redfield, pp. 311, adding ten Charades, and two political songs.

In 1860, a new edition in two volumes was edited by W. H. Whitmore, of Boston, and fifty copies were printed in quarto form. This edition of 310 pages and 304 pages, contained a number of poems from the "Etonian," and "Knight's Magazine," as "Gog," "The County Ball," "Changing Quarters," &c., and some other poems, of which the most important was "The Legend of the Drachenfels."

The present edition, being the fifth issued in

America, contains a number of poems furnished to the English editor by the relatives and friends of the poet. The poems wrongly attributed to Praed, in the fourth edition, consist of productions which appeared in the "New Monthly Magazine" in 1840. These are to be regarded as the work of some imitator, very probably of a Mr. Fitzgerald, who wrote at that time.

It may not be improper to state that, previous to the appearance of the authorized English edition, it had been decided by the present publisher to issue a new and corrected edition. Considerable progress had been made when the English edition was announced; and this collection, an exact reprint of Dr. Coleridge's new English edition, is offered to the public, as that by which the family of the poet expeet his fame will be preserved.

It is unnecessary to dwell upon the merits of the poems here presented. Not only has the American public called for these successive editions, but it is in some degree owing to this trans-Atlantic appreciation that Praed's name has been kept before the literary public at home. Such of his friends and admirers as have seen these collections have been urgent in their demand for an authorized edition; and it is most pleasant to find the task has been placed in the hands of one so competent as the Rev. Derwent Coleridge.

NEW YORK, *November* 1, 1864.

ADVERTISEMENT.

The Poems of Winthrop Mackworth Praed were prepared for publication after his decease by his widow, and were to have been carried through the press, at her request, by the Rev. Derwent Coleridge, to whom the publication of an introductory Memoir was also intrusted. By her death the prosecution of this undertaking has devolved upon her daughters, under whose direction the present collected edition is now, in accordance with their lamented mother's design, presented to the public.

Their acknowledgments are gratefully offered to the many kind friends by whose contributions and suggestions the work has from time to time been assisted.

To Lady Young, the author's sister, the collection is indebted for many interesting pieces in her possession. These are chiefly of early date, and are now published for the first time. She has added to the obligation by placing in the hands of the compiler of the Memoir a number of Mr. Praed's letters, and has materially contributed, by her recollections of his early life, to the interest and accuracy of the record.

The Rev. John Moultrie, the Rev. B. H. Kennedy, D. D., the Rev. C. H. Hartshorne, Charles Knight, Esq., with other of Mr. Praed's valued friends, have also furnished important aid; and with these must be named the late Rev. E. C. Hawtrey, D. D., the late Robert Hildyard, Esq., Q. C., and the late Alaric Watts, Esq.

More recently the editor of the last American edition of Mr Praed's Poems has shown the interest which he continues to take in the subject—an interest largely shared by a numerous body of his countrymen—by his kind and valuable communications.

It only remains to add that, in bringing out these Poems, the Rev. Derwent Coleridge has had the assistance and co-operation of Sir George Young, Bart., the author's nephew, who has carefully verified the text of the Poems, collating them with the author's manuscript copies, from which many important corrections, and several large additions, have been derived, and to whom is due the arrangement adopted in the present edition.

CONTENTS OF VOL. I.

TALES.

POEMS OF LOVE AND FANCY.

MISCELLANEOUS POEMS.

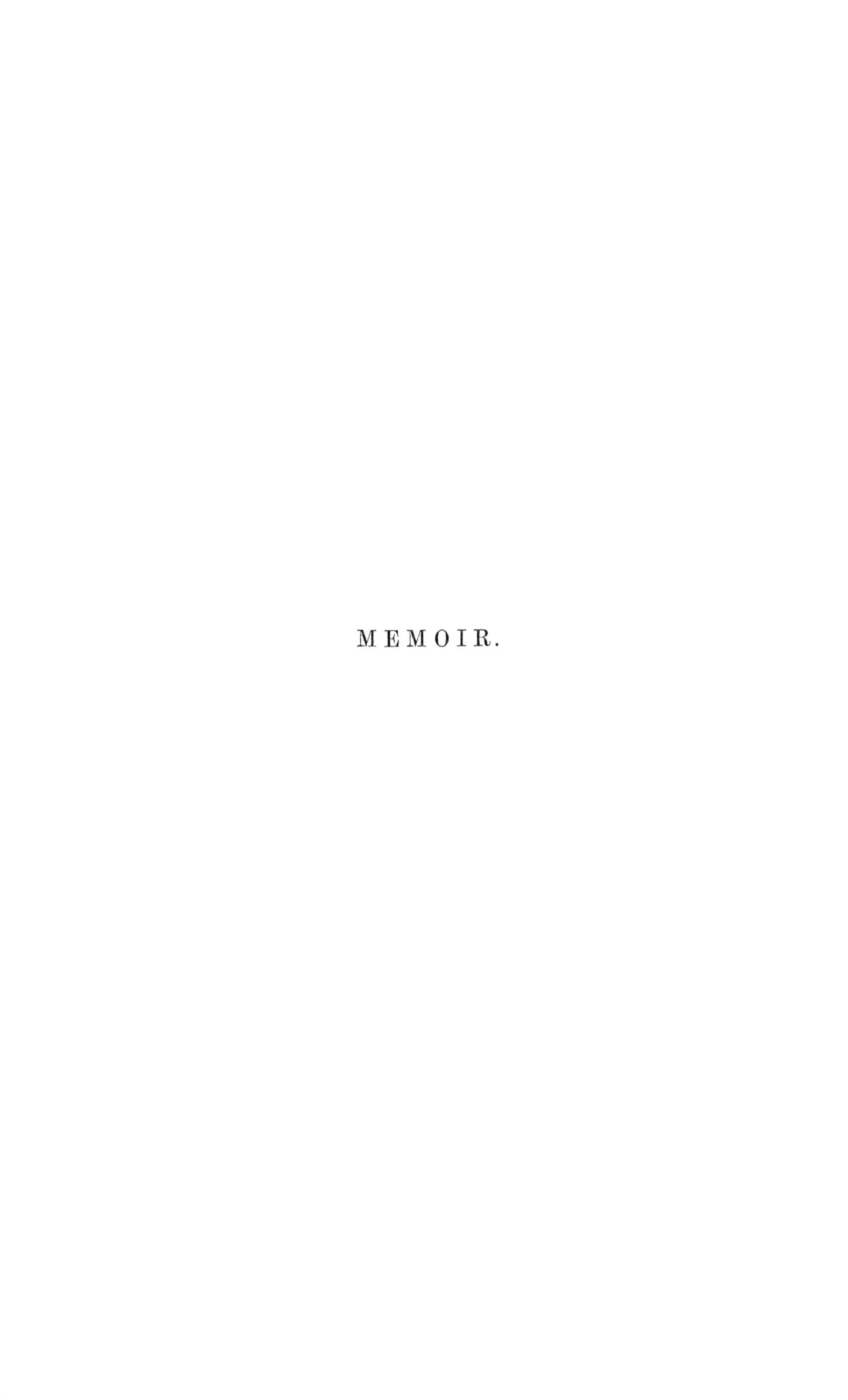

MEMOIR.

MEMOIR.

The literary productions of Winthrop Mackworth Praed, though given to the world many years ago, in publications more or less of an ephemeral character, continue to excite considerable interest. Of the Poems, three separate collections have appeared in America, neither of them complete or accurate, yet reflecting credit on the taste and enterprise of our transatlantic brethren. In this country, an authorized edition has for some time been announced, not before it had been long expected and desired. The delay has been occasioned by no want of zeal on the part of those more immediately concerned in the undertaking, who may rather be charged with too anxious a sense of duty, than with any indifference of feeling. Though well aware that there is a tide in the affairs of books, no less than of men, and that a debt is due to the generation which is passing away for which the next can give no acquittance, they have been willing to forego the advantage of a timely appearance, and even to be held defaulters in a matter of admitted obligation, rather than bring out what seemed to them an imperfect work, or do less than justice to him whose memory as a man, no less than an author, it is intended to preserve.

The life of an individual may be written for various reasons, and the undertaking in each case be fairly justified. He may have been sufficiently distinguished in the world whether of thought or action, in literature or in public life, to draw the eyes of men to his private fortunes and character,—what he has done leading them to inquire what he was; or there may have been something in the man himself, some rare excellence, or strange peculiarity, which may impart a special interest to his portraiture; or, lastly, by a certain felicity of nature, aided perhaps by an advantageous position, he may have drawn around him so large a circle of admiring friends, that the ordinary monuments of regret and affection have been deemed inadequate. Thus the pen has been called in to make up the deficiencies of the statuary and the painter. Each of these motives might readily be illustrated by appropriate examples, but they more commonly act in combination; and so it is in the present instance. If one should be deemed weak and insufficient, it may yet add strength to the plea which it cannot support alone. Not unknown, nor without mark in the arena of political conflict, the name of PRAED is still remembered as at least that of a forward pupil in the school of statesmanship; and though his literary honors, won in earliest manhood, and sustained by the casual productions of a leisure hour, were worn carelessly, while he was preparing for higher distinctions and more serious duties, yet, now that years have gone by, and we have to audit the past with no expectation of any future account, we find that he has left behind him a permanent expression of wit and grace, of refined and tender feeling, of inventive fancy and acute observation, unique in character, and his own by an undisputed title. Some brief record, if not of the rising orator and politician, yet of the accomplished poet and sparkling essayist, may surely accompany his writings, and join in whatever welcome they may receive. Such at least may be taken as the pretext and occasion of the following biography: but it need not be concealed that the work has been undertaken from feelings of a more personal nature, and with somewhat of a higher aim. So marked and individual a character, so full both in its moral and intellectual endowments, so fine in modification, so peculiar in the interchange and play of light and shade, if happily depicted, might, it was thought, be studied with pleasure and advantage on its own account. And if this language be criticised as the heightened utterance of partial friendship, it will yet be repeated by many voices. To his contemporaries, to all by whom he was intimately known, to very many who knew him mainly by report, and who perhaps cherish the remembrance of a casual meeting, the name of WINTHROP PRAED is still as the sound of music. The depths of his nature were indeed opened but to few; not often or willingly to them: but he had a special faculty and privilege, better than any craft of will, by which he attracted even when he seemed to repel,—and was more than popular even when, in his younger and gayer days, he appeared to court animadversion and defy dislike.

Winthrop Mackworth Praed, the subject of the present Memoir, was the third and youngest son of William Mackworth Praed, Sergeant-at-law, and for many years chairman of the Audit Board. He was born in London, in the house then occupied by his father, 35 John Street, Bedford Row, on the 26th of July, 1802. Bitton House, at Teignmouth, in the county of Devon, his father's country seat, is however to be regarded as his paternal home. He was called Winthrop from the maiden name of his mother, a branch of whose family emigrated to America, and rose to eminence in the time of Charles the First; and Mackworth from his father, whose family originally bore that name, but had taken the name of Praed some generations earlier. His constitution was delicate, and when about six years of age he passed through a severe illness, which threatened his life. On this occasion a copy of verses was written in his name by his father, a man of highly cultivated mind, by whom the poetic faculty which early developed itself in his youngest son was carefully fostered and directed. As these verses, in addition to their intrinsic merit, have a biographical interest, they are here preserved.

AUGUST, 1808.

LITTLE WINTHROP'S MEDITATION ON HIS RECOVERY FROM A DANGEROUS ILLNESS.

To Thee, Almighty God! who from the bed
Of sickness hast vouchsafed to raise me up
To health and strength renewed, with grateful heart
I offer up my praises and thanksgivings,
And I beseech Thee that my life preserved
May through Thy grace be constantly employed
In goodly works, and keeping Thy commandments!
  You next, my dearest mother, I approach
With thankfulness and joy! You gave me birth,
You fostered me in infancy, and taught
My dawning mind to seek our heavenly Father,
To trust in Him, to love and to adore Him.
You through my lingering illness wakeful sat,
The tedious nights beside me, while your voice,
Sweeter than Zephyr's breath, soothed my complaints,
Assuaged my pains, and lulled me to repose.
Whate'er of medicine passed my feverish lips,
What little food my stomach would admit,
Your hand administered. Oh! if at times
I answered crossly, or in froward mood
Seemed to reject the help you fondly tendered,
Impute to the disorder all the blame,
And do not think your darling was ungrateful.
Not for the riches of the East, the power
Of mightiest emperors, nor all the fame
Conquest bestows on warriors most renowned,
Would I offend you—kindest, best of mothers!
May all your days be blest with many comforts,
The last of them far distant! and the close,
When it shall come, be smoothed by resignation,
And welcomed by the hope of bliss eternal!

That the child should have been made thus early to express the tender and solemn thoughts and feelings here imputed to him in the language of poetry, may perhaps have been no more than a striking coincidence; but there can be no doubt that his poetic faculty, in whatever degree it may have been inherited, was recognized at a very early period, and that it was developed under very favorable influences. His home education was, indeed, of the best kind in all respects. Ample evidence of this is afforded by his letters written from school at a very early age, and which not merely record an amount of attainment considerably beyond his years, but which exhibit a clearness and accuracy, both of thought and language, not less remarkable, and of far surer promise. The same remark applies with still greater force to his early verses. Indications of wit and fancy, afterwards so conspicuous in his writings, are not wanting; but the qualities by which they are most favorably distinguished are distinctness of thought and accuracy of expression. The metrical construction is always perfect; and if these fundamental excellences be due in the first instance to the character of his own mind, there can be no doubt that they were brought out and strengthened by his father's strict and judicious criticism. He never spared the pruning-knife, preferring that the literary exercises of a boy should be stiff and formal, rather than loose and careless. He required plain sense plainly spoken, and would tolerate no extravagances. But to return.

The prayer which the child was made to utter in his father's verses, "that the last of his mother's days might be far distant," was not granted. She died about a year afterwards, too soon for the loss to be severely felt by the younger children. It can, however, scarcely be doubted that the remembrance of his own loss was present to the mind of the poet, and acted as a stimulus to his imagination on more than one occasion. The readers of "The Troubadour" will remember, in this connection, the beautiful passage—

"My mother's grave, my mother's grave," &c. (See p. 60.)

Her place was indeed well supplied by the care of an elder sister, under whose superintendence his education was carried on at home till he had completed his eighth year, when he was sent, in 1810, to Langley Broom School, near Colnbrook, where he remained under the care of Mr. Atkins, the gentleman by whom it was then conducted, about four years. Such a boy could hardly fail to engage the particular attention of his master; and it appears that he made considerable progress under the teaching which he there received, however much may be ascribed to his own talent, and the careful preparation which he had received at home. His vacations, moreover, were put to full account, not only in the way of rest and recreation, but of mental culture. His physical powers were not strong, and he was thus led to prefer the amusement and quiet employments of which he could partake in-doors to more vigorous and active sports. He delighted in reading of a more profitable kind than is common with young people, Plutarch's lives being one of his chief favorites: Shakespeare he would read aloud to his sisters. Young as he was, he already took much pleasure in chess, of which he continued fond during the whole of his life, and soon became a very good player. He also amused himself with the composition of short dramas, too unripe, as may well be supposed, for publication, but in which he already displayed that talent for drollery which he afterwards exhibited in so elegant and refined a form.

From Langley Broom School he was sent to Eton, where his father had been educated, and where he had been preceded by his eldest brother, William Mackworth. This important event took place on the 28th of March, 1814, before he had completed his twelfth year.

Of the feelings with which he found himself denizened among the inhabitants of this new world—new and strange to him, and he for a while, it would appear, strange to them—we have no distinct record. His countenance at this time, as remembered by one of his surviving schoolfellows, was grave, his complexion pale, and his person slight. His appearance and manners, eventually so attractive, were already marked and peculiar. A studious and retiring boy, of delicate bodily frame, he was neither inclined, nor from want of physical power enabled, to enter warmly or vigorously into active sports. His intellectual superiority was however speedily recognized, and received the fullest and most appropriate encouragement.

He was placed under the charge of the late Rev. J. F. Plumptre, then one of the Assistant Masters, afterwards one of the Fellows, of Eton College, to whose personal kindness and careful tuition he was under deep obligation. His first debt of gratitude was however due to his elder brother, who for some time directed his studies with a care and ability of which he was duly sensible. His progress was rapid, and in little more than a year he was "sent up for good," as it is termed, for a copy of Latin lyrics, the first of a series of similar distinctions, numerous beyond all previous example.

Meanwhile his poetic faculty was exercised not alone in the usual routine of school exercises, distinguished in his case by a sparkling vein of thought more than commonly original and characteristic. Poetry, in his mother-tongue, was his recreation. His ready pen sported with equal ease whether in verse or prose composition.

It has been said that his poetic faculty was carefully watched and cultivated at home; the same advantage attended him at school. His tutor, Mr. Plumptre, made it a practice to train such of his pupils, as showed any talent in that direction, in the composition of English verse, offering prizes for voluntary competition on given subjects. Five or six poems, some of considerable length, attest the ardor with which Praed entered into these contests. Together with the present Lord Carlisle, he carried off most of the honors; and, besides the encouragement thus given, his style in all probability acquired much of its classical elegance and remarkable facility, as well from the practice thus afforded, as by the judicious criticism to which his pieces were subjected. Some of these exercises, with other early "buds of promise," dating from the fourteenth year of his age, have been printed in the following collection. However immature, they will, it is believed, be read with pleasure, if only as throwing light upon the formation of the author's mind.

It was not long before his productions were to be submitted to a wider public. In the year 1819 there appeared in print a selection from the pages of two school periodicals, "The College Magazine," and "Horæ Otiosæ,"* which had previously been circulated in manuscript, and had obtained considerable celebrity among the Etonians of that day, but to which Praed, being somewhat junior to the principal writers, had contributed nothing. Some time after the discontinuance of these miscellanies, in the year 1820, Praed set on foot the "Apis Matina," a manuscript journal, conducted with at least equal ability, of which one

* The writers in the "College Magazine" and "Horæ Otiosæ" were Howard, now Lord Carlisle, H. N. Coleridge, W. Sidney Walker, Moultrie, Curzon Neech, Trower, and C. H. Townshend, all of whom, except Howard, afterwards contributed to the "Etonian."

copy only is known to have been preserved entire, but in which several pieces, afterwards printed in the "Etonian," originally appeared. It was in copying out the pages of the "Apis Matina"* for circulation that Praed acquired his peculiar handwriting, of which Mr. Charles Knight, in his "Autobiography of a Working Man," observes, "It was the most perfect calligraphy I ever beheld. No printer could mistake a word or a letter. It was not what is called a running hand, yet was written with rapidity, as I have witnessed." Though in the strictest sense a voluntary enterprise on the part of the boys, yet their performances were not regarded without interest by the masters. The Rev. E. C. Hawtrey—then an Assistant—afterwards Head Master, and eventually Provost of Eton—to whom Praed was indebted for many personal attentions, the more gratifying as he had no special connection with him in the school, addressed a letter of advice to him on the occasion of this his first effort at editorship, which was inserted in the

* The "Apis Matina" consisted of six numbers, written in the months of April May, June, and July, 1820. The principal contributors, after Praed, who wrote about half of it, were Trower (now Bishop of Gibraltar) and F. Curzon. The latter left Eton at Election, 1820. The following pieces, afterwards printed in the "Etonian," first appeared in the "Apis Matina." The lines "To Julio," "To Julia," "To Florence," "Laura," and "The Invocation to the Deities," by Praed. "The Temple of Diana at Ephesus," and "The Lapland Sacrifice," by Curzon. "Edith," "Genius," by Trower. The rest of Praed's poetical pieces, and nearly all his prose, were of a satirical cast, very amusing, but not suited for republication.

second number. This pleasant relation continued during the whole of his school life, and ripened into a lasting friendship.*

The "Apis Matina" was immediately succeeded by the "Etonian." It is upon his contributions to the latter periodical that the brilliancy of Praed's early reputation was founded, and by which it is still maintained. The first number of this work was printed and published in October, 1820, from which time it continued to appear monthly till July, 1821, when, upon Praed's leaving Eton, it was brought to a close.

Of this publication Praed, together with his friend Walter Blunt, was the projector and editor, and there can be no doubt that it was he whose genius impressed upon it its distinctive character, and chiefly contributed to obtain for it the reputation which it still retains above all other juvenile periodicals. It has been questioned in what sense this term is to be understood, and whether this miscellany is to be attributed in main part to the School or to the University. Certainly in main part to the School. The publication was indeed arranged in concert with a few under-graduates who had recently left Eton, young men already of high mark, whose contributions were of distinguished excellence.† These,

* It was at Dr. Hawtrey's request that the paper in the "Etonian," vol. ii., p. 74, on the death of a schoolfellow, was written. He had himself written some elegant Latin lines on the same subject, which were translated by Praed. See vol. ii., p. 276.

† Among the contributors appear the names of Henry Nelson

however, in the aggregate, hardly exceeded one-fourth part of each number. The remainder was the work of actual schoolboys, by far the largest portion being due to Praed himself. His was the guiding spirit; and as his productions exceeded those of his associates, whether in the School or at the University, in quantity, so they ranked among the very best in quality.

The work is agreeably characterized by the buoyancy of youthful spirits, the grave portions being upon the whole of considerably less value than the gay. The writers, while they give themselves out as boys, appear throughout under feigned names, the whole being wrought up into a sort of drama. The leading articles, in which the plot or action, if it may be so called, is carried on, bore the title of the

Coleridge, William Sidney Walker, John Moultrie, and John Louis Petit, to which that of Chauncey Hare Townshend, omitted in the printed list ("Etonian," vol. ii., p. 483), and who wrote the sonnet to "Ada," which is there attributed to Praed, ought to have been added; all of whom have become known in the world of letters. The only name in the list supplied by Oxford, is that of Henry Neech. Of the youthful aspirants thus early associated with Praed in the career of literary enterprise, the two first named belong with him to the past. The Hon. William Ashley, Edmund Beales, William Chrichton, The Hon. Francis Curzon, Richard Durnford, William Henry Ord, Thomas Powys Outram, and Walter Trower, who, with others, contributed to the "Etonian," were still at school. Among the anonymous contributors were R. Streatfield, and J. A. Kinglake,

"dear to poetry,
And dearer to his friends."—*Surly Hall.*

King of Clubs. These, with the exception of a few pages here and there, in which the principal dramatis personæ are severally introduced, were uniformly written by Praed, sometimes in prose, sometimes in verse, which presented no obstacle to the rapid flow of his thoughts. It has indeed been said that his talent exhibited itself to most advantage in the latter form; and perhaps his early prose compositions have been unduly depreciated by the comparison. That they should not possess the same permanent interest as his poems, is no more than was to be expected. Many of his prose articles, more particularly his "leaders," are of an occasional character, and the fashion of this kind of writing passes away; but there is little or no inferiority in point of power. He displays the same facility of expression, the same lively observation, and very much of the same wit and fancy, whether he writes in prose or verse.

The possessors of the "Etonian" are referred to the articles "Old Boots," "Reminiscences of my Youth," "Yes and No," "Lovers' Vows," "The Knight and the Knave," "On the Poems of Homer,"—compositions as various in style and subject as they are finished in execution, and surely displaying far more of the spirit and vigor, than of the immaturity of youth.

The work was brought out by Mr. Charles Knight, the well-known publisher, himself distinguished by those literary talents and accomplishments which he has subsequently turned to such valuable account.

As the testimony of a contemporary, personally engaged in the transactions recorded, no apology is needed for here introducing the following extract from his very interesting "Autobiography of a Working Man," to which a reference has already been made. After speaking of the manifest delight taken by Mr. Blunt in doing what he calls the "editorial drudgery," he proceeds to say: "Mr. Praed came to the printing-office less frequently. But during the ten months of the life of this Miscellany—which his own productions were chiefly instrumental in raising to an eminence never before attained by schoolboy genius similarly exerted—I was more and more astonished by the unbounded fertility of his mind and the readiness of his resources. He wrote under the signature of 'Peregrine Courtenay,' the President of 'The King of Clubs,' by whose members the magazine was assumed to be conducted. The character of Peregrine Courtenay, given in 'An Account of the Proceedings which led to the Publication of the "Etonian,"' furnishes no satisfactory idea of the youthful Winthrop Mackworth Praed, when he is described as one 'possessed of sound good sense, rather than of brilliance of genius.' His 'general acquirements and universal information' are fitly recorded, as well as his acquaintance with 'the world at large.' But the kindness that lurks under sarcasm; the wisdom that wears the mask of fun; the half-melancholy that is veiled by levity;—these qualities very soon struck me as far out of the ordinary indications of precocious talent.

"It is not easy to separate my recollections of the Praed of Eton from those of the Praed of Cambridge. The Etonian of 1820 was natural and unaffected in his ordinary talk; neither shy nor presuming; proud, without a tinge of vanity; somewhat reserved, but ever courteous; giving few indications of the susceptibility of the poet, but ample evidence of the laughing satirist; a pale slight youth, who had looked upon the aspects of society with the keen perception of a clever manhood; one who had, moreover, seen in human life something more than follies to be ridiculed by the gay jest or scouted by the sarcastic sneer. I had many opportunities of studying his complex character. His writings then, especially his poems, occasionally exhibited that remarkable union of pathos with wit and humor which attested the originality of his genius, as it was subsequently developed in maturer efforts. In these blended qualities, a superficial inquirer might conclude that he was an imitator of Hood. But Hood had written nothing that indicated his future greatness, when Praed was pouring forth verse beneath whose gayety and quaintness might be traced the characteristics which his friend Mr. Moultrie describes as the peculiar attributes of his nature—

'drawing off intrusive eyes
From that intensity of human love,

And that most deep and tender sympathy,
Close guarded in the chambers of his heart.'—
The Dream of Life."

This record of a schoolboy's life, rich in actual achievement as well as in promise for the future, would be incomplete if a word were not added of the part he took in those recreations which form no unimportant feature of a schoolboy's career.

His amusements were indeed for the most part of an intellectual character. As a chess-player, he found no equal among boys of his own age; and it is remembered that he was selected, when comparatively young, by a schoolfellow in the upper part of the school—the celebrated Dr. Pusey—as an antagonist who could meet him on equal terms.

In school theatricals, then in high vogue at Eton, he was a distinguished performer. He was not, however, altogether a stranger to more active sports. Though from the delicacy of his constitution he took no part in the leading athletic exercises by which Eton has always been distinguished, yet in the variety of the game of fives, then peculiar to that school, an exercise in which the dexterity and grace of the player are exhibited to much advantage, he was unrivalled. He afterwards became an excallent tennis-player. He was also fond of whist, and played very well. It was not till the last year of his Eton life that he entered the Debating Society, of which he at once became a distinguished member.

One other circumstance remains to be recorded,

of which he was justly proud, and for which, to employ the language of the valued friend by whom the information has been communicated, "the thanks of Etonians are no less due than for the brilliant legacy of 'The Etonian' itself." By his efforts, with some assistance from the masters and other friends, the "Boys' Library" was founded at Eton. This, the first institution of the kind, was established in an upper room at the college bookseller's, as a society to which a few of the senior boys might belong, and to which they might present an occasional volume on leaving or on revisiting Eton, to testify their sympathy with the studies of their successors. Under Dr. Hawtrey's superintendence, and aided by his magnificent liberality, it became what it is, the sanctuary of learning, and the refuge of quiet to many a boy for whom a public school would else afford small opportunity of satisfying a desire for knowledge, beyond the mere routine of school-work. If Eton has no longer to lament the injury done within her walls to the organization of a Shelley, or a Sydney Walker, she owes it in great measure to the public library which was founded by Praed.*

* At the back of one of the stalls in Eton College Chapel, erected by Mr. W. Mackworth Praed, as a fitting tribute to the memory of his brother in that place, is the following inscription, from the pen of Dr. Hawtrey:—

"Winthropo Mackworth Praed olim Coll. SS. Trin. apud Cantabrigiam socio literis humanioribus senatoriis numeribus et Bibliothecæ in puerorum Etonensium frugem inchoatæ laude felicissimè ornato posuit frater maximus natu."

The summer of 1821 terminated Praed's brilliant career at Eton, and in the October of the same year he commenced his residence as an undergraduate at Trinity College, Cambridge. Since the days of Canning, no Etonian had brought with him so high a reputation, and large expectations were formed with respect to his academical career. It was indeed soon apparent that neither his time nor his talents would be devoted exclusively, or even mainly, to the pursuit of university distinction. His disposition was eminently social, his company gladly welcomed wherever he was pleased to bestow it, whether by his immediate contemporaries or by men of higher standing. In a word, his habits were by no means those of a severe or regular student, while, as we shall see presently, it was not long before he found himself literary employment foreign to his academical pursuits, and sufficient of itself to occupy almost any pen but his own. For scientific studies he had no peculiar liking or aptitude, though he acquired without difficulty the modicum of mathematical knowledge which was then required from the candidate for classical honors.

His scholarship was pre-eminently of the Etonian cast, as it was commonly exhibited at that day—elegant, refined and tasteful, characterized by an unconscious, and, as it were, living sympathy with the graces and proprieties of diction, rather than by a minute analysis of its laws, or careful collation of its facts. It must be understood, however, that this is spoken comparatively. Though his scholarship was distinguished for its grace and finish rather than by its depth, it was far indeed from superficial, and his mastery over the resources of the classical tongues, as displayed in his composition, was in particular most remarkable. The following critical remarks, for which the compiler of this Memoir is indebted to a friend, are so much to the point that they are given in his own words: "The character of Praed's Latin and Greek verse is peculiar. It is the exact translation for the most part of the same style and diction which he wielded with hardly greater ease in his native language. The same sparkling antithesis, the same minute elaboration of fancy, whether employed in depicting natural or mental objects, and the same ever-present under-current of melancholy, are found in both. Of a certain kind of Greek, adapted to the curious production called at Cambridge a Sapphic Ode, and of a certain degree of Latin scholarship, competent to express all the ideas necessary to his verse, but not to sound the depths or exhaust the capacities of the language, he was master. His epigrams are perhaps the most scholarlike of his productions in classic verse; but it may be said of them all, what cannot be said of many such exercises, that they were Greek and Latin poetry."*

There can be no doubt, indeed, that he might have

* Specimens of these remarkable compositions will be found in vol. ii. of this collection.

attained still higher distinction as a scholar by a course of systematic study, for he showed in after life both the power of thorough investigation and a sense of its value; but the bent of his genius, and perhaps the state of his bodily health, inclined him to more discursive occupation. As it was, though he failed as a competitor for the University Scholarship,* the long and shining list of his academic honors bore full testimony not merely to his extraordinary talent, but to the high character of his scholastic attainments.

In 1822 he gained Sir William Browne's medal for the Greek Ode, and for the Epigrams; in 1823 the same medal a second time for the Greek Ode, with the first prizes for English and Latin declamation in his College. In 1824 Sir William Browne's medal a second time for Epigrams. In 1823 and 1824 he also gained the Chancellor's medal for English verse, "Australasia" being the subject in the former year, and "Athens" in the latter. In the classical tripos his name appeared third in the list, a high position, yet scarcely adding to the reputation which he already enjoyed. In 1827 he was successful in the examination for a Trinity Fellowship, and in 1830 he completed his University triumphs by gaining the Seatonian prizes.

* He had been second in the examination for the Pitt Scholarship, beating all competitors of his own standing, and sat again the following year for the Battie Scholarship, when it appears that three votes out of seven were recorded in his favor.

Prize poems, even when written by true poets, are for the most part of ephemeral interest, and do scant justice to the genius of their authors. It is one thing to perform a set task with skill, another to obey a spontaneous impulse, and give expression to "thoughts that voluntary move harmonious numbers." These exercises are properly intended as tests and encouragements of academic scholarship and literary culture—taste, judgment, and the art of composition, with an especial reference to established models—rather than as opportunities for the display of original power. In Praed's case, however, these poems rise so far above the ordinary level, and display such clear evidence of poetic faculty, in him always equal to the occasion, even when exercised at a disadvantage, that they have been deemed worthy of preservation, and will be found in the second volume of this collection.

Such a career might well be supposed to have demanded all the time and strength that could be given to serious effort, and doubtless it bore evidence to very unusual energy, and very strenuous exertion. It was not, however, in the senate-house or the schools, nor in the rigid course of intellectual discipline prescribed to the candidate for academic distinction, that Praed was mainly occupied, or that his powers were chiefly, or perhaps most advantageously, exercised. Without undervaluing, or professing himself indifferent to, University honors, or to College preferment and emoluments, by far the larger portion of his time was devoted to the exercise and improvement of his oratorical powers, to the cultivation of his literary talents, and to the enjoyment of social intercourse, itself a means of culture of prime necessity as a preparation for the more active walks of life, and, in the present instance, far more than commonly stimulating and instructive. To the circle in which he moved belonged many who became subsequently among the most distinguished men of their time, and who were certainly not less remarkable in the spring and promise of their powers, than in the maturity and fulfilment of after life. The discussions which occurred at the frequent meetings of these friends—*noctes cœnæque deum*—were conducted with a force of argument, a readiness of illustration, and a command of language on the part of more than one of the disputants, which the compiler of this memoir has seldom heard equalled, surpassed perhaps never, except among the worthies of an earlier generation. It may readily be supposed that the war of words was not exclusively aroused by matters of taste or literary judgment; the graver questions of social, political, and mental philosophy were debated with at least equal interest, and with scarcely less ability. If the scale and purpose of this memoir admitted of any discursion, it might not be without interest, or out of place, to speak more in detail of the life with which Praed was then associated, and which cannot have been without influence on the formation of his mind and character.

Suffice it to say, that in these delightful meetings Praed ever held a foremost place, his social qualities, now fully called out, not merely procuring him a welcome, but enabling him to take a lead on every festive occasion. It was not, however, his habit to commit himself decidedly and seriously to one or the other side in the matters of debate—if, indeed, he had made up his own mind, and were not waiting for further and more mature reflection. Even to his most intimate friends he did not readily disclose his deeper thoughts and feelings. If an attempt were made to involve him in argument, or to extort from him an expression of opinion, it was promptly parried by a playful witticism, or retorted with good-humored satire.*

It is probable that he felt more keenly than most others that apparent contradiction between the life within, and the outward conditions under which it has to be developed—not uncommonly experienced by young men of high aspirations and deep sensi-

* "He then a youth
Fresh from Etonian discipline, well skilled
In all her classic craft, and therewithal
Known, ere his sun in Granta's sky arose,
In many a boyish feat, unlike a boy's,
Of sparkling prose and verse,—he graced our board
With that rich vein of fine and subtle wit—
That tone of reckless levity—that keen
And polished sarcasm—armed with which he waged
A war of dexterous sword-play, wherein few
Encountered, none o'ercame him."

bility in a sense of perplexity and dissatisfaction, which under various forms appears in their first efforts, and modifies their behavior for a while. In Praed, if the interpretation here offered be correct, this showed itself in a habit of banter, by which he kept serious words at bay, and seemed to drive away all serious thoughts. This humor, which he long continued to affect, both in his conversation and in his writings, led to some misapprehension as to his real character. It was in reality both earnest and tender in a remarkable degree. This became more apparent as he advanced in life; yet his vein of sportive irony remained unexhausted to the last, and the impression produced upon his contemporaries by his wit, his gayety, and his social talents, is ineffaceable.

The above remarks are not offered merely in illustration of character, as suggested by that cherished remembrance, preserved by living memory, but of which a faint outline is all that can be transferred to these pages. They have a bearing upon the course of Praed's subsequent conduct as it became known to the world. Too much importance is commonly attached to the expressed opinions, and more particularly to the political opinions, of very young men. Thus they have to bear the reproach of inconsistency if, as may well happen, they afterwards see occasion to change their views. In the case of Praed, this spirit of retrospective criticism was exercised with more than ordinary severity, yet with less than ordinary justice. His early opinions were for the most part undecided, and merely tentative; eventually they ripened into settled convictions, from which he never swerved. Although it is not the object of this memoir to enter with any particularity upon the details of Praed's public life, it must yet be mentioned that, during the years which he passed at the University, he was in active training for the professional and, as it turned out, the political career on which he was about to enter, and to which his most serious efforts were directed. The Union Debating Society, of which, soon after his matriculation, Praed became a member, and in which he took a leading part, was then in its most high and palmy state. It was here that Mr. (afterwards Lord) Macaulay first became known as an orator, many of his speeches in this mimic arena being little inferior in rhetorical skill or in force of argument to his most splendid achievements in Parliament. Scarcely less remarkable, in a different style, was the clear and commanding eloquence of Mr. Charles Austin, then equipping himself for the very high position which he afterwards obtained as an advocate and parliamentary lawyer. After these, amid a large number of promising speakers, destined to attain celebrity either at the bar or in the senate, there was no third name that could be put in competition with that of Praed. His style of speaking was indeed wholly different from that of the distinguished orators above mentioned. He rather shunned than sought to carry away his hearers by rhetorical display. It was his ambition to make himself an accomplished debater, to excel in reply, for which his rapid apprehension, ready wit, and racy diction, gave him singular advantages. It has been said that he was not an "impassioned orator." Perhaps not. He did not care to affect an earnestness which he did not feel. He carried with him into the heat of debate the sparkling gayety, and light careless manner, by which he was generally distinguished. In after life, when he had made up his mind to the part which he was to take, and was contending for what he believed to be the truth, his oratory was not merely serious, but on all suitable occasions fervid. His temperament was indeed warm and excitable, and when his passions were really roused, as at a contested election, he spoke with remarkable force and vehemence.

It may be worthy of a passing notice, that in the debates of the Union Society both Macaulay and Praed commonly appeared as the advocates of opinions more or less opposed to those of the political party with which they were associated in after life. Then as afterwards they stood face to face as opponents, but each on the other side. We are not, however, to conclude that either the one or the other made, or would have cared to make, a serious profession of political principles. They were engaged in sportive conflict, following the bent of their minds at the time, but without the sense of public responsi bility, or any direct object beyond the exercise of their oratorical powers.

We now return to the topic with which we are more immediately concerned, and to which, as it has fallen out, contrary to his own expectations and those of his friends, a more general as well as a more permanent interest has become attached than to his political training,—his literary avocations—avocations in the proper sense of the term. He had not made, he was not prepared to make, literature his *vocation*. It was but an occasional diversion, which called him away from more serious pursuits.

In the autumn of 1822, about the commencement of his second year at Cambridge, proposals were made to him, and through him to some of his most distinguished contemporaries, by Mr. Charles Knight, for the establishment and support of a new periodical to be brought out by the latter, then commencing business in London as a publisher. Such was the origin of Knight's "Quarterly Magazine," of which the proprietor was himself the responsible editor,—Praed, as in the case of the "Etonian," and scarcely in an inferior degree, the animating and directing spirit.

Of this periodical a full and interesting account has recently been given by Mr. Knight himself in his "Autobiography," already more than once quoted; a much briefer notice is all that would be consistent with the limits of the present memoir. In its general character the periodical may be regarded as a continuation of the "Etonian." Praed wrote the leading article, in which the plan of the work was set forth, the several contributors being introduced under feigned names. "Some eight or ten of these *noms de guerre*," as we learn from Mr. Knight, "clung to the real men during their connection with the Magazine. Take," he says, "as the more distinguished examples—

PEREGRINE COURTENAY.. VYVYAN JOYEUSE......	... WINTHROP MACKWORTH PRAED.
GERARD MONTGOMERY	JOHN MOULTRIE.
DAVENANT CECIL	DERWENT COLERIDGE.
TRISTRAM MERTON..........	THOMAS BABINGTON MACAULAY
EDWARD HASELFOOT........	WILLIAM SIDNEY WALKER.
HAMILTON MURRAY	HENRY MALDEN.
JOSEPH HALLER............	HENRY NELSON COLERIDGE."

To these must be added Paterson Aymer, by which signature Mr. Knight's own contributions were distinguished.

The work was carried on with considerable vigor, and a fair prospect of success, for three or four numbers, in which are to be found the whole of the papers contributed by Praed. It was hardly to be anticipated that a set of undergraduates would continue their contributions with the required regularity, or submit without a murmur to the curtailments or alterations required, it may well be, by editorial prudence, but not in their opinion by any means enhancing the literary value of their productions.

However this may be, it is pleasant to record that the temporary disagreement thus occasioned between the editor and his leading contributor was of very short duration. "Within two manths," to use Mr. Knight's own words, "Mr. Praed spontaneously called upon me, and never afterwards lost an opportunity of testifying his good-will towards me." An attempt was made to revive the work, chiefly with the assistance of another set of contributors. In this continuation Praed took no part, and accordingly the publication assumed an entirely new character. Many articles of high merit were contributed. Mr. Macaulay, Mr. Malden, Mr. Henry Nelson Coleridge, and Mr. De Quincey lent their powerful aid; but it had lost the life and spirit to which its previous popularity had been owing, and after the appearance of the sixth number the work was closed, and brought out as a whole in three octavo volumes. It is now scarce, and may be pronounced curious, many of the most interesting papers, some of them by authors who afterwards attained high eminence, not having been republished.*

* The following papers were contributed by Praed: "Castle Vernon.—No. I.;" "What you will.—No. I.;" "Castle Vernon —No. II.;" "My First Folly;" "Points;" "Damasippus;" and "Leonora;" together with several enigmas and short poems. Here also appeared the two first cantos of the "Troubadour," each complete in itself, yet leaving with the reader the wish and the hope that more should follow. A third canto was actually in preparation, and far advanced towards completion. It is of fully

Mr. Knight, who had already earned the character of a man of letters, has since won for himself the more enviable distinction of a national benefactor by his admirable series of popular works, as well of amusement as of instruction. He has himself recorded the fact, which he evidently remembers with pleasure, that to him the subject of this memoir owed his first introduction to the world of letters, first at Eton, and afterwards at Cambridge. In 1826, after Praed had left the University, they were again associated in the production of a periodical entitled "The Brazen Head," which, however, notwithstanding the talent which Praed brought to its support, failed to attract public attention, and was abandoned after it had reached the third number. "Lidian's Love," with one or two shorter poems republished in this collection, first appeared in the ephemeral pages of this miscellany.

The following is Mr. Knight's account of this publication: "In the spring of 1826, St. Leger and I—at a time when there was little prospect of publishing books with any success—thought that a smart weekly sheet might have some hold upon the London public, who were sick of all money questions, and wanted

equal merit with its predecessor, and is now published for the first time as a fragment. It was doubtless intended for the pages of the "Quarterly Magazine." The discontinuance of Praed's connection is indeed much to be regretted, if only for the abrupt conclusion of this charming poem, to which perhaps a fourth canto might have been added.

something like fun in the gloomy season of commercial ruin. We went to Eton to consult Praed. He entered most warmly and kindly into the project. We settled that 'The Brazen Head' should be the title; and that the Friar and the Head should discourse upon human affairs, chiefly under the management of our brilliant associate. * * * We had four weeks of this pleasantry, and, which was not an advantage, we had nearly all the amusement to ourselves, for the number of our purchasers was not 'Legion.' Yet in 'The Brazen Head' there are poems of Praed (unknown from the scarcity of these sixty-four pages to the Americans, who have printed three editions of his poems) which are every way worthy of that genius which his countrymen will soon be permitted more fairly to appreciate in an edition of all his poetical pieces, issued by an English publisher."

The autumn of 1825 saw Praed once more established at Eton, as Private Tutor to Lord Ernest Bruce, a younger son of the Marquis of Ailesbury. The circumstances under which he obtained this appointment, with his motives for accepting it, may be given in his own words, extracted from a letter written from Paris, where he first joined his young pupil, in the spring of the year.

"About a week before the Senate House debate, Dobree* called upon me to know whether I was

* The late eminent Greek scholar.

willing to take a private tutorship to which he had the power of recommending me. A negotiation took place which ended satisfactorily. * * * I am to be with Lord Ernest two or three years, during which period I am to spend two years in preparing for a Trinity fellowship, and the rest in keeping terms at Lincoln's Inn, and preparing for the bar. With many men the accepting of such employment would be a virtual resignation of all hopes of advancement from an active profession; but for myself I have lived, during the last two years, a life of such continued and violent excitement, that I believe a period of retirement and abstraction will do more for me than any thing; and I have acquired, from a chain of circumstances and feelings that I cannot detail, a strong and enduring ambition in place of the frivolous longing for temporary notoriety which is all that you remember in me."

It will be obvious from this specimen that a far more lively impression of Praed's mind—his way of thinking and feeling—might have been conveyed from a connected series of his familiar letters than from any mere description, or literary portrait. But from this course the compiler of this biography has been withheld, first by the narrow limits within which an introductory memoir must necessarily be confined, and secondly by the character of the letters themselves. They are exactly what such letters should be, written as they were without the slightest expectation of their being preserved; records, for the most part, of passing trifles, interspersed with lively comments, not without an occasional touch of satire, but without a vestige of ill-nature. Taken as a whole, they represent clearly and faithfully the heart and mind from which they flowed; but the scanty selection which could alone find place in these pages would not merely be inadequate for this purpose, but might even do the writer some injustice. He was a diligent, as he was a most delightful correspondent, and in every letter may be found some grace of expression, some witty turn of thought, a keen observation of men and manners; but they rarely touch, and never can be said to treat, on subjects of general interest, while the very warmth and tenderness of feeling which constitute their peculiar charm, entitle them to the sacred privacy for which they were originally intended.

The two years which he spent at Eton, amid scenes so much endeared to him by the associations of his schoolboy days, formed a pleasant sequel to his University life. The system of private tuition, as subsidiary to the regular instruction of the school, had about that period reached its climax, and a number of accomplished young men were thus added to the society of the place. Of the many distinguished scholars and clergymen with whom he was thus brought into contact, none who yet survive can have forgotten the grace and amenity of his manner, the charm of his good humor and vivacious spirits, the heartiness and zest with which he shared and promoted the social recreations with which the labors of tuition were relieved. Those who knew him more intimately will remember, above all, his unvarying kindness of heart. There can be no doubt that he shared largely in the pleasure to which he so freely contributed. It was during this, his second residence at Eton, that he commenced the brilliant series of poetical contributions to the magazines and annuals of the day which fills a large portion of the succeeding pages.

At the close of the year 1827 his connection with the Marquis of Ailesbury terminated. Hereupon he took his final leave of Eton—with mingled feelings. He had been for some time anxious to bring his tutorial engagement to a close, and enter upon the more active career to which he felt himself called; yet he could not take leave of so many kind friends without regret, or quit without a struggle a place in which, at two different periods of his life, he had found so much enjoyment. He now established himself at one of the Inns of Court, and devoted himself earnestly for some years to the professional study, and subsequently to the practice of the law.

He was called to the bar at the Middle Temple, May 29, 1829. He went the Norfolk circuit, and was rapidly rising in reputation and practice. But the main current of his mind had run from the first in another direction. Even when engaged on the circuit he would post up to London to attend a parliamentary debate, hurrying back to his legal engagements as soon as it was concluded; and when, as we shall presently see, he obtained a seat in the House of Commons, his senatorial duties more than divided, and eventually threatened to engross, his time and thoughts.

We have now arrived at a turning point of Praed's life—the commencement of his public career as a Member of Parliament, of which, however, it would be foreign to the purpose of this memoir to record more than the leading facts. No man, it is believed, ever entered the service of his country with a more ardent zeal, or with a deeper sense of duty. To this he devoted, during the whole remainder of his life, his time, his talents, and his strength; for this he was ready to make any sacrifice; but he had from the first to contend with adverse circumstances, and with failing health, and if we would raise a monument to his patriotic efforts, it must, alas! be a broken column.

It has already been intimated that his political sentiments during his residence at Cambridge, so far as he had cared to express them, had been of a liberal character, and his associations, for some years after he left the University, had been with the Liberal party. Thus, in the summer of the year 1829 we find him engaged as a member of Mr. Cavendish's committee, the Whig candidate for the representation of Cambridge; and so late as the autumn of the following year, he expressed in a letter to a friend a very lively satisfaction in Mr. Brougham's election for Yorkshire.

Up to this time, then, it would seem that he retained his sympathies with his old friends on the liberal side of politics. His appearance, therefore, shortly afterwards, as a member of the Conservative party in the House of Commons, occasioned considerable surprise. The change was, however, more apparent than real; a change in his political associations, rather than a change in sentiments. He had never sided with the extreme views of the so-called Radical Reformers, and to the last he continued the friend of social progress, and was by no means opposed to such changes in the constitutional arrangements of the country, as altered circumstances and the advancement of political science appeared to require. He was the zealous and active friend of national education; he was attached to the doctrines of free trade, and hailed with pleasure the relief of religious opinion from political restrictions. But important changes in this direction had already taken place. The Test and Corporation Act had been rescinded; the bill for Catholic Emancipation had been passed; and as, on the one hand, the leaders of Conservative opinions were becoming more and more identified with liberal measures, so, on the other hand, the reforming party, at that critical period, were tending to what he considered to be a revolutionary extreme. Such at least was the view taken by Praed, as appears from his own statement, conveyed in a letter to an old college friend (the Rev. Charles Hartshorne), bearing date January 17, 1831:

"Your kind and friendly letter gratified me very much, and amused me not a little; in the first place I was delighted to find yourself, with many old familiars, welcoming my arrival at a goal I had long strained for; and, in the next place, I could not but smile to think of the face you will make when you read in the 'Court Journal' that I am to be introduced to political life by the Duke of Wellington, or in the 'Age' that I am pledged to vote against the Whigs. There is as much truth in one as in the other; none in either. I am not acquainted with the Duke, and I am not pledged to vote this way or that way, on any one subject. I believe there is no man in the House more at liberty to follow his own inclinations. My old college opinions have, however, been considerably modified by subsequent acquaintance with the world, and more observation of things *as they are*. I am not going to stem a torrent, but I confess I should like to confine its fury within some bounds. I am in no small degree an alarmist, and I would readily give a cart-load of abstract ideas for a certainty of fifty years' peace and quietness. So my part in political matters will probably expose me to all sorts of abuse for ratting, and so forth. I abandon the party, if ever I belonged to it, in which my friends and my interests are both to be found, and I adopt one where I can hope to earn nothing but a barren reputation, and the consciousness of meaning well. If all I hear be correct, your friends the Whigs find the machine going a little too fast, and are not sorry that some should be found to put on the drag."

This interesting statement, the sincerity of which will be questioned by no one acquainted with the straightforward truthfulness of the writer, needs no comment. The nature, the extent, and the reasons of the change, which occasioned so much animadversion at the time, and which is not yet forgotten, are clearly set before us. In common with other men of note, by whom his example was speedily followed, he had persuaded himself that the safety of the country, and with it the hope of improvement and real progress, were endangered by the haste and violence displayed by the advocates of Parliamentary Reform at that stirring period; and, accordingly, when the time for action was come, his early prepossessions gave way. Doubtless in thus obtaining a seat in the British Senate he satisfied the yearnings, long cherished, of an honorable ambition; and while he was clearly aware that his worldly interests were rather compromised than promoted by the step which he had taken, he was full of hope, and the resolution which it engenders. He entered Parliament, as we have seen, on the most independent footing, which he preserved to the last; yet he served the party to which he had united himself with no wavering allegiance. He devoted himself to the business of the House with indefatigable zeal; and though he had an up-hill path to climb, associated as he was with an unpopular cause, and confronted by antagonists of the most brilliant talent, yet he did more than enough to prove that, had not his health given way, he would have eventually obtained high and permanent distinction as a statesman.

The first difficulty with which his parliamentary career was commenced arose from the high expectations which he had to satisfy. That this anticipation was not immediately realized may be explained partly from the fact, that the qualities for which he was most desirous of gaining credit, and in which he was fitted to excel, required time for their exercise. Though he possessed an easy command of language, he wanted the physical power requisite for oratorical display, and rather sought to acquire distinction by his intimate acquaintance with the subject, and his ability to deal with it in detail. His maiden speech on the cotton duties, uninviting as the subject might appear to a young member, and foreign to his previous habits of thought and study, was, however, eminently successful, and created a considerable sensation even among his political opponents. In his next effort, to which he had looked forward with extreme anxiety, he was not so fortunate. He did not again address the House till the Reform Bill came on for discussion. The speech which he delivered on this occasion is still extant. It is temperate, firm, and argumentative, but was delivered under most unfavorable circumstances, and barely obtained a hearing. He was suffering at the time from a severe cold, and as he did not catch the Speaker's eye till past midnight, he was unable to command the attention of the House, which had already exhibited symptoms of impatience.

It cannot be doubted that Praed for some time after this check labored under a sense of discouragement, to which, however, he did not give way. He continued from time to time to take a part in the discussions of the House, and steadily rose in general estimation, not merely as a ready and skilful debater, but for the higher qualities of political intelligence and sagacity. After his death he was designated as a "rising statesman" by Lord John Russell, in allusion to a scheme which he had propounded, for giving proportional weight to the opinions of the minority in the representation of the country.* He was first returned to Parliament for

* This project was to the following effect: In the Reform Bill of 1831, it was provided that certain counties should be represented by three members. The opportunity was thus afforded of giving weight to the opinions of a minority of voters, by restricting the number of votes to be given by each of the electors to two only; by which certain anomalies of representation—greater then, when party spirit was high, than now, when such irregularities have partially corrected themselves under the influence of time and the spirit of compromise—were to some extent remedied and avoided. The scheme was proposed in the form of an amendment in committee, and received but slight attention at the time; but it has since, more than once, been noticed with praise by the philosophical observers of the working of our parliamentary constitution.

Another amendment was moved by Praed to the Reform Bill

the borough of St. Germains, in November, 1830, and again for the same place at the general election of 1831. In 1832, after the passing of the Reform Bill, by which St. Germains had lost its franchise, he contested the borough of St. Ives, in Cornwall, where his relative, Mr. Praed of Trevethow, a country seat in the neighborhood, possessed considerable influence. Party spirit, however, ran high at the time, and notwithstanding a vigorous canvass, in which his oratorical powers were displayed to great advantage, he lost his election; and during the interim between this and the following Parliament, he resumed his practice at the bar with his wonted vigor and with no inconsiderable success. But his mind could not be turned aside from the active struggle of political life, and though no longer in Parliament, he was present night after night at its debates, as an interested spectator. To this period are to be referred many of the political squibs, still remembered as the productions of his pen, though published anonymously. Of this species of composition he was a consummate master, and though it has not been thought expedient to incorporate these

of 1832, which, if carried, would have forestalled the measure upon which the last Derby Government practically staked its existence. It was, "that freeholds situate within boroughs should in all cases confer votes for the borough, and not for the county." The proposal was of course rejected; but the speech in which it was advocated contains a store of valuable hints as to the principal defects in the Reform Bill of 1832, and fully deserves consideration by future reformers.

monuments of party strife in the present edition of his poems, if indeed the time be yet fully come for their reappearance, it is not improbable that they may hereafter be reproduced in a collected form, as revised by the author, by whom they were printed in a small volume for private circulation.

It was not long before he was again enabled to compete as an active candidate for parliamentary honors. In 1834 he was returned, with Mr. T. Baring, for Yarmouth. He always regarded his success on this occasion as a signal triumph, which, however, was dearly purchased. The exertions which he used to secure his seat overtasked the powers of his constitution, and, it is believed, first developed, if they did not lay the foundation, of that fatal disease to which a few years afterwards he fell a victim. But his energy was irrepressible; and now his merit was publicly recognized by the leaders of his party. He had already formed the acquaintance of the Duke of Wellington, to whom, as he truly said, he was personally unknown at his first entrance into political life. In the year 1833 the Duke became the subject of a malicious attack in the newspapers, connected with the distribution of certain places of small value which had been bestowed upon deserving officers of long service in the field. At this time Praed was a regular contributor to the "Morning Post." The Duke sent for him, intrusted him with the facts upon which he rested his defence, and requested him to undertake an answer to the attacks of the Liberal papers in the columns of the "Post." The defence was considered complete and satisfactory, and the acquaintance thus formed between the statesman and the young writer was further extended during a visit to Walmer Castle, of which Praed writes the following account, dated Aylesbury, October 15, 1833:—"My time at Walmer Castle was spent very agreeably. On the first morning I had a long interview with his Grace on 'business,' in which he opened to me all his views, personal and political, with a frankness which was most flattering and most delightful. To be put on terms of the most intimate confidence with the greatest man of his time, was what indeed I should scarcely have dreamed of a few years ago. He seemed at least to keep nothing from me; his judgment of measures, and his opinions of men; his fears, which are manifold, and his hopes, which are few or none, were all expounded. I can scarcely be too proud of such a reception, or too much pleased with the prospect it affords of future intercourse with such a man. It was made the more satisfactory to me from the candor with which he spoke of the permanent exclusion of the Tories from political power—a promise which he would scarcely have held out to an adherent of whose motives he thought meanly."

This "promise" was not however literally or immediately fulfilled; and under the ministry of Sir Robert Peel, 1834–1835, Praed held the office of Secretary to the Board of Control, the terms in which the offer was made to him being scarcely less gratifying than the appointment itself. The following is Sir Robert Peel's letter on this occasion: —

"WHITEHALL, *Dec.* 13, 1834.

"MY DEAR SIR,

"Your name has occurred to me among the first in my consideration of those appointments which, in point of fact (whatever their name or rank in point of precedence may be), are of the first importance from the nature of the duties attached to them. Among those there is not one affording greater opportunities of distinction, or requiring more ability and prudence, than the office of Secretary of the Board of Control, when the Head of that Board is in the House of Lords.

"I do not make the offer of this appointment to you without previous communication with Lord Ellenborough, the future President, and having ascertained his entire concurrence in my opinion as to your high qualifications for it.

"Believe me, my dear sir,
"Most faithfully yours,
"ROBERT PEEL.

"W. MACKWORTH PRAED, ESQ.,
Great Yarmouth."

In 1837, having received an invitation from the Aylesbury electors, he was induced by prudential considerations to retire from Yarmouth, when he was presented with a silver cup by the Conservative electors of that borough, with whom he had rendered himself extremely popular, in recognition of his services as their representative. At Aylesbury he gained his election, and was Member for that borough at the time of his death.

It only remains to add, that during the latter years of his life he held the office of Deputy High Steward of the University of Cambridge. To this most appropriate distinction he attached a peculiar value. It renewed a connection of which he was justly proud, and which he was always desirous to preserve and cherish. If, indeed, his life had been spared, and the opportunity had presented itself, it is not impossible that he might have offered himself as a candidate for the representation of that seat of learning. Such at least is known to have been his own wish, and the hope of his friends.

In the party conflicts in which Praed engaged with so much zeal, and in which it will appear, even from this brief summary, that he played no undistinguished part, it was impossible that he should avoid all collision with his former associates, who sat with him in Parliament, but on the opposite side of the House. Rarely, indeed, did any approach to personal animosity mingle with the strife; and it would be worse than idle, after the lapse of so many years, to recall the expressions of transient irritation which he may on any occasion have had to encounter in the heat of debate. To his friends, of whatever political opinion, he remained to the last what he had been from the first; and the affectionate admiration with which he is remembered by his surviving contemporaries is without alloy.

But one other incident connected with his public life remains to be recorded. In 1838 he was engaged, with Mr. T. D. Acland, Mr. Mathison, Mr. H. N. Coleridge, and other friends, in and out of Parliament, in preparing a scheme of education for the children of the laboring classes, to be carried out under the auspices of the National Society, in accordance with the religious requirements of the country. This scheme, which included an effectual provision for the instruction and training of the National Schoolmaster, was ably seconded, on the part of the Government, by Sir James Kaye Shuttleworth, and remains a monument—it is to be hoped an enduring monument—of the enlightened zeal of its authors and promoters.

On Praed's domestic life we must, for obvious reasons, touch lightly. In the opening pages of this memoir it has been mentioned that on the death of his mother he was indebted to the care of an elder sister. Her decease, which took place in 1830, made a deep impression on his mind, and contributed, with the advance of years and the experience of life, to that greater earnestness and seriousness of character which marked his later years. The greater part of that year was passed in the most tender attendance in the sick-room, and afterwards in endeavoring to cheer the home made desolate by her removal. He gave up the Summer Circuit that he might devote himself more fully to this object; and the unselfishness with which he set aside his own stirring occupations for the claims of family affection, can never be forgotten by those who shared the sorrow and partook of the sympathy.

In 1835 he lost his father, to whom he was affectionately and reverentially attached, and whose memory deserves on every account to be handed down with that of the son whose mind he did so much to form, and who profited so largely by his precept and example.

It may well be supposed that his legal and parliamentary engagements left him little time for literary pursuits. He continued, however, from time to time to contribute poems to the "Literary Souvenir" and other periodicals, from which they have now been collected. His political squibs have been already mentioned, and, besides these, articles from his pen appeared from time to time in the "Morning Post." To the last his poetical talent was exercised with no decrease of power, and with even increasing refinement of taste, whether for the amusement of his friends, in pieces of playful fancy, or in the tender service of family affection; to the last—when sickness had at length completely incapacitated him from every other occupation; and it is scarcely possible to repress a feeling of regret that he had not sooner withdrawn from the toils and excitement, whether of the bar or the senate, before it was too late, and devoted the full power of his mind to that genial art in which his success was incontestable, and to which, as it is, he owes his permanent reputation.

But it was not so to be. The uncontrollable energy of his nature carried him on year after year, while the disease was yet only nascent; and month after month, long after he had received unmistakable warning of its increasing growth.

But there is a bright side to this picture. His latter years, amid all the trials which he had to pass through, aggravated as they were by bodily infirmity and suffering, were cheered and solaced by the best earthly consolation—that of the domestic hearth. In the summer of 1835, while his hopes of public advancement were yet high, and no suspicion of the uncertainty of his bodily health had dawned upon his mind, he was happily united in marriage to Helen, daughter of George Bogle, Esq., a lady to whose virtues and accomplishments a respectful allusion is all that can here be permitted. Suffice it to say, that during the four years of their companionship, she devoted to her husband, whose high qualities, intellectual and moral, she was every way qualified to appreciate, all the resources of the most assiduous affection; and that, during the four-and-twenty years of her widowhood, she never ceased to mourn his loss. Her own decease occurred early in the autumn of the past year.

Little remains to be told. The winter of 1838–9 was spent by Praed, with his wife and two infant daughters, at St. Leonard's-on-Sea, when aggravated symptoms of the disorder under which he had in reality long labored, and in particular an increased difficulty of breathing when taking exercise, began to force themselves upon his attention. Nevertheless, upon his return to London for the meeting of Parliament, in the February of 1839, his general health appeared to have improved, when he entered upon the discharge of his public duties with undiminished energy, neither entertaining himself, nor, it would appear, leading those about him to entertain, any unusual alarm for the probable consequences of his exertions. It was not till the termination of the debate on the Corn Laws, which lasted seven nights, that any serious apprehensions were entertained. Dr. James Johnson, who had attended him in the earlier stages of his illness, was now called in; but though he appeared, on the cessation of the easterly wind—to the long continuance of which he had attributed the increase of his ailments—to rally a little, no real improvement took place. Still he remained full of hope and resolution; and, taking advantage of an adjournment of Parliament, consequent upon a transient change of Government in the May of that year, paid a visit to Cambridge in his official capacity of Deputy High Steward. The letter from which the following is taken is dated the 29th of May, the last which the writer of this Memoir received from his beloved friend:—"Helen went with me to Cambridge on the 17th instant, where I was to have held my court last week; but to my amazement I found my supposed sinecure up to its chin in points of disputed jurisdiction, so that I was forced to dismiss my Leet Jury *re infectâ*, and return to town to study opinions of counsel, and refer the matters in discussion, or at least my cause thereanent, to the attention of the Vice-Chancellor and Heads, whose attention to the subject I took care to bespeak. We might have passed our week's holiday agreeably enough at Cambridge, Helen having never visited it before, but for the severity of the weather, which from Tuesday the 21st to Saturday the 25th was winter in bleak earnest. I could do little in the way of lionizing. Helen, however, saw much of what is sight-worthy. The hospitalities of our old friends in Trinity and elsewhere were of course boundless."

The buoyancy of his mind, and the interest which he continued to take in public affairs, appears from what follows. "This morning, with your letter, I duly received your four petitions, which I shall be very glad to present. Our London meeting on the Education question was magnificent." In fact, he continued, notwithstanding the remonstrances of his friends, to attend in his place in Parliament till nearly the middle of June, when he paired off with Lord Arundel for the rest of the session. This step he was at length induced to take by the advice of Dr. Paris, to whom his case had been referred. On the 17th of June, he was removed to Sudbury Grove, a villa in the neighborhood of Harrow, kindly placed at his disposal by a friend. But it was too late to hope even for a partial restoration. He grew rapidly worse, and his return to London was not accomplished without difficulty.

He entered into his rest on the 15th of July, 1839, at his own house in Chester Square, and was interred, on the 23d of the same month, in the cemetery at Kensal Green, his funeral being attended by his widow, his two brothers, and a considerable number of his relations and private friends; and among these, by the writer of the present sketch, who had also the melancholy but valued privilege of attending him in his last hours.

He left two daughters, Helen Adeline Mackworth, and Elizabeth Lillian Mackworth, under whose authority the present collection of their father's poems is given to the public.

A monumental Tablet at Kensal Green bears the following inscription from the pen of the Reverend James Hildyard:—

JUXTA HOC MARMOR CONDITUM EST
QUICQUID MORTALE FUIT EGREGII VIRI ET SENATORIS,
WINTHROP MACKWORTH PRAED, A. M.,
COLL. SS. TRIN. CANTAB. OLIM SOCII: EJUSDEMQUE ACADEMIÆ PROSENESCALLI
TER AD CURIAM BRITANNICAM A TRIBUS MUNICIPIIS DELEGATI,
ALIISQUE TUM PRIVATIS TUM PUBLICIS HONORIBUS INSIGNITI.
NAT. VII. KAL. SEXTIL. MDCCCII. OBIIT ID. JUL. MDCCCXXXIX.
JUVENTUTEM OPTIMIS LITTERIS, ÆTATEM MATURIOREM REIPUBLICÆ,
UNIVERSAM VITAM INGENIUM VIRES ELOQUENTIAM PATRIÆ DICAVIT.
RARO SIMUL CONJUNCTÆ SUNT TOT NATURÆ DOTES,
TAM DOCTRINÆ ARTIUMQUE LIBERALIUM SUBSIDIIS EXCULTÆ:
RARISSIME TAM GENERIS HUMANI UTILITATI TAM CHRISTI HONORI SUBJECTÆ.
IMMATURA EHEU MORTE CORREPTUS TRISTE SUI AMICIS DESIDERIUM,
AH QUANTO TRISTIUS CONJUGI DILECTISSIMÆ AMANTISSIMÆ RELIQUIT.
ILLA SICUT HOC TESTIMONIO DEFLETAM MEMORIAM PIE PROSECUTA EST,
ITA GRATO TAMEN ANIMO DEUM DATOREM,
SUBMISSO ADEMPTOREM VENERATUR.

Beneath a marble bust in the possession of his widow were engraved the following lines by the Rev. John Moultrie, a last tribute paid by his valued friend and brother-poet to the memory of Winthrop Mackworth Praed.

Not that in him, whom these poor praises wrong,
  Gifts, rare themselves, in rarest union dwelt;
Not that, revealed through eloquence and song,
  In him the Bard and Statesman breathed and felt;—

Not that his nature, graciously endued
  With feelings and affections pure and high,
Was purged from worldly taint, and self-subdued,
  Till soul o'er sense gained perfect mastery;

Not for this only we lament his loss,—
  Not for this chiefly we account him blest;
But that all this he cast beneath the Cross,
  Content for Christ to live, in Christ to rest.

TALES.

LILLIAN.

A FAIRY TALE.

THE reader is requested to believe that the following statement is literally true; because the writer is well aware that the circumstances under which LILLIAN was composed are the only source of its merits, and the only apology for its faults.

At a small party at Cambridge some malicious belles endeavored to confound their sonneteering friends, by setting unintelligible and inexplicable subjects for the exercise of their poetical talents. Among many others, the thesis was given out which is the motto of LILLIAN—

"A dragon's tail is flayed to warm
A headless maiden's heart,"

and the following poem was an attempt to explain the riddle.

The partiality with which it has been honored in manuscript, and the frequent applications which have been made to the author for copies, must be his excuse for sending it to the press.

It was written, however, with the sole view of amusing the friends in whose circle the idea originated; and to them, with all due humility and devotion, it is inscribed.

TRINITY COLLEGE, CAMBRIDGE,
October 26, 1822.

POEMS

BY

WINTHROP MACKWORTH PRAED.

LILLIAN.

"A dragon's tail is flayed to warm
A headless maiden's heart."—*Miss* ——.

"And he's cleckit this great muckle bird out o' this wee egg! he could wile the very flounders out o' the Frith!"
Mr. Saddletree.

CANTO I.

There was a dragon in Arthur's time,
When dragons and griffins were voted "prime,"
  Of monstrous reputation:
Up and down, and far and wide,
He roamed about in his scaly pride;
And ever, at morn and eventide,
He made such rivers of blood to run
As shocked the sight of the blushing sun,
  And deluged half the nation.

It was a pretty monster, too,
With a crimson head, and a body blue,
And wings of a warm and delicate hue,
Like the glow of a deep carnation:
And the terrible tail that lay behind,
Reached out so far as it twisted and twined,
That a couple of dwarfs, of wondrous strength
Bore, when he travelled, its horrible length,
Like a Duke's at the coronation.

His mouth had lost one ivory tooth,
Or the dragon had been, in very sooth,
No insignificant charmer;
And that—alas! he had ruined it,
When on new-year's day, in a hungry fit,
He swallowed a tough and a terrible bit—
Sir Lob, in his brazen armor.
Swift and light were his steps on the ground,
Strong and smooth was his hide around,
For the weapons which the peasants flung
Ever unfelt or unheeded rung,
Arrow, and stone, and spear,
As snow o'er Cynthia's window flits,
Or raillery of twenty wits
On a fool's unshrinking ear.

In many a battle the beast had been,
Many a blow he had felt and given:
Sir Digore came with a menacing mien,

But he sent Sir Digore straight to Heaven;
Stiff and stour were the arms he wore,
Huge the sword he was wont to clasp;
But the sword was little, the armor brittle,
Locked in the coil of the dragon's grasp.

He came on Sir Florice of Sesseny Land,
Pretty Sir Florice from over the sea,
And smashed him all as he stepped on the sand,
Cracking his head like a nut from the tree.
No one till now, had found, I trow,
Any thing good in the scented youth,
Who had taken much pains to be rid of his brains,
Before they were sought by the dragon's tooth.

He came on the Sheriff of Hereford,
As he sat him down to his Sunday dinner;
And the Sheriff he spoke but this brief word:
"St. Francis, be good to a corpulent sinner!"
Fat was he, as a Sheriff might be,
From the crown of his head to the tip of his toe;
But the Sheriff was small, or nothing at all,
When put in the jaws of the dragon foe.

He came on the Abbot of Arnondale,
As he kneeled him down to his morning devotion;

But the dragon he shuddered, and turned his tail
  About, "with a short uneasy motion."
Iron and steel, for an early meal,
  He stomached with ease, or the Muse is a liar;
But out of all question, he failed in digestion,
  If ever he ventured to swallow a friar!

Monstrous brute!—his dread renown
Made whispers and terrors in country and town;
Nothing was babbled by boor or knight,
But tales of his civic appetite.
At last, as after dinner he lay,
Hid from the heat of the solar ray,
By boughs that had woven an arbor shady,
He chanced to fall in with the Headless Lady.
Headless! alas! 't was a piteous gibe;
I'll drink Aganippe, and then describe.

Her father had been a stout yeoman,
Fond of his jest and fond of his can,
  But never over-wise;
And once, when his cups had been many and deep,
He met with a dragon fast asleep,
  'T was a fairy in disguise:
In a dragon's form she had ridden the storm,
  The realm of the sky invading;
Sir Grahame's ship was stout and fast.
But the fairy came on the rushing blast,

And shivered the sails, and shivered the mast,
And down went the gallant ship at last,
With all the crew and lading.
And the fay laughed out to see the rout,
As the last dim hope was fading;
And this she had done in a love of fun,
And a love of masquerading.
She lay that night in a sunny vale,
And the yeoman found her sleeping;
Fiercely he smote her glittering tail,
But oh! his courage began to fail,
When the fairy rose all weeping.
"Thou hast lopped," she said, "beshrew thine hand!—
The fairest foot in fairy land!

"Thou hast an infant in thine home!
Never to her shall reason come,
For weeping or for wail,
Till she shall ride with a fearless face
On a living dragon's scale,
And fondly clasp to her heart's embrace
A living dragon's tail."
The fairy's form from his shuddering sight
Flowed away in a stream of light.

Disconsolate that youth departed,
Disconsolate and poor;
And wended, chill and broken-hearted,
To his cottage on the moor;

Sadly and silently he knelt
  His lonely hearth beside;
Alas! how desolate he felt
  As he hid his face and cried.
The cradle where the babe was laid
  Stood in its own dear nook,
But long—how long! he knelt, and prayed,
  And did not dare to look.
He looked at last; his joy was there,
And slumbering with that placid air
Which only babes and angels wear.
Over the cradle he leaned his head;
The cheek was warm, and the lip was red:
And he felt, he felt, as he saw her lie,
A hope—which was a mockery.
The babe unclosed her eye's pale lid:—
Why doth he start from the sight it hid?
He had seen in the dim and fitful ray,
That the light of the soul hath gone away!
Sigh nor prayer he uttered there,
In mute and motionless despair,
But he laid him down beside his child,
And LILLIAN saw him die—and smiled.
The mother? she had gone before;
And in the cottage on the moor,
With none to watch her and caress,
No arm to clasp, no voice to bless,
The witless child grew up alone,
And made all Nature's book her own.

If, in the warm and passionate hour
When Reason sleeps in Fancy's bower,
If thou hast ever, ever felt
A dream of delicate beauty melt
  Into the heart's recess,
Seen by the soul, and seen by the mind,
  But indistinct its loveliness,
Adored, and not defined;
A bright creation, a shadowy ray,
Fading and flitting in mist away,
Nothing to gaze on, and nothing to hear,
But something to cheat the eye and ear
With a fond conception and joy of both,
So that you might, that hour, be loth
To change for some one's sweetest kiss
Thy vision of unenduring bliss,
Or lose for some one's sweetest tone,
The murmur thou drinkest all alone—
If such a vision hath ever been thine,
Thou hast a heart that may look on mine!

For, oh! the light of my saddened theme
Was like to naught but a poet's dream,
Or the forms that come on the twilight's wing,
Shaped by the soul's imagining.
Beautiful shade with her tranquil air,
And her thin white arm, and her flowing hair,
And the light of her eye so coldly obscure,
And the hue of her cheek so pale and pure!
Reason and thought she had never known,
Her heart was as cold as a heart of stone;

So you might guess from her eyes' dim rays,
And her idiot laugh, and her vacant gaze.
She wandered about all lone on the heather,
She and the wild heath-birds together;
For Lillian seldom spoke or smiled,
But she sang as sweet as a little child.
Into her song her dreams would throng,
  Silly, and wild, and out of place;
And yet that wild and roving song
  Entranced the soul in its desolate grace.
And hence the story had ever run,
That the fairest of dames was a headless one.

The pilgrim in his foreign weeds
  Would falter in his prayer;
And the monk would pause with his half told beads
  To breathe a blessing there;
The knight would loose his vizor-clasp,
And drop the rein from his nerveless grasp,
And pass his hand across his brow
With a sudden sigh, and a whispered vow,
And marvel Flattery's tale was told,
From a lip so young to an ear so cold.
She had seen her sixteenth winter out,
When she met with the beast I was singing about:
The dragon, I told you, had dined that day;
So he gazed upon her as he lay,
Earnestly looking, and looking long,
With his appetite weak and his wonder strong.
Silent he lay in his motionless coil;
And the song of the lady was sweet the while:—

"Nonny Nonny! I hear it float,
Innocent bird, thy tremulous note:
It comes from thy home in the eglantine,
And I stay this idle song of mine,
Nonny Nonny! to listen to thine!

"Nonny Nonny! 'LILLIAN sings
The sweetest of all living things!'
So Sir Launcelot averred;
But surely Sir Launcelot never heard
Nonny Nonny! the natural bird!"

The dragon he lay in mute amaze,
Till something of kindness crept into his gaze;
He drew the flames of his nostrils in,
He veiled his claws with their speckled skin,
He curled his fangs in a hideous smile;
And the song of the lady was sweet the while:—

"Nonny Nonny! who shall tell
Where the summer breezes dwell?
Lightly and brightly they breathe and blow,
But whence they come and whither they go,
Nonny Nonny! who shall know?

"Nonny Nonny! I hear your tone,
But I feel ye cannot read mine own;
And I lift my neck to your fond embraces,
But who hath seen in your resting-places,
Nonny Nonny! your beautiful faces?"

A moment! and the dragon came
Crouching down to the peerless dame,
With his fierce red eye so fondly shining,
And his terrible tail so meekly twining,
And the scales on his huge limbs gleaming o'er,
Gayer than ever they gleamed before.
She had won his heart, while she charmed his ear,
And Lillian smiled, and knew no fear.
And see, she mounts between his wings;
  (Never a queen had a gaudier throne,)
And fairy-like she sits and sings,
  Guiding the steed with a touch and a tone,
Aloft, aloft in the clear blue ether,
The dame and the dragon they soared together;
He bore her away on the breath of the gale—
The two little dwarfs held fast by the tail.

Fanny! a pretty group for drawing;
My dragon like a war-horse pawing,
My dwarfs in a fright, and my girl in an attitude,
Patting the beast in her soulless gratitude.
There; you may try it if you will,
While I drink my coffee and nib my quill.

CANTO II.

The sun shone out on hill and grove;
  It was a glorious day,
The lords and the ladies were making love,
  And the clowns were making hay;

But the town of Brentford marked with wonder
A lightning in the sky, and thunder,
And thinking ('t was a thinking town)
Some prodigy was coming down,
A mighty mob to Merlin went,
To learn the cause of this portent;
And he, a wizard sage, but comical,
Looked through his glasses astronomical,
And puzzled every foolish sconce
By this oracular response:

"*Now the slayer doth not slay,*
Weakness flings her fear away,
Power bears the powerless,
Pity rides the pitiless;
Are ye lovers? are ye brave?
Hear ye this, and seek, and save!
He that would wed the loveliest maid,
Must don the stoutest mail,
For the rider shall never be sound in the head,
Till the ridden be maimed in the tail.
Hey diddle diddle! the cat and the fiddle!
None but a lover can read me my riddle!"

How kind art thou, and oh! how mighty,
Cupid! thou son of Aphrodite!
By thy sole aid in old romance,
Heroes and heroines sing and dance;
Of cane and rod there's little need;
They never learn to write or read;

Yet often, by thy sudden light,
Enamored dames contrive to write;
And often, in the hour of need,
Enamored youths contrive to read.
I make a small digression here:
I merely mean to make it clear,
That if Sir Eglamour had wit
To read and construe, bit by bit,
All that the wizard had expressed,
And start conjectures on the rest,
Cupid had sharpened his discerning,
The little god of love and learning.
He revolved in his bed what Merlin had said,
 Though Merlin had labored to scatter a veil on't;
And found out the sense of the tail and the head,
 Though none of his neighbors could make head or
  tail on't.
Sir Eglamour was one o' the best
 Of Arthur's table round;
He never set his spear in rest,
 But a dozen went to the ground.
Clear and warm as the lightning flame,
His valor from his father came,
 His cheek was like his mother's;
And his hazel eye more clearly shone
Than any I ever have looked upon,
 Save Fanny's and two others!

With his spur so bright, and his rein so light,
 And his steed so swift and ready;

And his skilful sword, to wound or ward,
  And his spear so sure and steady;
He bore him like a British knight
  From London to Penzance;
Avenged all weeping women's slight,
  And made all giants dance.
And he had travelled far from home,
  Had worn a mask at Venice,
Had kissed the Bishop's toe at Rome,
  And beat the French at tennis:
Hence he had many a courtly play,
  And jeerings and jibes in plenty,
And he wrote more rhymes in a single day
  Than Byron or Bowles in twenty.

He clasped to his side his sword of pride,
His sword, whose native polish vied
  With many a gory stain;
Keen and bright as a meteor-light;
But not so keen and not so bright,
  As Moultrie's* jesting vein.
And his shield he bound his arm around,
His shield, where glowing saffron wound
  About a field of blue;
Heavy and thick as a wall of brick,
But not so heavy and not so thick
  As the Edinburgh Review.

* Rev. John Moultrie, who, in 1823, (when many manuscript copies of "Lillian" were in circulation,) wrote some beautiful and pathetic lyrics, some of which appeared in Knight's Quarterly Magazine.

With a smile and a jest he set out on the quest,
  Clad in his stoutest mail,
With his helm of the best, and his spear in the rest,
  To flay the dragon's tail.
  The warrior travelled wearily,
  Many a league and many a mile;
And the dragon sailed in the clear blue sky;
  And the song of the lady was sweet the while:—

"My steed and I, my steed and I,
  On in the path of the winds we fly,
  And I chase the planets that wander at even,
  And bathe my hair in the dews of heaven!
  Beautiful stars, so thin and bright,
  Exquisite visions of vapor and light,
  I love ye all with a sister's love,
  And I rove with ye wherever ye rove,
  And I drink your changeless, endless song,
  The music ye make as ye wander along!
  Oh! let me be, as one of ye,
  Floating for aye on your liquid sea;
  And I'll feast with you on the purest rain,
  To cool my weak and wildered brain,
  And I'll give you the loveliest lock of my hair
  For a little spot in your realm of air!"

The dragon came down when the morn shone bright
  And slept in the beam of the sun;
Fatigued, no doubt, with his airy flight,
  As I with my jingling one.

With such a monstrous adversary
Sir Eglamour was far too weary
  To think of bandying knocks;
He came on his foe as still as death,
Walking on tiptoe, and holding his breath,
And instead of drawing his sword from his sheath,
  He drew a pepper-box!
The pepper was as hot as flame,
  The box of a wondrous size;
He gazed one moment on the dame,
Then, with a sure and a steady aim
Full in the dragon's truculent phiz
He flung the scorching powder—whiz!
  And darkened both his eyes!

Have you not seen a little kite
  Rushing away on its paper wing,
  To mix with the wild wind's quarrelling?
Up it soars with an arrowy flight,
    Till, weak and unsteady,
    Torn by the eddy,
It dashes to earth from its hideous height?
Such was the rise of the beast in his pain,
Such was his falling to earth again;
Upward he shot, but he saw not his path,
Blinded with pepper, and blinded with wrath;
One struggle—one vain one—of pain and emotion!
And he shot back again, like "a bird of the ocean!"
Long he lay in a trance that day,

And alas! he did not wake before
The cruel knight with skill and might,
Had lopped and flayed the tail he wore.

Twelve hours by the chime he lay in his slime,
More utterly blind, I trow,
Than a Polypheme in the olden time,
Or a politician now.
He sped, as soon as he could see,
To the Paynim bowers of Rosalie;
For there the dragon had hope to cure,
By the tinkling rivulets, ever pure,
By the glowing sun, and fragrant gale,
His wounded honor and wounded tail!
He hied him away to the perfumed spot:
The little dwarfs clung—where the tail was not!
The damsel gazed on that young knight,
With something of terror, but more of delight;
Much she admired the gauntlets he wore,
Much the device that his buckler bore,
Much the feathers that danced on his crest,
But most the baldrick that shone on his breast.
She thought the dragon's pilfered scale
Was fairer far than the warrior's mail,
And she lifted it up with her weak white arm.
Unconscious of its hidden charm,
And round her throbbing bosom tied,
In mimicry of warlike pride.

Gone is the spell that bound her!
The talisman hath touched her heart,
And she leaps with a fearful and fawn-like start

As the shades of glamory depart—
Strange thoughts are glimmering round her;
Deeper and deeper her cheek is glowing,
Quicker and quicker her breath is flowing,
And her eye gleams out from its long dark lashes,
Fast and full, unnatural flashes;
For hurriedly and wild
Doth Reason pour her hidden treasures,
Of human griefs, and human pleasures,
Upon her new-found child.
And "oh!" she saith, "my spirit doth seem
To have risen to-day from a pleasant dream;
A long, long dream—but I feel it breaking!
Painfully sweet is the throb of waking;"
And then she laughed, and wept again:
While, gazing on her heart's first rain,
Bound in his turn by a magic chain,
The silent youth stood there:
Never had either been so blest;—
You that are young may picture the rest,
You that are young and fair.
Never before, on this warm land,
Came Love and Reason hand in hand.

When you were blest, in childhood's years
With the brightest hopes and the lightest fears,
Have you not wandered in your dream,
Where a greener glow was on the ground,
And a clearer breath in the air around,
And a purer life in the gay sunbeam.
And a tremulous murmur in every tree,
And a motionless sleep on the quiet sea?

And have you not lingered, lingered still,
All unfettered in thought and will,
A fair and cherished boy ;
Until you felt it pain to part
From the wild creations of your art,
Until your young and innocent heart
Seemed bursting with its joy?
And then, oh then, hath your waking eye
Opened in all its ecstacy,
And seen your mother leaning o'er you.
The loved and loving one that bore you,
Giving her own, her fond caress,
And looking her eloquent tenderness?
Was it not heaven to fly from the scene
Where the heart in the vision of night had been,
And drink, in one o'erflowing kiss,
Your deep reality of bliss?
Such was LILLIAN's passionate madness,
Such the calm of her waking gladness.

Enough! my tale is all too long:
Fair children, if the trifling song,
That flows for you to-night,
Hath stolen from you one gay laugh,
Or given your quiet hearts to quaff
One cup of young delight,
Pay ye the rhymer for his toils
In the coinage of your golden smiles,
And treasure up his idle verse,
With the stories ye loved from the lips of your nurse

GOG.

CANTO I.

"A most delicate monster!"—*Shakspeare.*

King Arthur, as the Legends sing,
Was a right brave and merry King,
And had a wondrous reputation
Through this right brave and merry nation.
His ancient face, and ancient clothes,
His Tables Round, and rounder Oaths,
His crown and cup, his feasts and fights,
His pretty Queen, and valiant Knights,
Would make me up the raciest scene
That is, or will be, or has been.
These points, and others not a few,
Of great importance to the view,—
As, how King Arthur valued Woman,
And, how King Arthur threshed the Roman,
And, how King Arthur built a Hall,
And, how King Arthur play'd at ball—

I'll have the prudence to omit,
Since Brevity's the soul of Wit.
Oh! Arthur's days were blessed days,
When all was wit, and worth, and praise;
And planting thrusts, and planting oaks,
And cracking nuts, and cracking jokes,
And turning out the toes, and tiltings,
And jousts, and journeyings, and jiltings;
Lord! what a stern and stunning rout,
As tall Adventure strode about,
Rang through the land! for there were duels
For love of Dames, and love of Jewels;
And steeds, that carried Knight and Prince
As never steeds have carried since,
And heavy Lords and heavy lances;
And strange, unfashionable dances;
And endless bustle and turmoil,
In vain disputes for fame or spoil.
Manners, and roads, were very rough,
Armour, and beeves, were very tough;
And then,—the brightest figures far
In din or dinner, peace or war,—
Dwarfs sang to Ladies in their teens,
And Giants grew as thick as beans!

One of these worthies, in my verse,
I mean, Oh! Clio, to rehearse:
He was much talk'd of in his time,
And sung of, too, in monkish rhyme;

So, lest my pen should chance to err,
I'll quote his ancient chronicler.
Thus Friar Joseph paints my hero:

Addictus cædibus et mero,
Impavidus, luxuriosus.
Preces, jejuniaque perosus,
Metum ubique vultu jactans,
Boves ubique manu mactans,
Tauros pro cœna vorans, post hos
Libenter edens pueros tostos,
Anglorum, et (ni fallit error)
Ipsius Regis sæpe terror,
Equorum equitumque captor,
Incola rupis, ingens raptor,
Episcopalium honorum,—
Damnatus hostis monachorum!

Such was his eulogy! The fact is,
He had a most outrageous practice
Of running riot, bullying, beating,
Behaving rudely, killing, eating;
He wore a black beard, like a Jew's,
And stood twelve feet without his shoes
He used to sleep through half the day,
And then went out to kill and slay;
At night he drank a deal of grog,
And slept again;—his name was Gog.

He was the son of Gorboduc,
And was a boy of monstrous pluck;

For once, when, in a morning early,
He happened to be bruising barley,
A Knight came by with sword and spear
And halted in his mid career:
The youngster look'd so short and pliant,
He never dreamed he was a giant,
And so he pulled up with a jerk,
And called young bruiser from his work:—
"Friend, can you lead me by the rein
To Master Gordobuc's domain?
I mean to stop the country's fears,
And knock his house about his ears!"
The urchin chuckled at the joke,
And grinned acutely as he spoke:
"Sir Knight, I'll do it if I can,
Just get behind me in my pan,
I'm off,—I stop but once to bait,
I'll set you down before the gate."
Sir Lolly swallowed all the twang,
He leaped into the mortar—bang!
And when he saw him in the vessel,
Gog beat his brains out with the pestle.

This was esteemed a clever hit,
And showed the stripling had a wit;
Therefore his father spared no arts
To cultivate such brilliant parts.
No giant ever went before
Beyond his "two and two made four,"

But Gog possess'd a mind gigantic,
And grasp'd a learning quite romantic.
'Tis certain that he used to sport
The language that they spoke at court;
Had something of a jaunty air,
That men so tall can seldom wear;
Unless he chanc'd to need some victuals,
He was a pleasant match at skittles;
And if he could have found a horse
To bear him through a single course,
I think he might have brought the weight
'Gainst all that Britain counted great.
In physic he was sage indeed,
He used to blister and to bleed,
Made up strange plasters—had been known
To amputate, or set a bone,
And had a notable device
For curing colic in a trice,
By making patients jump a wall,
And get a most salubrious fall.
Then in philosophy, 'twas said,
He got new fancies in his head;
Had reckonings of the sea's profundity,
And dreams about the earth's rotundity;
In argument was quite a Grecian,
And taught the doctrine of cohesion.
This knowledge, as one often sees,
Softened his manners by degrees;
He came to have a nicer maw,
And seldom ate his mutton raw;

And if he had upon his board
At once a Peasant and a Lord,
He call'd the Lord his dainty meat,
And had him devill'd for a treat.

Old Gordobuc, the Legends say,
Happen'd to go to pot one day;
The how and why remains a question
Some say he died of indigestion,
From swallowing a little boat,
In drinking dry Sir Toby's moat.
Others assert that Dame Ulrica
(Whom he confined beneath a beaker,
Having removed her from her cottage
To stew her in a mess of pottage;)
Upset her prison in the night,
And played Ulysses out of spite,
So that he woke, in great surprise,
With two sharp needles in his eyes.
Perhaps Ulrica may have lied;
At all events—the giant died,
Bequeathing to his son and heir,
Illustrious Gog, the pious care
To lord it o'er his goods and chattels,
And wield his club, and fight his battles.

Twould take an Iliad, Sirs, to tell
The numerous feats on flood and fell
At which my hero tried his hand;
He was the terror of the land,

And did a thousand humorous things
Fit to delight the ear of Kings;
I cull what I consider best,
And pass in silence o'er the rest.

There was a Lady sent from Wales,
With quiet sea, and favouring gales,
To land upon the English shore,
And marry with Sir Paladore.
It seems she sail'd from Milford Haven,
On board the Bittern, Captain Craven,
And smiles, and nods, and gratulation,
Attended on her embarkation.
But when the ship got out from land,
The Captain took her by the hand,
And, with a brace of shocking oaths,
He led her to her chest of clothes.
They paused! he scratching at his chin,
As if much puzzled to begin;
She o'er the box in stupor leaning,
As if she couldn't guess his meaning;
Then thus the rogue the silence broke—
His whiskers wriggled as he spoke:—
"Look out an extra gown and shift;
You're going to be turned adrift;
As many gewgaws as you please,
Only don't bounce upon your knees;
It's very fine, but don't amuse,
And isn't of the smallest use.

Ho! there—above!—put down the boat,—
In half an hour you'll be afloat;—
I wouldn't have you lose a minute—
There—put a little victuals in it;
You think I'm playing off a sham,
But—split my vitals if I am!"
Struggling and tears in vain were tried,
He haul'd her to the vessel's side,
And still the horrid brute ran on,
Exclaiming in ferocious tone—
"You needn't hollow to the crew,
Be quiet, it will never do;
Pray, spare your breath;—come wind and
weather,
We all are sworn to this together!
Don't talk us round!—'cause why?—you can't!
Oh! sink my timbers if we an't!
So—gently!—mind your footing—there!
You'll find the weather very fair;
You'd better keep a sharp look-out,
There are some ugly reefs about;
Stay!—what provision have they made ye?
I wouldn't have ye famished, Lady!
Dick! lend a hand, ye staring oaf,
And heave us down another loaf;
Here are two bustards—take 'em both;
You've got a famous pot of broth;
You'd better use the sculls—you'll find
You've got a deucèd little wind;

Now!—don't stand blubbering at me,
But trim the boat, and put to sea."
He spoke! regardless of her moan,
They left her in the boat, alone!
According to our modern creed,
It was a cruel thing, indeed;
Unless some villain bribed them to it,
I can't conceive what made them do it.
It was a very cruel thing!—
She was the daughter of a king;
Though it appears that kings were then
But little more than common men.
She was a handsome girl, withal,
Well-formed, majestic, rather tall;
She had dark eyes—(I like them dark,)
And in them was an angry spark
That came, and went, and came again,
Like lightning in the pause of rain;
Her robe adorn'd, but not conceal'd
The shape it shrouded, yet reveal'd;
It chanc'd her ivory neck was bare,
But clusters rich of jetty hair
Lay like a garment scatter'd there;
She had upon her pale, white brow,
A look of pride, that, even now,
Gazed round upon her solitude,
Hopeless, perhaps, but unsubdued,
As if she thought the dashing wave
That swell'd beneath, was born her slave.

She felt not yet a touch of fear,
But didn't know which way to steer;
She thought it prudent to get back:
The wind due East!—she said she'd tack;
And though she had a tinge of doubt,
She laugh'd, and put the helm about.
The wind went down—a plaguy calm;
The Princess felt a rising qualm;
The boat lay sleeping on the sea,
The sky look'd blue,—and so did she!
The night came on, and still the gale
Breath'd vainly on her leather sail;
It scarcely would have stirr'd a feather;—
Heaven and her hopes grew dark together;
She slept! I don't know how she dined,—
And light returned, and brought no wind;
She seized her oars at break of day,
And thought she made a little way;
The skin was rubbed from off her thumb,
And she had no Diaculum.
(Diaculum, my story says,
Was not invented in those days.)
At last, not being used to pull,
She lost her temper,—and her scull.

A long, long time becalm'd she lay,
And still untir'd from day to day,
She formed a thousand anxious wishes,
And bit her nails, and watch'd the fishes;

To give it up she still was loth;
She ate the bustards and the broth;
And when they fail'd, she sigh'd, and said,
"I'll make my dinner on the bread!"
She ate the bread, and thought with sorrow,
"There's nothing left me for to-morrow!"
She pull'd her lover's letter out,
And turn'd its vellum leaves about;
It was a billet-doux of fire,
Scarce thicker than a modern quire;
And thus it ran:—"I never suppe,
Because mine heatte dothe eatte me uppe;
And eke, dear Loue, I never dine,
Nor drinke atte Courte a cuppe of wine;
For daye and nighte—I telle you true,—
I feede uponne my Loue for you."
Alas! that Lady fair, who long
Had felt her hunger rather strong,
Said (and her eye with tears was dim),
"I've no such solid love for him!"
And so she thought it might be better
To sup upon her Lover's letter.

She ate the treasure quite, or nearly,
From "Beauteous Queen!" to "Yours sincerely!"
She thought upon her Father's crown,
And then Despair came o'er her!—down
Upon the bottom-boards she lay,
And veil'd her from the look of day;

The sea-birds flapp'd their wings, and she
Look'd out upon the tumbling sea;
And there was nothing on its face
But wide, interminable space,
And so she gave a piteous cry—
The murmuring waters made reply!
Alas! another morning came,
And brought no food! the hapless Dame
Thought, as she watch'd the lifeless sail,
That she should die "withouten fail!"
Another morn,—and not a whiff!
The lady grew so weak and stiff
That she could hardly move her stumps;
At last she fed upon her pumps!
And call'd upon her absent Lord,
And thought of going overboard:
As the dusk evening veil'd the sky
She said, "I'm ready now to die!"
She saw the dim light fade away,
And fainted as she kneel'd to pray.

I sing not where and how the boat
With its pale load contrived to float,
Nor how it struck off Hartland Point,
And 'gan to leak at every joint;
'Twill be enough, I think, to tell ye
Linda was shaken to a jelly,
And, when she woke from her long sleep,
Was lying in the Giant's keep,

While at a distance, like a log,
Her Captor snored—prodigious Gog!

He spared, as yet, his captive's life;
She wasn't ready for the knife,
For toil, and famine, and the sun,
Had worn her to a skeleton;
He kept her carefully in view,
And fed her for a week or two;
Then, in a sudden hungry freak,
He felt her arm, and neck, and cheek,
And, being rather short of meat,
Cried out that she was fit to eat.
The monster saw the bright dark eye
That met his purpose fearlessly;
He saw the form that did not quail,
He saw the look that did not fail,
And the white arm, that tranquil lay,
And never stirred to stop or stay;
He changed his mind—threw down the knife,
And swore that she should be his wife.

Linda, like many a modern Miss,
Began to veer about at this;
She feared not roasting!—but a ring!
Oh Lord! 'twas quite another thing;
She'd rather far be fried than tied,
And make a sausage than a bride;

She had no hand at argument,
And so she tried to circumvent.*
"My Lord," said she, "I know a plaster,
The which, before my sad disaster,
I kept most carefully in store
For my own Knight, Sir Paladore.
It is a mixture mild and thin;
But when 'tis spread upon the skin
It makes a surface white as snow—
Sword-proof thenceforth from top to toe;
I've sworn to wed with none, my Lord,
Who can be harm'd by human sword.
The ointment shall be yours! I'll make it,
Mash it and mix it, rub and bake it;
You look astonish'd!—you shall see,
And try its power upon me."

She bruised some herbs; to make them hot,
She put them in the Giant's pot;
Some mystic words she uttered there,
But whether they were charm or prayer
The Convent Legend hath not said;—
A little of the salve she spread

* The latter part of Linda's history,
In Ariosto's work is an ingredient;
I can't imagine how my monks and he
Happen'd to hit upon the same expedient;
You'll find it in "Orlando Furioso;"
But Mr. Hoole's Translation is but so so.

Upon her neck, and then she stood
In reverential attitude,
With head bent down, and lips compress'd,
And hands enfolded on her breast;—
"Strike!"—and the stroke in thunder fell
Full on the neck that met it well;
"Strike!"—the red blood started out
Like water from a water-spout;
A moment's space—and down it sunk,—
That headless, pale, and quivering trunk,
And the small head with its gory wave
Flew in wild eddies round the cave.
You think I shouldn't laugh at this;
You know not that a scene of bliss
To close my song is yet in store;
For Merlin to Sir Paladore
The head and trunk in air convey'd,
And spoke some magic words, and made,
By one brief fillip of his wand,
The happiest pair in all the land:—
The Giant—but I think I've done
Enough of him for Canto One.

GOG.

CANTO II.

"A most delicate monster!"—*Shakspeare.*

The morn is laughing in the sky,
The sun hath risen jocundly,
Brightly the dancing beam hath shone
On the cottage of clay, and the abbey of
stone;
As on the redolent air they float,
The songs of the birds have a gayer note,
And the fall of the waters hath breathed
around
A purer breath and a sweeter sound;
And why is Nature so richly drest
In the flowery garb she loveth best?
Peasant and Monk will tell you the tale,—
There is a wedding in Nithys-dale!

With his green vest around him flung,
His bugle o'er his shoulders hung,
And roses blushing in his hair,
The Minstrel-Boy is waiting there!
O'er his young cheek and earnest brow
Pleasure hath spread a warmer glow,
And Love his fervid look hath dight
In something of etherial light:
And still the Minstrel's pale blue eye
Is looking out impatiently
To see his glad and tender bride
Come dancing o'er the hillock's side.
For look! the sun's all-cheering ray
Shines proudly on a joyous day;
And, ere his setting, young Le Fraile
Shall wed the Lily of Nithys-dale!

A moment, and he saw her come,—
That maiden, from her latticed home,
With eyes all love, and lips apart,
And faltering step, and beating heart.
She came, and joined her cheek to his
In one prolonged and rapturous kiss;
And while it thrilled through heart and limb,
The world was nought to her or him.
Fair was the boy; a woman's grace
Beam'd o'er his figure and his face;
His red lips had a maiden's pout,
And his light eyes look'd sweetly out,

Scattering a thousand vivid flashes
Beneath their long and jetty lashes;—
And she, the still and timid bride,
That clung so fondly to his side,
Might well have seem'd, to Fancy's sight,
Some slender thing of air or light!
So white an arm, so pale a cheek,
A look so eloquently meek,
A neck of such a marble hue,
An eye of such transparent blue,—
Could never, never take their birth
From parentage of solid earth!
He that had searched fair England round
A lovelier pair had never found,
Than that minstrel boy, the young Le Fraile,
And Alice, the Lily of Nithys-dale!

Hark! hark! a sound! it flies along,
How fearfully! a trembling throng
Come round the Bride in wild amaze,
All ear and eye to hear and gaze;
Again it came—that sound of wonder—
Rolling along like distant thunder;
"That barbarous growl—that horrid noise—
Was it indeed a human voice?
The man must have a thousand tongues,
And bellows of brass, by way of lungs!"
Each to his friend, in monstrous fuss,
The staring peasants whispered thus:—

"Hark! hark! another echoing shout!"
And, as the boobies stared about,
Just leaping o'er a mountain's brow,
They saw the Brute that made the row;—
Two meadows and a little bog
Divided them from cruel Gog!

Maiden and matron, boy and man,
You can't conceive how fast they ran!
And as they scampered, you might hear
A thousand sounds of pain and fear.
"I get so tired"—"Where's my son?"—
"How fast the horrid beast comes on!"—
"What plaguy teeth!"—"You heard him
roar?"—
"I never puffed so much before!"—
"I can't imagine what to do!"–
"Whom has he caught?"—"I've lost my shoe!"
"Oh! I'm a sinful——" "Father Joe,
Do just absolve me as we go!"–
"Absolve you here? pray hold your pother;
I wouldn't do it for my mother!
A pretty time to stop and shrive,
Zounds! we shall all be broiled alive!
I feel the spit!"—"Nay, father, nay,
Don't talk in such a horrid way!"—
"Oh! mighty Love, to thee I bow!
Oh give me wings and save me now!"—
"A fig for Love!"—"Don't talk of figs!
He'll stick us all like sucking pigs!

Or skin us like a dish of eels—"
"Run—run—he's just upon your heels!"
"I promise the Abbey a silver cup!
Holy St. Jerome, trip him up!"
"I promise the Abbey a silver crown!
Holy St. Jerome, knock him down!"
The Monster came, and singled out
The tenderest bit in all the rout;
Spite of her weeping and her charms,
He tore her from her Lover's arms.
Woe for that hapless Minstrel-Boy!
Where is his pride, his hope, his joy?
His eye is wet, his cheek is pale;
He hath lost the Lily of Nithys-dale.

It chanc'd that day two travelling folk
Had spread their cloth beneath an oak,
And sat them gayly down to dine
On good fat buck, and ruddy wine.
One was a Friar, fat and sleek,
With pimpled nose, and rosy cheek,
And belly, whose capacious paunch
Told tales of many a buried haunch.
He was no Stoic! in his eye
Frolic fought hard with Gravity;
And though he strove, in conversation,
To talk as best beseemed his station,
Yet did he make some little slips;
And in the corners of his lips

There were some sly, officious dimples,
Which spake no love for roots and simples.
The other was a hardy Knight,
Caparison'd for instant fight;
You might have deemed him framed of stone,
So huge he was of limb and bone:
His short black hair, unmixed with grey,
Curl'd closely on his forehead lay;
His brow was swarthy, and a scar,
Not planted there in recent war,
Had drawn one long and blushing streak
Over the darkness of his cheek.
The Warrior's voice was full and bold,
His gorgeous arms were rich with gold;
But weaker shoulders soon would fail
Beneath that cumbrous mass of mail;
Yet, from his bearing, you might guess
He oft had worn a softer dress,
And laid aside that nodding crest,
To lap his head on lady's breast.

The meal, of course, was short and hasty,
And they had half got through the pasty,
When hark! a shriek rung loud and shrill;—
The Churchman jump'd, and dropp'd the gill;
The Soldier started from the board,
And twined his hand around his sword.
While they were wondering at the din,
The Minstrel-Boy came running in;

With trembling frame, and rueful face,
He bent his knee, and told his case :—
" The Monster's might away hath riven
My bliss on Earth, my hope in Heaven ;
And there is nothing left me now
But doubt above, and grief below !
My heart and hers together fly,
And she must live, or I must die !
Look at the Caitiff's face of pride;
Look at his long and haughty stride ;
Look how he bears her o'er hill and vale—
My Beauty, the Lily of Nithys-dale !"

They gazed around them !—Monk and Knight
Were startled at that awful sight;
They never had the smallest notion
How vast twelve feet would look in motion.
Dark as the midnight's deepest gloom—
Swift as the breath of the Simoom,—
That hill of flesh was moving on ;
And oh ! the sight of horror won
A shriek from all our three beholders ;
He bore the maid upon his shoulders !
" Now," said the Knight, " by all the fame
That ever clung to Arthur's name,
I'll do it,—or I'll try, at least,
To win her from that monstrous Beast !"
"Sir," said the Friar to the Knight,
" Success will wait upon the right ;

I feel much pity for the youth,
And though, to tell the honest truth,
I'm rather used to drink than slay,
I'll aid you here as best I may!"
They bade the Minstrel blow a blast
To stop the monster as he passed;
Gog was quite puzzled!—"Zounds—I' feg!
My friend—*piano!*—let me beg!"
Then in a rage towards the place
He strode along a rattling pace;
Firm on the ground his foot he planted,
And "wonder'd what the deuce they wanted!"

No blockhead was that holy man—
He clear'd his throat and thus began:—
"*O Pessime*—that is, I pray,
Discede—signifying stay!
Damno—that is, before you go,
Sis comes in convivio:
Abi—that is, set down the Lass;
Monstrum—that is, you'll take a glass?
Oh, holy church!—that is, I swear
You never looked no nicer fare;
Informe—horridum—immane!
That is, the wine's as good as any;
Apage! exorcizo te!
That is, it came from Burgundy;
We both are anxious—*execrande!*
To drink your health—*abominande!*

And then my comrade means to put
His falchion through your occiput!"
The Giant stared (and who would not?)
To find a monk so wondrous hot;
So fierce a stare you never saw;
At last the Brute's portentous jaw
Swung, like a massy creaking hinge,
And then, beneath its shaggy fringe
Rolling about each wondrous eye,
He scratched his beard, and made reply:—
"Bold is the Monk, and bold the Knight
That wishes with Gog to drink or fight,
For I have been from east to west,
And battled with King Arthur's best,
And never found I friend or foe
To stand my cup—or bear my blow!"
"Most puissant Gog! although I burst,"
Exclaimed the Monk, "I'll do the first;"
And ere a moment could be reckoned,
The Knight chimed in—"I'll try the second!"

The Giant, ere he did the job,
Took a huge chain from out his fob;
He bound his captive to a tree!
And young Le Fraile came silently,
And marked how all her senses slept,
And leaned upon her brow, and wept;
He kissed her lip, but her lip was grown
As coldly white as a marble stone;

He met her eye, but its vacant gaze
Had not the light of its living rays;
Yet still that trembling lover pressed
The maiden to his throbbing breast,
Till consciousness returned again,
And the tears flowed out like summer rain.
There was the bliss of a hundred years
In the rush of those delicious tears!

The helm from off the warrior's head
Is doffed to bear the liquor red;
That casque, I trow, is deep and high,
But the Monk and the Giant shall drain it dry;
And which of the two, when the feat is done,
Shall keep his legs at set of sun?

They filled to the brim that helm of gold,
And the Monk hath drained its ample hold;
Silent and slow the liquor fell,
As into some capacious well:
Tranquilly flowing down it went,
And made no noise in its long descent;
And it leaves no trace of its passage now
But the stain on his lip, and the flush on his
brow.

They filled to the brim that helm of gold,
And the Giant hath drained its ample hold;
Through his dark jaws the purple ocean
Ran with a swift and restless motion,

And the roar that heralded on its track
Seemed like the burst of a cataract.
Twice for each was the fountain filled—
Twice by each was the red flood swilled;
The Monk is as straight as a poplar tree,—
Gog is as giddy as Gog may be!

"Now try we a buffet!" exclaimed the Knight,
And rose collected in his might,
Crossing his arms, and clenching his hand,
And fixing his feet on their firmest stand.
The Giant struck a terrible stroke,
But it lighted on the forest-oak;
And bough and branch of the ancient tree
Shook, as he smote it, wondrously:
His gauntleted hand the Warrior tried;
Full it fell on the Giant's side;
He sank to earth with a hideous shock,
Like the ruin of a crumbling rock;
And that quivering mass was senseless laid
In the pit its sudden fall had made.

That stranger Knight hath gone to the tree
To set the trembling Captive free;
Thrice hath he smitten with might and main,
And burst the lock, and shivered the chain;
But the knotty trunk, as the warrior strove,
Wrenched from his hand the iron glove,
And they saw the gem on his finger's ring,
And they bent the knee to England's King.

"Up! up!" he said, "for the sun hath past
The shadows of night are falling fast,
And still the wedding shall be to-day,
And a King shall give the bride away!"

The Abbey-bells are ringing
With a merry, merry tone;
And the happy boors are singing
With a music all their own;
Joy came in the Morning, and fled at Noon;
But he smiles again by the light of the Moon;
That Minstrel-Boy, the young Le Fraile,
Hath wedded the Lily of Nithys-dale!

(Eton, 1821.)

THE TROUBADOUR.

Le Troubadour
Brulant d'amour.

French Ballad.

CANTO I.

In sooth it was a glorious day
For vassal and for lord,
When Cœur de Lion had the sway
In battle and at board.
He was indeed a royal one,
A Prince of Paladins;
Hero of triumph and of tun,
Of noisy fray and noisy fun,
Broad shoulders and broad grins:
You might have looked from east to west,
And then from north to south,
And never found an ampler breast,
Never an ampler mouth,
A softer tone for lady's ear,
A daintier lip for syrup,
Or a ruder grasp for axe and spear,
Or a firmer foot in stirrup.

A ponderous thing was Richard's can,
  And so was Richard's boot,
And Saracens and liquor ran,
  Where'er he set his foot.
So fiddling here, and fighting there,
  And murdering time and tune,
With sturdy limb, and listless air,
And gauntleted hand, and jeweled hair,
  Half monarch, half buffoon,
He turned away from feast to fray,
  From quarreling to quaffing,
So great in prowess and in pranks,
So fierce and funny in the ranks,
That Saladin the Soldan said,
Whene'er that mad-cap Richard led,
Alla! he held his breath for dread,
  And burst his sides for laughing!

At court, the humor of a king
Is always voted "quite the thing;"
Morals and cloaks are loose or laced
According to the Sovereign's taste,
And belles and banquets both are drest
Just as his majesty thinks best.
Of course in that delightful age,
  When Richard ruled the roast,
Cracking of craniums was the rage,
  And beauty was the toast.
Ay! all was laugh, and life, and love;
  And lips and shrines were kiss'd;
And vows were ventured in the grove,
  And lances in the list;

And boys roamed out in sunny weather
To weave a wreath and rhyme together:
While dames, in silence, and in satin,
Lay listening to the soft French-Latin,
And flung their sashes and their sighs
From odor-breathing balconies.

From those bright days of love and glory,
I take the hero of my story.
A wandering Troubadour was he;
He bore a name of high degree,
And learned betimes to slay and sue,
As knights of high degree should do.
While vigor nerved his buoyant arm,
And youth was his to cheat and charm,
Being immensely fond of dancing,
And somewhat given to romancing,
He roamed about through towers and towns,
Apostrophizing smiles and frowns,
Singing sweet staves to beads and bonnets,
And dying, day by day, in sonnets.
Flippant and fair, and fool enough,
And careless where he met rebuff,
Poco-curante in all cases
Of furious foes, or pretty faces,
With laughing lip, and jocund eye,
And studied tear, and practised sigh,
And ready sword, and ready verse,
And store of ducats in his purse,
He sinned few crimes, loved many times,
And wrote a hundred thousand rhymes!

Summers twice eight had passed away,
Since in his nurse's arms he lay,
  A rosy, roaring child,
While all around was noisy mirth,
And logs blazed up upon the hearth,
  And bonfires on the wild;
And vassals drank the brown bowl dry,
And cousins knew "the mother's eye,"
And wrinkled crones spoke prophecy,
  And his brave father smiled.
Summers twice eight had passed away;
His sire's thin locks grew very gray;
He lost his song, and then his shout,
And seldom saw his bottle out.
Then all the menials straight began
To sorrow for "the poor old man,"
Took thought about his shirts and shoe-ties
And pestered him with loves and duties:
Young Roger laced a crimson row
Of cushions on his saddle-bow;
Red Wyke at Christmas mingled up
More sugar in the wassail-cup;
Fair Margaret laid finer sheets;
Fat Catharine served richer sweets;
And all, from scullion up to squire,
Who stirred his cup or kitchen fire,
Seemed by their doings to determine
The knight should ne'er be food for vermin.
All would not do; the knight grew thinner,
And loved his bed, and loathed his dinner;

And when he muttered—"Becket—beast,
Bring me the posset—and a priest,"
Becket looked grave, and said "good lack!"
And went to ask the price of black.

Masses and medicines both were bought,
Masses and medicines both were naught;
  Sir Hubert's race was run;
As best beseemed a warrior tall,
He died within his ancient hall:
And he was blest by Father Paul,
  And buried by his son.
'Twere long to tell the motley gear,
That waited on Sir Hubert's bier;
  For twenty good miles round,
Maiden and matron, knave and knight,
All rode or ran to see the sight;
  Yeomen with horse and hound,
Gossips in grief and grogram clad,
Young warriors galloping like mad,
Priors and peddlers, pigs and pyxes,
Cooks, choristers, and crucifixes,
Wild urchins cutting jokes and capers,
And taper shapes, and shapely tapers.
The mighty barons of the land
Brought pain in heart, and four-in-hand;
And village maids, with looks of woe,
Turned out their mourning, and their toe.
The bell was rung, the hymn was sung,
On the oak chest the dust was flung;

And then, beneath the chapel-stones,
With a gilt 'scutcheon o'er his bones,
Escaped from feather-beds and fidget,
Sir Hubert slept with Lady Bridget.

The mob departed: cold and cloud
Shed on the vault their icy shroud,
  And night came dark and dreary
But there young Vidal lingered still,
And kept his fast and wept his fill,
Though the wind in the chapel was very chill,
  And Vidal very weary.
Low moaned the bell; the torch-light fell
  In fitful and faint flashes;
And he lay on the stones, where his father's bones
  Were mouldering now to ashes;
And vowed to be, on earth and sea,
  Whatever stars shone o'er him,
A trusty knight, in love and fight,
  As his father had been before him.
Then in the silence of the night
Passionate grief was his delight;
He thought of all the brave and fair
Who slept their shadowy slumber there;
And that sweet dotage held him long,
Ere sorrow found her voice in song.

It was an ancient thing; a song
  His heart had sung in other years,
When boyhood had its idle throng
  Of guiltless smiles, and guileless tears;

But never had its music seemed
  So sweet to him, as when to-night
All lorn and lone, he kneeled and dreamed,
  Before the taper's holy light,
Of many and mysterious things,
His cradle's early visitings,
The melancholy tones, that blest
The pillow of his sinless rest,
The melody, whose magic numbers
Broke in by snatches on his slumbers,
When earth appeared so brightly dim,
And all was bliss, and all for him,
And every sight and every sound
Had heaven's own day-light flowing round.

"My mother's grave, my mother's grave!
  Oh! dreamless is her slumber there,
And drowsily the banners wave
  O'er her that was so chaste and fair;
Yea! love is dead, and memory faded!
  But when the dew is on the brake,
    And silence sleeps on earth and sea,
  And mourners weep, and ghosts awake,
    Oh! then she cometh back to me,
In her cold beauty darkly shaded!

"I cannot guess her face or form;
  But what to me is form or face?
I do not ask the weary worm
  To give me back each buried grace

Of glistening eyes, or trailing tresses!
I only feel that she is here,
And that we meet, and that we part;
And that I drink within mine ear,
And that I clasp around my heart,
Her sweet still voice, and soft caresses!

"Not in the waking thought by day,
Not in the sightless dream by night,
Do the mild tones and glances play,
Of her who was my cradle's light!
But in some twilight of calm weather,
She glides, by fancy dimly wrought,
A glittering cloud, a darkling beam,
With all the quiet of a thought,
And all the passion of a dream,
Linked in a golden spell together!"

Oh! Vidal's very soul did weep
Whene'er that music, like a charm,
Brought back from their unlistening sleep
The kissing lip and clasping arm.
But quiet tears are worth, to some,
The richest smiles in Christendom;
And Vidal, though in folly's ring
He seemed so weak and wild a thing,
Had yet an hour, when none were by,
For reason's thought, and passion's sigh.
And knew and felt, in heart and brain,
The Paradise of buried pain!

And Vidal rose at break of day,
  And found his heart unbroken;
And told his beads, and went away,
  On a steed he had bespoken;
His bonnet he drew his eyelids o'er,
  For tears were like to blind him;
And he spurred Sir Guy o'er mount and moor,
With a long dull journey all before,
  And a short gay squire behind him.
And the neighborhood much marvel had;
  And all who saw did say,
The weather and the roads were bad,
And either Vidal had run mad,
  Or Guy had run away!
Oh! when a cheek is to be dried,
  All pharmacy is folly;
And Vidal knew, for he had tried,
There's nothing like a rattling ride
  For curing melancholy!
Three days he rode all mad and mute;
  And when the sun did pass,
Three nights he supp'd upon dry fruit,
  And slept upon wet grass.
Beneath an oak, whose hundred years
Had formed fit shade for talk or tears,
On the fourth day he lay at noon,
And put his gilt guitar in tune;
  When suddenly swept by,
In gold and silver all arrayed,
A most resplendent cavalcade;

Baron and Beauty, Knave and Knight,
And lips of love, and eyes of light,
All blended dazzlingly.
Ah! all the world that day came out,
With horse and horn, and song and shout;
And belles and bouquets gayly bloomed,
And all were proud, and all perfumed,
And gallants, as the humor rose,
Talked any nonsense that they chose,
And damsels gave the reins for fun
Alike to palfrey and to pun.
It chanced no lady had been thrown,
No heir had cracked his collar-bone,
So pleasure laughed on every cheek,
And naught, save saddles, dreamed of pique.
And brightest of that brilliant train,
With jeweled bit, and gilded rein,
And pommel clothed in gorgeous netting,
And courser daintily curvetting,
Girt round with gallant Cavaliers,
Some deep in love, and some in years,
Half exquisites and half absurds,
All babbling of their beasts and birds,
Quite tired of trumpeting and talking,
The Baroness returned from hawking.

The lady halted; well she might;
For Vidal was so fair,
You would have thought some god of light
Had walked to take the air;

Bare were both his delicate hands,
  And the hue on his cheek was high,
As woman's when she understands
  Her first fond lover's sigh;
And desolate very, and very dumb,
  And rolling his eyes of blue,
And rubbing his forehead, and biting his thumb,
  As lyrists and lovers do.
Like Queen Titania's darling pet,
  Or Oberon's wickedest elf,
He lay beside a rivulet,
  And looked beside himself;
And belles full blown, and beaux full drest,
  Stood there with smirk and smile,
And many a finger, and many a jest,
  Were pointed all the while.

Then Vidal came, and bent his knees
  Before the lady there,
And raised his bonnet, that the breeze
  Might trifle with his hair;
And said, he was a nameless youth,
Had learned betimes to tell the truth,
Could greet a friend, and grasp a foe,
Could take a jest, and give a blow,
Had no idea of false pretences,
Had lost his father, and his senses,
Was travelling over land and sea,
Armed with guitar and gallantry;
And if her will found aught of pleasure
In trifling soul, and tinkling measure,

He prayed that she would call her own
His every thought, and every tone.

"Bonne grace, good Mary, and sweet St. John!"
That haughty dame did say;
"A goodly quarry I have won,
In this our sport to-day!
A precious page is this of mine,
To carve my meat and pour my wine,
To loose my greyhound's ringing chain,
And hold my palfrey's gaudy rein,
And tell strange tales of moody sprites,
Around the hearth, on winter nights.
Marry! a wilful look, and wild!
But we shall tame the wayward child,
And dress his roving locks demurely,
And tie his jesses on securely."

She took from out her garment's fold
A dazzling gaud of twisted gold;
She raised him from his knee;
The diamond cross she gravely kiss'd,
And twined the links around his wrist
With such fine witchery,
That there he kneeled, and met her glance
In silence and a moveless trance,
And saw no sight, and heard no sound,
And knew himself more firmly bound
Than if a hundred weight of steel
Had fettered him from head to heel!

And from that moment Vidal gave
His childish fancy up,
Became her most peculiar slave,
And wore her scarf, and whipped her knave,
And filled her silver cup.
She was a widow: on this earth
It seemed her only task was mirth;
She had no nerves and no sensations,
No troubling friends nor poor relations;
No gnawing grief to feel a care for,
No living soul to breathe a prayer for.
Ten years ago her lord and master
Had chanced upon a sad disaster;
One night his servants found him lying
Speechless or senseless, dead or dying,
With shivered sword and dabbled crest,
And a small poniard in his breast,
And nothing further to supply
The slightest hint of how or why.
As usual, in such horrid cases,
The men made oath, the maids made faces;
All thought it most immensely funny
The murderer should have left the money,
And showed suspicions in dumb crambo,
And buried him with fear and flambeau.

Clotilda shrieked and swooned, of course,
Grew very ill, and very hoarse,
Put on a veil, put off a rout,
Turned all her cooks and courtiers out,

And lived two years on water-gruel,
And drank no wine, and used no fuel.
At last, when all the world had seen
How very virtuous she had been,
She left her chamber, dried her tears,
Kept open house for Cavaliers,
New furnished all the cob-webbed rooms,
And burned a fortune in perfumes.
She had seen six-and-thirty springs,
And still her blood's warm wanderings
Told tales in every throbbing vein
Of youth's high hope, and passion's reign,
And dreams from which that lady's heart
Had parted, or had seemed to part.
She had no wiles from cunning France,
Too cold to sing, too tall to dance;
But yet, where'er her footsteps went,
She was the Queen of Merriment:
She called the quickest at the table,
For Courcy's song, or Comine's fable,
Bade Barons quarrel for her glove,
And talked with Squires of ladie-love,
And hawked and hunted in all weathers,
And stood six feet—including feathers.

Her suitors, men of swords and banners,
Were very guarded in their manners,
And e'en when heated by the jorum
Knew the strict limits of decorum.
Well had Clotilda learned the glance
That checks a lover's first advance;

That brow to her was given
That chills presumption in its birth,
And mars the madness of our mirth,
And wakes the reptile of the earth
From the vision he hath of Heaven.
And yet for Vidal she could find
No word or look that was not kind,
With him she walked in shine or shower,
And quite forgot the dinner hour,
And gazed upon him, till he smiled,
As doth a mother on a child.
Oh! when was dream so purely dreamed!
A mother and a child they seemed:
In warmer guise he loved her not;—
And if, beneath the stars and moon,
He lingered in some lonely spot
To play her fond and favorite tune,
And if he fed her petted mare,
And made acquaintance with her bear,
And kissed her hand whene'er she gave it
And kneeled him down, sometimes, to crave it,
'Twas partly pride, and partly jest,
And partly 'twas a boyish whim,
And that he liked to see the rest
Look angrily on her and him.
And that—in short he was a boy,
And doted on his last new toy.

It chanced that late, one summer's gloaming,
The lady and the youth were roaming,

In converse close of those and these,
Beneath a long arcade of trees;
Tall trunks stood up on left and right,
Like columns in the gloom of night,
Breezeless and voiceless; and on high,
  Where those eternal pillars ended,
  The silent boughs so closely blended
Their mirk, unstirring majesty,
That superstition well might run,
To wander there from twelve to one,
And call strange shapes from heaven or hell,
Of cowl and candle, book and bell,
And kneel as in the vaulted aisle
Of some time-honored Gothic pile,
To pay her weary worship there
Of counted beads, and pattered prayer.

Clotilda had, for once, the vapors,
And when the stars lit up their tapers,
She said that she was very weary—
She liked the place, it was so dreary—
The dew was down on grass and flower,
  'Twas very wet—'twas very wrong—
But she must rest for half an hour,
  And listen to another song.

Then many a tale did Vidal tell
Of warrior's spear, and wizard's spell;
How that Sir Brian le Bleu had been
Cup-bearer to a fairy queen;

And how that a hundred years did pass,
And left his brow as smooth as glass;
Time on his form marked no decay,
He stole not a single charm away,
He could not blight
That eye of light,
Nor turn those raven ringlets gray.

But Brian's love for a mortal maid,
Was written and read in a magic sign,
When Brian slipped on the moonlight glade,
And spilled the fairy's odorous wine;
And she dipped her fingers in the can,
And sprinkled him with seven sprinkles,
And he went from her presence a weary man,
A withering lump of rheum and wrinkles.

And how that Satan made a bond
With Armonell of Trebizond—
A bond that was written at first in tears,
And torn at last in laughter—
To be his slave for a thousand years,
And his sovereign ever after.

And oh! those years, they fleeted fast,
And a single year remained at last,
A year for crouching and for crying,
Between his frolic and his frying.

"Toil yet another toil," quoth he,
"Or else thy prey I will not be,

Come hither, come hither, servant mine,
And call me back
The faded track
Of years nine hundred and ninety-nine!"
And Satan hied to his home again
On the wings of a blasting hurricane,
And left old Armonell to die,
And sleep in the odor of sanctity.

In mockery of the Minstrel's skill
The Lady's brow grew darker still;
She trembled as she lay,
And o'er her face, like fitful flame,
The feverish color went and came,
And, in the pauses of the tune,
Her black eyes stared upon the moon
With an unearthly ray.

"Good Vidal,"—as she spoke she leant
So wildly o'er the instrument
That wondering Vidal started back,
For fear the strings should go to wrack—
"Good Vidal, I have read and heard
Of many a haunted heath and dell,
Where potency of wand or word,
Or chanted rhyme, or written spell,
Hath burst, in such an hour as this,
The cerements of the rotting tomb,
And waked from wo, or torn from bliss,
The heritors of chill and gloom,

Until they walked upon the earth,
Unshrouded, in a ghastly mirth,
And frightened men with soundless cries,
And hueless cheeks, and rayless eyes.
Such power there is!—if such be thine,
Why, make to-night that sound or sign;
And while the vapory sky looks mirk
In horror at our midnight work,
We two will sit on two green knolls,
And jest with unembodied souls,
And mock at every moody sprite
That wanders from his bed to-night."

The boy jumped up in vast surprise,
And rubbed his forehead and his eyes,
And quite unable to reflect,
Made answer much to this effect:
"Lady!—the saints befriend a sinner!
Lady!—she drank too much at dinner!
I know a rhyme, and—ghosts forsooth!
I used to sing it in my youth;
'Twas taught me—curse my foolish vanity!
By an old wizard—stark insanity!
Who came from Tunis—'tis the hock!
At a great age and—twelve o'clock!
He wore—oh, Lord!—a painted girdle,
For which they burnt him on a hurdle;
He had a charm, but—what the deuce!
It wasn't of the slightest use;
There's not a single ghost that cares
For—mercy on me! how she stares!"

And then again he sate him down,
For fiercer fell Clotilda's frown,
And played, abominably ill,
And horribly against his will.

"Spirits, that walk and wail to-night,
I feel, I feel that ye are near;
There is a mist upon my sight,
There is a murmur in mine ear.
And a dark, dark dread
Of the lonely dead,
Creeps through the whispering atmosphere!

"Ye hover o'er the hoary trees,
And the old oaks stand bereft and bare;
Ye hover o'er the moonlight seas,
And the tall masts rot in the poisoned air;
Ye gaze on the gate
Of earthly state,
And the ban-dog shivers in silence there.

"Come hither to me upon your cloud,
And tell me of your bliss or pain,
And let me see your shadowy shroud,
And colorless lip, and bloodless vein;
Where do ye dwell,
In heaven or hell,
And why do ye wander on earth again?

"Tell to me where and how ye died,
Fell ye in darkness, or fell ye in day,
On lorn hill-side, or roaring tide,
In gorgeous feast, or rushing fray?
By bowl or blow,
From friend or foe,
Hurried your angry souls away?

"Mute ye come, and mute ye pass,
Your tale untold, your shrift unshriven;
But ye have blighted the pale grass,
And scared the ghastly stars from heaven;
And guilt hath known
Your voiceless moan,
And felt that the blood is unforgiven!"

He paused; for silently and slow
The lady left his side;
It seemed her blood had ceased to flow,
For her cheek was as white as the morning snow,
And the light of her eyes had died.
She gazed upon some form of fright—
But it was not seen of Vidal's sight;
She drank some sound of hate or fear—
But it was not heard of Vidal's ear;
"Look! look!" she said; and Vidal spoke—
"Why! zounds! it's nothing but an oak!"

"Valence!" she muttered, "I will rise;
Ay! turn not those dead orbs on mine;
Fearless to-night are these worn eyes,
And nerveless is that arm of thine.

Thrice hast thou fleeted o'er my path ;
  And I would hear thy dull lips say,
Is it in sorrow, or in wrath,
  That thou dost haunt my lonely way ?
Ay ! frown not ! heaven may blast me now,
  In this dark hour, in this cold spot ;
And then—I can but be as thou,
  And hate thee still, and fear thee not !"
She strode two steps, and stretched her hand,
In attitude of stern command ;
The tremor of her voice and tread
Had more of passion than of dread,
The net had parted from her hair,
The locks fell down in the powerless air,
Her frame with strange convulsion rocked—
And Vidal was intensely shocked.
The lady drew a long low sigh,
As if some voice had made reply,
Though Vidal could not catch a word,
And thought it horribly absurd.
"Remember it ?—avenging power !
  I ask no word, I need no sign,
To teach me of that withering hour,
  That linked this wasted hand in thine !
He was not there !—I deemed him slain—
And thine the guilt—and mine the pain !
There are memorials of that day
Which time shall never blot away,
Unheeded prayer, unpardoned sin,
And smiles without, and flames within,

And broken heart, and ruined fame
And glutted hate, and dreaded shame,
And late remorse, and dreams, and fears,
And bitter and enduring tears!"

She listened there another space,
And stirred no feature of her face,
Though big drops, ere she spoke again,
Fell from her clammy brow like rain:
At last she glanced a wilder stare,
And stamped her foot, and tore her hair.
"False fiend! thou liest, thou hast lied!
  He was, what thou couldst never be—
In anguish true, in danger tried—
  Their friend to all—my god to me!
He loved—as thou couldst never love—
  Long years—and not, till then, in guilt;
Nay! point not to the wailing grove,
  I know by whom the blood was spilt,
I saw the tomb, and heard the knell,
  And life to me was lorn and blighted,
He died—and vengeance watches well!
  He died—and thou wert well requited!"

Again she listened:—full five score
You might have counted duly o'er—
And then she laughed; so fierce and shrill
That laughter echoed o'er the hill,
That Vidal deemed the very ground
Did shake at its unearthly sound.

"I do not tremble! be it so!—
Or here or there! in bliss or wo!—
Yea! let it be! and we will meet,
Where never——" and at Vidal's feet
She sank, as senseless and as cold
As if her death were two days old;
And Vidal, who an hour before
Had voted it a horrid bore,
His silken sash with speed unlaced,
And bound it round her neck and waist,
And bore her to her castle-gate,
And never stopped to rest or bait,
Speeding as swiftly on his track
As if nine fiends were at his back.

Then rose from fifty furious lungs
A Babel of discordant tongues:
"Jesu! the Baroness is dead!—
Shouldn't her Ladyship be bled?—
Her fingers are as cold as stone!—
And look how white her lips are grown!
A dreadful thing for all who love her!
'Tis ten to one she won't recover!—
Ten?—did you ever, Mrs. Anne?
Ten rogues against one honest man!—
How master Vidal must have fought!
It's what I never should have thought;
He seems the sickliest thing alive;—
They say he killed and wounded five!—
Is master Vidal killed and wounded?
I trust the story is unfounded!—

I saw him on his legs just now,—
What! sawed his legs off? well, I vow—
Peace, babbler, peace! you see you've shocked her!
Help! ho!—cold water for the Doctor!
Her eyes are open!—how they blink!
Why, Doctor, do you really think,——
My Lord, we never think at all;
I'll trouble you to clear the Hall,
And check all tendency to riot,
And keep the Castle very quiet;
Let none but little Bertha stay;
And—try to keep the Friar away!"
Poor Vidal, who, amid the rout,
Had crept in cautious silence out,
Reeled to his chamber in the staggers,
And thought of home, and dreamed of daggers.

Day dawned: the Baroness was able
To beam upon the breakfast table,
As well as could be well expected,
Before the guests were half collected.
'A fainting fit;—a thing of course;—
In sooth it might have ended worse;
Exceedingly obliged to Vidal;—
Pray, had the groom repaired her bridle?
She walked too late;—it was a warning;
And—who was for the chase this morning?"

Days past, and weeks: Clotilda's mien
Was gay as it before had been,

And only once or twice her glance
Fell darkly on his countenance,
And gazed into his eyes of blue,
As if she read his young heart through:
At length she mildly hinted—"Surely
Vidal was looking very poorly—
He never talked—had parted quite
With spirits, and with appetite—
She thought he wanted change of air,
It was a shame to keep him there—
She had remarked the change with sorrow,
And——well, he should set out to-morrow."

The morrow came, 't was glorious weather,
And all the household flocked together
To hold his stirrup and his rein,
And say, "Heaven speed!" with might and main.
Clotilda only said "Farewell!"
  And gave her hand to kiss and clasp;
He thought it trembled, as it fell
  In silence from his lip and grasp,
And yet upon her cheek and brow
There dwelt no flush of passion now;
Only the kind regret was there
Which severed friends at parting wear,
And the sad smile and glistening eye
Seemed naught to shun, and naught defy.

"Farewell!" she said, and so departed;
And Vidal from his reverie started,
And blessed his soul, and cleared his throat,
And crossed his forehead—and the moat.

CANTO II.

All milliners who start from bed
To gaze upon a coat of red,
  Or listen to a drum,
Know very well the Paphian Queen
Was never yet at Paphos seen,
  That Cupid's all a hum,
That minstrels forge confounded lies,
About the Deities and skies,
That torches all go out sometimes,
That flowers all fade except in rhymes,
That maids are seldom shot with arrows
And coaches never drawn by sparrows.

And yet, fair cousin, do not deem
  That all is false which poets tell
Of Passion's first and dearest dream,
  Of haunted spot, and silent spell,
Of long low musing, such as suits
  The terrace on your own dark hill,
Of whispers which are sweet as lutes,
  And silence which is sweeter still;
Believe, believe—for May shall pass,
  And summer sun and winter shower
Shall dim the freshness of the grass,
  And mar the fragrance of the flower—
Believe it all, whate'er you hear
  Of plighted vow, and treasured token,
And hues which only once appear,
  And words which only once are spoken,

And prayers whose natural voice is song,
  And schemes that die in wild endeavor.
And tears so pleasant, you will long
  To weep such pleasant tears for ever.
Believe it all, believe it all!
  Oh! Virtue's frown is all divine;
And Folly hides his happy thrall
  In sneers as cold and false as mine;
And Reason prates of wrong and right,
  And marvels hearts can break or bleed,
And flings on all that's warm and bright
  The winter of his icy creed;
But when the soul has ceased to glow,
  And years and cares are coming fast,
There's nothing like young love! no, no!
  There's nothing like young love at last!

The Convent of St. Ursula
Has been in a marvellous fright to-day;
The nuns are all in a terrible pother
Scolding and screaming at one another;
Two or three pale, and two or three red,
Two or three frightened to death in bed,
Two or three waging a wordy war
With the wide-eared Saints of the Calendar.
Beads and lies have both been told,
Tempers are hot, and dishes are cold;
Celandine rends her last new veil,
Leonore babbles of horns and tail;
Celandine proses of songs and slips,
Violette blushes and bites her lips:

Oh! what is the matter, the matter to-day,
With the Convent of St. Ursula?
But the Abbess has made the chiefest din,
  And cried the loudest cry;
She has pinned her cap with a crooked pin,
And talked of Satan and of sin,
  And set her coif awry;
And she can never quiet be;
  But ever since the Matins,
In gallery and scullery,
And kitchen and refectory,
  She tramps it in her pattens;
Oh! what is the matter, the matter to-day
With the Abbess of St. Ursula?

Thrice in the silence of eventime
A desperate foot has dared to climb
  Over the Convent gate;
Thrice a venturous voice and lute
Have dared to wake their amorous suit,
Among the Convent flowers and fruit,
  Abominably late:
And thrice, the beldames know it well,
From out the lattice of her cell,
To listen to that murmured measure
Of life, and love, and hope, and pleasure,
With throbbing heart and eyelid wet,
Hath leaned the novice Violette;
And oh! you may tell from her mournful gaze,
Her vision hath been of those dear days,

When happily o'er the quiet lawn,
  Bright with the dew's most heavenly sprinkles,
She scared the pheasant, and chased the fawn,
  Till a smile came o'er her father's wrinkles,
Or stood beside that water fair,
  Where moonlight slept with a ray so tender,
That every star which glistened there,
  Glistened, she thought, with a double splendor,
And oh! she loved the ripples' play,
  As to her feet the truant rovers
Wandered and went with a laugh away,
  Kissing but once, like wayward lovers.
And oh! she loved the night-wind's moan,
  And the dreary watch-dog's lonely yelling,
And the sentinel's unchanging tone,
  And the chapel chime so sadly knelling,
And the echoes from the Castle hall,
  Of circling song and noisy gladness,
And, in some silent interval,
  The nightingale's deep voice of sadness.
Alas! there comes a winter bleak
  On the lightest joy, and the loveliest flower:
And the smiles have faded on Violette's cheek,
  And the roses have withered in Violette's bower,
But now by the beautiful turf and tide
  Poor Violette's heart in silence lingers;
And the thrilling tears of memory glide
  Thro' the trembling veil and the quivering fingers.
Yet not for these, for these alone,
  That innocent heart beats high to-day;

And not for these the stifled moan
Is breathed in such thick passionate tone,
  That not the lips appear to pray.
But you may deem those murmurs start
Forth from the life-strings of the heart,
So wild and strange is that long sigh,
So full of bliss and agony!

She thinks of him, the lovely boy,
Sweet Vidal, with his face of joy—
The careless mate of all the glee
That shone upon her infancy—
The baby-lover, who had been
The sceptred King, where she was Queen,
On Childhood's dream-encircled strand,
The undisputed Fairy-land!
She thinks of him, she thinks of him,
The lord of every wicked whim,
Who dared Sir Prinsamour to battle,
And drove away De Clifford's cattle,
And sang an Ave at the feast,
And made wry faces at the Priest,
And ducked the Duchess in the sea,
And tore Sir Roland's pedigree.

She thinks of him—the forehead fair,
The ruddy lip, and glossy hair—
The mountains, where they roved together,
In life's most bright and witching weather—
The wreck they watched upon the coast—
The ruin where they saw the ghost—

The fairy tale he loved to tell—
The serenade he sang so well;
And then she turns and sees again
The naked wall, and grated pane,
And frequent winks and frequent frowns,
And 'broidered books, and 'broidered gowns,
And plaster saints and plaster patrons,
And three impracticable matrons.

She was a very pretty Nun:
Sad, delicate, and five feet one;
Her face was oval, and her eye
Looked like the Heaven in Italy,
Serenely blue, and softly bright,
Made up of languish and of light!
And her neck, except where the locks of brown,
Like a sweet summer mist, fell droopingly down,
Was as chill and as white as the snow, ere the earth
Has sullied the hue of its heavenly birth;
And through the blue veins you might see
The pure blood wander silently,
Like noiseless eddies, that far below
In the glistening depths of a calm lake flow:
Her cold hands on her bosom lay;
And her ivory crucifix, cold as they,
Was clasped in a fearful and fond caress,
As if she shrank from its holiness,
And felt that hers was the only guilt
For which no healing blood was spilt:
And tears were bursting all the while;
Yet now and then a vacant smile

Over her lips would come and go—
A very mockery of wo—
A brief, wan smile—a piteous token
Of a warm love crush'd, and a young heart broken!

"Marry come up!" said Celandine,
  Whose nose was ruby red,
"From venomous cates and wicked wine
  A deadly sin is bred.
Darkness and anti-phlogistic diet,
These will keep the pulses quiet;
Silence and solitude, bread and water—
So must we cure our erring daughter!"
I have dined at an Alderman's board,
I have drunk with a German lord,
But richer was Celandine's own paté
Than Sir William's soup on Christmas day,
And sweeter the flavor of Celandine's flask
Than the loveliest cup from a Rhenish cask!

"Saints keep us!" said old Winifrede,
  "Saints keep and cure us all!
And let us hie to our book and bead,
  Or sure the skies will fall!
Is she a Heathen or is she a Hindoo,
To talk with a silly boy out of the window?
Was ever such profaneness seen?
Pert minx!—and only just sixteen!"
I have talked with a fop who has fought twelve duels,
Six for an heiress, and six for her jewels;

I have prosed with a reckless bard, who rehearses
Every day a thousand verses;
But oh! more marvellous twenty times
Than the bully's lies, or the blockhead's rhymes,
Were the scurrilous tales, which Scandal told
Of Winifrede's loves in the days of old!

The Abbess lifted up her eye,
And laid her rosary down,
And sigh'd a melancholy sigh,
And frown'd an angry frown.
"There's a cell in the dark cold ground,
Where sinful passions wither:
Vapory dews lie damp around,
And merriment of sight or sound
Can work no passage thither:
Other scene is there, I trow,
Than suits a love-sick maiden's vow;
For a death-watch makes a weary tune,
And a glimmering lamp is a joyless moon,
And a couch of stone is a dismal rest,
And an aching heart is a bitter guest!
Maiden of the bosom light,
There shall thy dwelling be to-night;
Mourn and meditate, fast and pray,
And drive the evil one away.
Axe and cord were fitter doom,
Desolate grave and mouldering tomb;
But the merciful faith that speaks the sentence,
Joys in the dawn of a soul's repentance,

And the eyes may shed sweet tears for them,
Whom the hands chastise, and the lips condemn!"
I have set my foot on the hallowed spot,
Where the dungeon of trampled France is not;
I have heard men talk of Mr. Peel;
I have seen men walk on the Brixton wheel;
And 'twere better to feed on frogs and fears,
Guarded by griefs and grenadiers,
And 'twere better to tread all day and night,
With a rogue on the left, and a rogue on the right,
Than lend our persons or our purses
To that old lady's tender mercies!

"Ay! work your will!" the young girl said;
And as she spoke she raised her head,
And for a moment turned aside,
To check the tear she could not hide;——
'Ay! work your will! —I know you all,
Your holy aims and pious arts,
And how you love to fling a pall
On fading joys, and blighted hearts;
And if these quivering lips could tell
The story of our bliss and wo,
And how we loved—Oh! loved, as well
As ever mortals loved below—
And how in purity and truth
The flower of early joy was nurst,
Till sadness nipp'd its blushing youth,
And holy mummery call'd it curst—

You would but watch my sobs and sighs,
  With shaking head, and silent sneers,
And deck with smiles those soulless eyes,
  When mine should swell with bitter tears!
But work your will! Oh! life and limb
  May wither in that house of dread,
Where horrid shapes and shadows dim
  Walk nightly round the slumberer's head;
The sight may sink, the tongue may fail,
  The shuddering spirit long for day,
And fear may make these features pale,
  And turn these boasted ringlets gray;
But not for this, oh! not for this,
  The heart will lose its dream of gladness;
And the fond thought of that last kiss
  Will live in torture—yea! in madness!
And look! I will not fear or feel
  The all your hate may dare or do;
And, if I ever pray and kneel,
  I will not kneel and pray to you!"

If you had seen that tender cheek,
  Those eyes of melting blue,
You would not have thought in a thing so weak,
  Such a fiery spirit grew.
But the trees which summer's breezes shake,
  Are shivered in winter's gale;
And a meek girl's heart will bear to break,
  When a proud man's truth would fail.

Never a word she uttered more;
 They have led her down the stair,
And left her on the dungeon floor,
 To find repentance there;
And naught have they set beside her bed,
 Within that chamber dull,
But a lonely lamp, and a loaf of bread,
 A rosary and skull.
The breast is bold that grows not cold,
 With a strong convulsive twinge,
As the slow door creeps to its sullen hold,
 Upon its mouldering hinge.
That door was made by the cunning hand
Of an artist from a foreign land;
Human skill and heavenly thunder
Shall not win its wards asunder.
The chain is fix'd, and the bolt is fast,
And the kind old Abbess lingers last,
To mutter a prayer on her bended knee,
And clasp to her girdle the iron key.

But then, oh then began to run
Horrible whispers from nun to nun:
"Sister Amelia,"—"Sister Anne,"
"Do tell us how it all began;"
"The youth was a handsome youth, that's certain,
For Bertha peeped from behind the curtain:"
"As sure as I have human eyes,
It was the devil in disguise;

His hair hanging down like threads of wire—
And his mouth breathing smoke, like a haystack
on fire—
And the ground beneath his footstep rocking,"—
"Lord! Isabel, how very shocking!"
"Poor Violette! she was so merry;
I'm very sorry for her!—very!"
"Well! it was worth a silver tester,
To see how she frown'd when the Abbess bless'd
her;"—
"Was Father Anselm there to shrive?
For I'm sure she'll never come out alive!"
"Dear Elgitha, don't frighten us so!"
"It's just a hundred years ago,
Since Father Peter was put in the cell
For forgetting to ring the vesper bell;
Let us keep ourselves from mortal sin!
He went not out as he went in!"
"No! and he lives there still, they say,
In his cloak of black, and his cowl of gray,
Weeping, and wailing, and walking about,
With an endless grief, and an endless gout,
And wiping his eyes with a kerchief of lawn,
And ringing his bell from dusk to dawn!"
"Let us pray to be saved from love and spectres!"—
"From the haunted cell!"—"And the abbess's lec-
tures!"
The garish sun has gone away,
And taken with him the toils of day;
Foul ambition's hollow schemes,
Busy labor's golden dreams,

Angry strife, and cold debate,
Plodding care, and plotting hate.
But in the nunnery sleep is fled
From many a vigilant hand and head;
A watch is set of friars tall,
Jerome and Joseph, and Peter and Paul;
And the chattering girls are all lock'd up;
And the wrinkled old abbess is gone to sup
On mushrooms and sweet muscadel,
In the fallen one's deserted cell.

And now 't is love's most lovely hour,
  And silence sits on earth and sky,
And moonlight flings on turf and tower
  A spell of deeper witchery;
And in the stillness and the shade
All things and colors seem to fade:
And the garden queen, the blushing rose,
Has bowed her head in a soft repose;
And weary zephyr is gone to rest
In the flow'ry grove he loves the best.
Nothing is heard but the long, long snore,
Solemn and sad, of the watchmen four,
And the voice of the rivulet rippling by,
And the nightingale's evening melody,
And the drowsy wing of the sleepless bat,
And the mew of the gard'ner's tortoise-shell cat.

Dear cousin! a harp like yours has power
Over the soul in every hour;

And after breakfast, when Sir G.
Has been discussing news and tea,
And eulogized his coals and logs,
And told the breeding of his dogs,
And hurl'd anathemas of pith
Against the sect of Adam Smith,
And handed o'er to endless shame
The voters for the sale of game,
'Tis sweet to fly from him and vapors,
And those interminable papers,
And waste an idle hour or two
With dear Rossini, and with you.

But those sweet sounds are doubly sweet,
  In the still nights of June,
When song and silence seem to meet,
  Beneath the quiet moon;
When not a single leaf is stirr'd,
By playful breeze or joyous bird,
And echo shrinks as if afraid
Of the faint murmur she has made.
Oh! then the spirit of music roves,
With a delicate step through the myrtle groves.
And still wherever he flits, he flings
A thousand charms from his purple wings.
And where is that discourteous wight,
Who would not linger through the night
Listening ever, lone and mute,
To the murmur of his mistress' lute,
And courting those bright phantasiès,
Which haunt the dreams of waking eyes?

He came that night, the Troubadour.
While the four fat friars slept secure,
And gazed on the lamp that sweetly glisten'd,
Where he thought his mistress listen'd;
Low and clear the silver note
On the thrill'd air seem'd to float;
Such might be an angel's moan,
Half a whisper, half a tone.

"So glad a life was never, love,
As that which childhood leads,
Before it learns to sever, love,
The roses from the weeds:
When to be very duteous, love,
Is all it has to do;
And every flower is beauteous, love,
And every folly true.

"And you can still remember, love,
The buds, that decked our play,
Though destiny's December, love,
Has whirled those buds away:
And you can smile through tears, love,
And feel a joy in pain,
To think upon those years, love,
You may not see again.

"When we mimick'd the Friar's howls, love,
Cared nothing for his creeds,
Made bonnets of his cowls, love,
And bracelets of his beads;

And gray-beards looked not awful, love,
  And grandames made no din,
And vows were not unlawful, love,
  And kisses were no sin.

"And do you never dream, love,
  Of that enchanted well,
Where under the moon-beam, love,
  The fairies wove their spell?
How oft we saw them greeting, love,
  Beneath the blasted tree,
And heard their pale feet beating, love,
  To their own minstrelsy!

"And do you never think, love,
  Of the shallop, and the wave,
And the willow on the brink, love,
  Over the poacher's grave?
Where always in the dark, love,
  We heard a heavy sigh,
And the dogs were wont to bark, love,
  Whenever they went by?

"Then gayly shone the heaven, love,
  On life's untroubled sea,
And Vidal's heart was given, love,
  In happiness to thee;
The sea is all benighted, love,
  The heaven has ceased to shine;
The heart is seared and blighted, love,
  But still the heart is thine!"

He paused and looked; he paused and sighed;
None appear'd, and none replied:
All was still but the water's wail,
And the tremulous voice of the nightingale,
And the insects buzzing among the briers,
And the nasal note of the four fat friars.

"Oh fly with me! 'tis passion's hour;
The world is gone to sleep;
And nothing wakes in brake or bower,
But those who love and weep:
This is the golden time and weather,
When songs and sighs go out together,
And minstrels pledge the rosy wine
To lutes like this, and lips like thine!

"Oh fly with me! my courser's flight
Is like the rushing breeze,
And the kind moon has said 'Good night!'
And sunk behind the trees:
The lover's voice—the loved one's ear—
There's nothing else to speak and hear;
And we will say, as on we glide,
That nothing lives on earth beside!

"Oh fly with me! and we will wing
Our white skiff o'er the waves,
And hear the tritons revelling,
Among their coral caves;
The envious mermaid, when we pass,
Shall cease her song, and drop her glass:

For it will break her very heart,
To see how fair and dear thou art.

"Oh fly with me! and we will dwell
Far over the green seas,
Where Sadness rings no parting knell
For moments such as these!
Where Italy's unclouded skies
Look brightly down on brighter eyes,
Or where the wave-wed city smiles,
Enthroned upon her hundred isles.

"Oh fly with me! by these sweet strings
Swept o'er by Passion's fingers—
By all the rocks, and vales, and springs—
Where Memory lives and lingers—
By all the tongue can never tell—
By all the heart has told so well—
By all that has been or may be—
And by Love's self—Oh fly with me!"

He paused again—no sight or sound!
The still air rested all around;
He look'd to the tower, and he look'd to the tree,
Night was as still as night could be;
Something he mutter'd of Prelate and Pope
And took from his mantle a silken rope;
Love dares much, and Love climbs well!
He stands by the Abbess in Violette's cell.

He put on a mask, and he put out the light;
The Abbess was dressed in a veil of white;

Not a look he gave, not a word he said;
The pages are ready, the blanket is spread;
He has clasped his arm her waist about,
And lifted the screaming Abbess out:
"My horse is fleet, and my hand is true,
And my Squire has a bow of deadly yew;
Away, and away, over mountain and moor!
Good luck to the love of the gay Troubadour!"

"What! rode away with the Abbess behind?
Lord! sister! is the Devil blind?"
"Full fourscore winters!"—"Fast and pray!
For the powers of darkness fight to-day!"
"I sha'nt get over the shock for a week!"—
"Did any one hear our Mother shriek?"—
"Do shut your mouth!"—"Do shut the cell!"
"What a villanous, odious, sulphury smell!"
"Has the Evil One taken the Mass-book too?"
"Ah me! what will poor little Violette do?
She has but one loaf since seven o'clock;
And no one can open that horrible lock;
And Satan will grin with a fiendish glee,
When he finds the Abbess has kept the key!"
"How shall we manage to sleep to-night?"
"I wouldn't for worlds put out my light!"
"I'm sure I shall die if I hear but a mole stir!"
"I'll clap St. Ursula under my bolster!"

But oh! the pranks that Vidal played,
When he found what a bargain his blindness had made!

Wilful and wild—half in fun, half on fire,
He stared at the Abbess, and storm'd at the Squire!
Consigned to perdition all silly romancers,
Ask'd twenty strange questions, and staid for no
answers,
Raving, and roaring, and laughing by fits,
And driving the old woman out of her wits.

There was a jousting at Chichester;
It had made in the country a mighty stir,
And all that was brave, and all that was fair,
And all that was neither, came trooping there;
Scarfs and scars, and frays and frowns,
And flow'ry speeches, and flow'ry crowns.
A hundred knights set spear in rest
For the lady they deemed the loveliest,
And Vidal broke a lance that day
For the Abbess of St. Ursula.

There was a feast at Arundel;
The town-clerk tolled a ponderous bell,
And nothing was there but row and rout,
And toil to get in, and toil to get out,
And sheriffs fatter than their venison,
And belles that never staid for benison.
The red, red wine was mantling there,
To the health of the fairest of the fair,
And Vidal drain'd the cup that day
To the Abbess of St. Ursula.
There was a wedding done at Bramber;
The town was full of myrrh and amber;

And the boors were roasting valorous beeves,
And the boys were gathering myrtle leaves,
And the bride was choosing her finest flounces,
And the bridegroom was scattering coin by ounces,
And every stripling danced on the green
With the girl he had made his idol queen;
And Vidal led the dance that day
With the Abbess of St. Ursula.

Three days had pass'd when the Abbess came back;
Her voice was out of tune,
And her new white veil was gone to wrack,
And so were her sandal shoon.
No word she said; they put her to bed,
With a pain in her heels, and a pain in her head,
And she talk'd in her delirious fever
Of a high-trotting horse, and a black deceiver;
Of music and merriment, love and lances,
Bridles and blasphemy, dishes and dances.

They went with speed to the dungeon-door;
The air was chill and damp;
And the pale girl lay on the marble floor,
Beside the dying lamp.
They kissed her lips, they called her name,
No kiss returned, no answer came;
Motionless, lifeless, there she lay,
Like a statue rent from its base away!
They said by famine she had died:
Yet the bread untasted lay beside;

And her cheek was as full, and fresh, and fair,
As it had been when warmth was there,
And her eyes were unclosed, and their glassy rays
Were fixed in a desolate, dreamy gaze,
As if before their orbs had gone
Some sight they could not close upon;
And her bright brown locks all gray were grown;
And her hands were clenched, and cold as stone;
And the veins upon her neck and brow——
But she was dead!—what boots it how?

In holy ground she was not laid;
For she had died in sin,
And good St. Ursula forbade
That such should enter in;
But in a calm and cold retreat
They made her place of rest,
And laid her in her winding-sheet,
And left her there unblest;
And set a small stone at her head,
Under a spreading tree;
"*Orate*"—that was all it said—
"*Orate hic pro me!*"

And Vidal came at night, alone,
And tore his shining hair,
And laid him down beside the stone,
And wept till day-break there.

"Fare thee well, fare thee well,
Most beautiful of earthly things,

I will not bid thy spirit stay,
Nor link to earth those glittering wings,
That burst like light away!
I know that thou art gone to dwell
In the sunny home of the fresh day beam,
Before Decay's unpitying tread
Hath crept upon the dearest dream
That ever came and fled;
Fare thee well, fare thee well;
And go thy way, all pure and fair,
Into the starry firmament;
And wander there with the spirits of air,
As bright and innocent!

"Fare thee well, fare thee well!
Strange feet will be upon thy clay,
And never stop to sigh or sorrow;
Yet many wept for thee to-day,
And one will weep to-morrow:
Alas! that melancholy knell
Shall often wake my wondering ear,
And thou shalt greet me, for a while,
Too beautiful to make me fear,
Too sad to let me smile!
Fare thee well, fare thee well!
I know that heaven for thee is won;
And yet I feel I would resign
Whole ages of my life, for one—
One little hour, of thine!

"Fare thee well, fare thee well!
See, I have been to the sweetest bowers,
And culled from garden and from heath
The tenderest of all tender flowers,
And blended in my wreath
The violet and the blue harebell,
And one frail rose in its earliest bloom;
Alas! I meant it for thy hair,
And now I fling it on thy tomb,
To weep and wither there!
Fare ye well, fare ye well!
Sleep, sleep, my love, in fragrant shade,
Droop, droop to-night, thou blushing token;
A fairer flower shall never fade,
Nor a fonder heart be broken!"

CANTO III.*

It is the hour, the lonely hour,
  Which desolate rhymers love to praise,
When listless they lie in brake or bower,
  In dread of their duns, or in dreams of their bays;
The glowing sun has gone away
To cool his face in the ocean spray,
  And the stars shine out in the liquid blue,
And the beams of the moon in silence fall
On rock and river, wood and wall,
Flinging alike on each and all
  A silver ray and a sober hue.
The village casements all are dark,
The chase is done in the princely park,
The scholar has closed the volume old,
And the miser has counted the buried gold;
There is not a foot and there is not a gale
To shake the roses in Ringmore Vale;
There is not a bird, the groves along,
To wake the night with his gushing song;
Nothing is heard but sounds that render
The rest which they disturb more tender;
The glassy river wanders still,
Making low music round the hill;

* The Troubadour was never finished. Fragments only of the Third Canto have been found, written upon stray leaves of paper.

And the last faint drops of the shower that fell
While the monks were ringing the vesper bell
Are trickling yet from leaf to leaf,
Like the big slow drops of an untold grief.

At that late hour a little boat
  Came dancing down the wave;
There were none but the Moon to see it float;
  And she, so very grave,
Looked down upon the quiet spot
As if she heard and heeded not
The eloquent vows which passion drew
From lips of beauty's tenderest hue,
And saw without the least surprise
The glances of the youthful eyes,
Which, in the warm and perilous weather,
Were gazing by night on the stream together.

* * * * * *

* * * * * *

Sometimes, upon a gala night,
Beneath the torches' festal light,
When I have seen your footsteps glance,
Sweet sister, through the merry dance,
Light as the wind that scarcely heaves
The softest of the soft rose-leaves
  In summer's sunniest hour,—
Sometimes, upon the level shore
Washed by the sea-wave just before,
When I have seen your palfrey glide

8

Along the margin of the tide,
As fleet as some imagined form
That smiles in calm, or frowns in storm,
Before the minstrel's bower,—
One moment I have ceased to doubt
The tales which poets pass about,
Of fairies and their golden wings,
Their earthward whims and wanderings,
The mummeries in which they traded,
The houses where they masqueraded,
The half unearthly tone they spoke,
The half unearthly thought they woke,
The rich they plagued, the poor they righted,
The heads they posed, the hearts they blighted!

So fancied Vidal, when he gazed
Upon a hundred glancing eyes,
While high in hall the torches blazed,
And all the blended witcheries
That clothe the revel of the night,
The dance's most voluptuous rounds,
And Beauty's most inthralling light,
And music's most entrancing sounds,
And many a tale, and many a song,
Which only passion sings and tells,
And dreams, most dazzling when most wrong,
Wove o'er him their delicious spells.
It was a long and spacious hall;
The limner's hand had wandered there,
And peopled half the lofty wall

With wondrous forms of great and fair;
And in small niches shapes of stone
Looked soft and white, like winter snow,
Queen Venus with her haunted zone,
Prince Cupid with his bended bow;
And there were brooks of essenced waters;
And mighty mirrors half a score
To tell the Baron's lovely daughters
What all their maids had told before;
And here an amorous lord was singing
Of honor's reign, or battle's rout;
And there a giggling page was flinging
Handfuls of odorous flowers about;
And wine and wit were poured together
From many a lip, from many a can;
And barons bowed beneath a feather,
And beauties blushed behind a fan;
And all were listening, laughing, chattering,
Playing the fiddle and the fool,
And metaphorically flattering,
According to established rule.
"If that bright glance did gleam on me,
How scarred and scorched my soul would be!
For even as the golden sun"—
"My Lord of Courcy, pray have done!"—
"I would I were a little bird,
That I might evermore be heard
Discoursing love, when morning's air"—
"Bonne grace, Sir Knight, I would you were!"—
"Mort de ma vie! the sea is deep,

And Dover cliffs are very steep,
And if I spring into the main,"—
"Sir Knight, you'll scarce spring out again!"
"This breast of mine is all a book;
And if her beauteous eyes would look
Upon the pale transparent leaves,
And mark how all the volume grieves,"—
"Sweet Count, who cares what tales it tells?
The title's all your mistress spells."—
"My faithful shield, my faithful heart!
Oh! both are pierced with many a dart;
And, Lady, both, through flood and flame,
Bear uneffaced thy beauteous name;
And both are stainless as a lake,"—
"And both are very hard to break!"

Thus deftly all did play their part,
  The valiant and the fair,
And Vidal's was the lightest heart
  Of all that trifled there.
Some six-and-twenty springs had passed
  In more of smiles than tears;
And boyhood's dreams had fleeted fast
  With boyhood's fleeting years!
His voice was sweet, but deeper now
  Than when its songs were new;
And o'er his cheek, and o'er his brow,
  There fell a darker hue;
His eye had learned a calmer ray,
  By browner ringlets shaded;

And from his lips the sunny play
  Of their warm smile had faded:
And, out alas! the perished thrill
  Of feeling's careless flashes,
The glistening flames, that now were chill
  In darkness, dust, and ashes,
The joys that wound, the pains that bless,
  Were all, were all departed;
And he was wise and passionless,
  And happy and cold-hearted.
It was not that the brand of sin
Had stamped its deadly blot within;
That riches had been basely won,
Or midnight murder darkly done;
That Valor's ardent glow had died,
Or Honor lost its truth and pride:
Oh, no! but Vidal's joy and grief
Had been too common, and too brief!
The weariness of human things
Had dried affection's silent springs,
And round his very heart had curled
The poisons of the drowsy world.
And he had conned the bitter lie
Of Fashion's dull philosophy;
How friendship is a schoolboy's theme,
And constancy a madman's dream,
And majesty a mouldering bust,
And loveliness a pinch of dust.
And so,—for when the wicked jest
The renegade blasphemes the best,—

He crushed the hopes which once he felt,
And mocked the shrines where once he knelt,
And taught that only fools endure
To find aught human good and pure.

And yet his heart was very light,
  His taste was very fine;
His rapier and his wit were bright,
  His attitudes divine:
He taught how snowy arms should rise,
  How snowy plumes should droop;
And published rhapsodies on sighs,
  And lectures upon soup;
He was the arbiter of bets,
  The fashioner of phrases;
And harpers sang his canzonets,
  And peeresses his praises.
And when, at some high dame's command,
Upon the lyre he laid his hand,
As now to-night, and flung aside
His silken mantle's crimson pride,
And o'er the strings so idly leant,
That you might think the instrument
Unwaked by any touch replied
To all its master said or sighed—
All other occupations ceased;
The revellers rose from cup and feast,
Young pages paused from scattering posies,
Old knights forgot to blow their noses,
And daughters smiled, and mothers frowned,

And peers beat time upon the ground;
And Beauty bowed her silent praise,
Which is so dear to minstrel lays;
And Envy dropped her whispered gall,
Which is the dearest praise of all.

That night, amid the motley crowd,
  In graver than his wonted mood,
When other lips were gay and loud,
  The Troubadour had silent stood:
Perhaps some dreams of those young hours
  Whose light was now all cold and dim,
Some visions of the faded flowers
  Whose buds had bloomed their last for him,
Came in their secret beauty back,
  Like fairy elves, whose footsteps steal
Unseen, unheard, upon their track,
  Except to those they harm or heal.
Oh! often will a look or sigh,
  Unmarked by other eyes or ears,
Recall, we know not whence or why,
  Sad thoughts that have been dead for years:
For sunset leaves the river warm
  Through evening's most benumbing chill;
And when the present cannot charm,
  The past can live and torture still!

Yet now, as if the secret spell
  That bound his inmost soul were broken,
He taught his harp a lighter swell

Than ever yet its strings had spoken;
And those who saw, and watched the while,
The smile that came, the frown that faded,
Could hardly tell if frown, or smile,
Or both, or neither, masqueraded.

"Clotilda! many hearts are light,
And many lips dissemble;
But I am thine till priests shall fight,
Or Cœur de Lion tremble!—
Hath Jerome burned his rosary,
Or Richard shrunk from slaughter?
Oh! no, no,
Dream not so!
But till you mean your hopes to die,
Engrave them not in water!

"Sweet Ida, on my lonely way
Those tears I will remember,
Till icicles shall cling to May,
Or roses to December!—
Are snow-wreaths bound on Summer's brow?
Is drowsy Winter waking?
Oh! no, no,
Dream not so!
But lances, and a lover's vow,
Were only made for breaking.

"Lenora, I am faithful still,
By all the saints that listen,

Till this warm heart shall cease to thrill,
  Or these wild veins to glisten !—
This bosom,—is its pulse less high ?
  Or sleeps the stream within it ?
        Oh ! no, no,
        Dream not so !
But lovers find eternity
  In less than half a minute.

" And thus to thee I swear to-night,
  By thine own lips and tresses,
That I will take no further flight,
  Nor break again my jesses :
And wilt thou trust the faith I vowed,
  And dream in spite of warning ?
        Oh ! no, no,
        Dream not so !
But go and lure the midnight cloud,
  Or chain the mist of morning.

" These words of mine, so false and bland,
  Forget that they were spoken !
The ring is on thy radiant hand,—
  Dash down the faithless token !
And will they say that Beauty sinned,
  That Woman turned a rover ?
        Oh ! no, no,
        Dream not so !
But lover's vows are like the wind,
  And Vidal is a Lover !"

Ere the last echo of the words
Died on the lip and on the chords,
The Baron's jester, who was clever
At blighting characters forever,
And whom all people thought delightful,
Because he was so very spiteful,
Stooped down to tie his sandal's string,
And found by chance a lady's ring;
So small and slight, it scarce had spanned
The finger of a fairy's hand,—
Or thine, sweet Rose, whose hand and wrist
Are much the least I ever kissed:—
Upon the ruby it enclosed
A bleeding heart in peace reposed,
And round was graved in letters clear:
"Let by the month, or by the year."
Young Pacolet, from ring and song,
Thought something might be somewhere wrong,
And round the room in transport flitted
To find whose hand the bawble fitted.

He was an ugly, dwarfish knave,
Most gravely wild, most wildly grave;
It seemed that Nature, in a whim,
Had mixed a dozen shapes in him;
One arm was longer than the other,
One leg was running from his brother,
And one dark eye, with fondest labor,
Coquetted with his fairer neighbor:
His color ever came and went,

Like clouds upon the firmament,
And yet his cheeks, in any weather,
Were never known to blush together:
To-day his voice was shrill and harsh,
Like homilies from Doctor Marsh;
To-morrow from his rosy lip
The sweetest of sweet sounds would trip;
Far sweeter than the song of birds,
Or the first lisp of Childhood's words,
Or Zephyrs soft, or waters clear,
Or Love's own vow to Love's own ear.
Such were the tones he murmured now,
As, wreathing lip and cheek and brow
Into a smile of wicked glee,
He begged upon his bended knee
That maid and matron, young and old,
Would try the glittering hoop of gold.

But then, as usual in such cases,
All sorts of pretty airs and graces
Were played by nymphs, whose hands and arms
Had, or had not, a host of charms:
And there were frowns, as wrists were bared,
And wonderings "how some people dared,"
And much reluctance and disdain,
Which some might feel, and all could feign;
And witty looks and whispered guesses,
And running into dark recesses,
And pointless gibes, and toothless chuckles,
And pinching disobedient knuckles,

And cunning thefts by watchful lovers,
Which filled the pockets of the glovers.
'Twas very vain; it seemed that all,
Except the mistress of the Hall,
Had done the utmost they could do,
And made their fingers black and blue,
And there they were, the gem and donor,
Without a mistress, or an owner.

But while the toy was vainly tried,
The ugly Baron's handsome bride
Had sate apart from that rude game
And listened to the sighs of flame,
Which followed her from night to morning,
In spite of frowning and of scorning.
Bred up from youth with naught before her
But humble slave and fond adorer,
Ill could that haughty Lady brook
A bantering phrase or brazen look;
* * * * * *
* * * * * *

Day passed, and Night came hurrying down
With her heaviest step, and her darkest frown;
Not witchingly mild, as when she hushes
The first warm thrill of woman's blushes;
Or mellows the eloquent murmur made
By some mad minstrel's serenade;
But robed in the clouds her anger flings
O'er the murderer's midnight wanderings,

The stealthy step, and the naked knife,
The sudden blow, and the parting life!—
On the snow that was sleeping its frozen sleep
Round cabin and castle, white and deep,
The love-stricken boy might have wandered far
Ere he found for his sonnet a single star;
And over the copse, and over the dell,
The mantle of mist so drearily fell,
That the fondest and bravest could hardly know
The smile of his queen from the sneer of his foe.
In the lonely cot on the lorn hill-side
The serf grew pale as he looked on his bride;
And oft, as the Baron's courtly throng
Were loud in the revel of wine and song,
The blast at the gate made such a din
As changed to horror the mirth within!

* * * * * *

(1823-1824.)

THE LEGEND OF THE HAUNTED TREE.

"Deep is the bliss of the belted knight,
When he kisses at dawn the silken glove,
And goes, in his glittering armor dight,
To shiver a lance for his Lady-love!

"Lightly he couches the beaming spear;
His mistress sits with her maidens by,
Watching the speed of his swift career,
With a whispered prayer and a murmured sigh

"Far from me is the gazing throng,
The blazoned shield, and the nodding plume;
Nothing is mine but a worthless song,
A joyless life, and a nameless tomb."

"Nay, dearest Wilfrid, lay like this
On such an eve is much amiss:
Our mirth beneath the new May moon
Should echoed be by a livelier tune.
What need to thee of mail and crest,
Of foot in stirrup, spear in rest?
Over far mountains and deep seas,
Earth hath no fairer fields than these;

And who, in Beauty's gaudiest bowers,
Can love thee with more love than ours?"

The minstrel turned with a moody look
From that sweet scene of guiltless glee;
From the old who talked beside the brook,
And the young who danced beneath the tree:
Coldly he shrank from the gentle maid,
From the chiding look and the pleading tone;
And he passed from the old elm's hoary shade,
And followed the forest path alone.
One little sigh, one pettish glance,
And the girl comes back to her playmates now,
And takes her place in the merry dance,
With a slower step and a sadder brow.

"My soul is sick," saith the wayward boy,
"Of the peasant's grief, and the peasant's joy;
I cannot breathe on from day to day,
Like the insects which, our wise men say,
In the crevice of the cold rock dwell,
Till their shape is the shape of their dungeon's cell;
In the dull repose of our changeless life,
I long for passion, I long for strife,
As in the calm the mariner sighs
For rushing waves and groaning skies.
Oh for the lists, the lists of fame!
Oh for the herald's glad acclaim;
For floating pennon and prancing steed,
And Beauty's wonder at Manhood's deed!"

Beneath an ancient oak he lay;
More years than man can count, they say,
On the verge of the dim and solemn wood,
Through sunshine and storm that oak had stood.
Yet were it hard to trace a sign
On trunk or bough of that oak's decline :
Many a loving, laughing sprite,
Tended the branches by day and by night;
Fettered the winds that would invade
The quiet of its sacred shade,
And drove in a serried phalanx back
The red-eyed lightning's fierce attack:
So the leaves of its age were as fresh and as green
As the leaves of its early youth had been.
Fretful brain and turbid breast
Under its canopy ill would rest;
For she that ruled the revels therein
Loved not the taint of human sin :
Moody brow with an evil eye
Would the Queen of the Fairy people spy;
Sullen tone with an angry ear
Would the Queen of the Fairy people hear.
Oft would she mock the worldling's care
E'en in the grant of his unwise prayer,
Scattering wealth that was not gain,
Lavishing joy that turned to pain.
Pure of thought should the mortal be
That would sleep beneath the Haunted Tree;
That night the minstrel laid him down
Ere his brow relaxed its peevish frown ;

And Slumber had bound his eyelids fast,
Ere the evil wish from his soul had passed.
And a song on the sleeper's ear descended,
  A song it was pain to hear, and pleasure,
So strangely wrath and love were blended
  In every note of the mystic measure.

"I know thee, child of earth;
The morning of thy birth
In through the lattice did my chariot glide;
I saw thy father weep
Over thy first wild sleep,
I rocked thy cradle when thy mother died.

"And I have seen thee gaze
Upon these birks and braes,
Which are my kingdoms, with irreverent scorn;
And heard thee pour reproof
Upon the vine-clad roof,
Beneath whose peaceful shelter thou wast born.

"I bind thee in the snare
Of thine unholy prayer;
I seal thy forehead with a viewless seal:
I give into thine hand
The buckler and the brand,
And clasp the golden spur upon thy heel.

"When thou hast made thee wise
In the sad lore of sighs,
When the world's visions fail thee and forsake,

Return, return to me,
And to my haunted tree;
The charm hath bound thee now; Sir Knight, awake!"

Sir Isumbras, in doubt and dread,
From his feverish sleep awoke,
And started up from his grassy bed
Under the ancient oak.
And he called the page who held his spear,
And, "Tell me, boy," quoth he,
"How long have I been slumbering here,
Beneath the greenwood tree?"—
"Ere thou didst sleep, I chanced to throw
A stone into the rill;
And the ripple that disturbed its flow
Is on its surface still;
Ere thou didst sleep, thou bad'st me sing
King Arthur's favorite lay;
And the first echo of the string
Has hardly died away."

"How strange is sleep!" the young knight said,
As he clasped the helm upon his head,
And, mounting again his courser black,
To his gloomy tower rode slowly back:
"How strange is sleep! when his dark spell lies
On the drowsy lids of human eyes,
The years of a life will float along
In the compass of a page's song.
Methought I lived in a pleasant vale,
The haunt of the lark and the nightingale,

Where the summer rose had a brighter hue,
And the noon-day sky a clearer blue,
And the spirit of man in age and youth
A fonder love, and a firmer truth.
And I lived on, a fair-haired boy,
In that sweet vale of tranquil joy;
  Until at last my vain caprice
  Grew weary of its bliss and peace.
And one there was, most dear and fair,
Of all that smiled around me there—
A gentle maid, with a cloudless face,
And a form so full of fairy grace;
Who, when I turned with scornful spleen
From the feast in the bower, or the dance on the green,
Would humor all my wayward will
And love me and forgive me still.
Even now, methinks, her smile of light
Is there before me, mild and bright;
And I hear her voice of fond reproof,
Between the beats of my palfrey's hoof.
'T is idle all: but I could weep;—
Alas!" said the knight, "how strange is sleep!"
He struck with his spear the brazen plate
That gleamed before the castle gate;
The torch threw high its waves of flame
As forth the watchful menials came;
They lighted the way to the banquet hall,
They hung the shield upon the wall,
They spread the board, and they filled the bowl,
And the phantoms passed from his troubled soul.

For all the ailments which infest
A solitary Briton's breast,
The peccant humors which defile
The thoughts in this fog-haunted isle,
Whatever name or style they bear—
Reflection, study, nerves, or care,
There's naught of such Lethean power
As dinner at the dinner-hour.
Sefton! the Premier, o'er thy plate,
Thinks little of last night's debate;
Cowan! the merchant, in thy hall,
Grows careless what may rise or fall;
The wit who feeds can puff away
His unsold tale, his unheard play;
And Mr. Wellesley Pole forgets,
At eight o'clock, his duns and debts.
The Knight approved the roasted boar,
And mused upon his dream no more:
The Knight enjoyed the bright champagne,
And deemed himself himself again.

Sir Isumbras was ever found
  Where blows were struck for glory;
There sate not at the Table Round
  A knight more famed in story:
The king on his throne would turn about
  To see his courser prancing;
And, when Sir Launcelot had gout,
  The queen would praise his dancing.

He quite wore out his father's spurs,
  Performing valor's duties—
Destroying mighty sorcerers,
  Avenging injured beauties,
And crossing many a trackless sand,
  And rescuing people's daughters
From dragons that infest the land,
  And whales that walk the waters.
He throttled lions by the score,
  And giants by the dozen;
And, for his skill in lettered lore,
  They called him "Merlin's Cousin."
A troop of steeds, with bit and rein,
  Stood ready in his stable;
An ox was every morning slain,
  And roasted for his table.
And he had friends, all brave and tall,
  And crowned with praise and laurel,
Who kindly feasted in his hall,
  And jousted in his quarrel;
And minstrels came and sang his fame
  In very rugged verses;
And they were paid with wine and game,
  And rings, and cups, and purses.

And he loved a Lady of high degree,
  Faith's fortress, Beauty's flower;
A countess for her maid had she,
  And a kingdom for her dower;

And a brow whose frowns were vastly grand,
  And an eye of sunlit brightness,
And a swan-like neck, and an arm and hand
  Of most bewitching whiteness;
And a voice of music, whose sweet tones
  Could most divinely prattle
Of battered casques, and broken bones,
  And all the bliss of battle.
He wore her scarf in many a fray,
  He trained her hawks and ponies,
And filled her kitchen every day
  With leverets and conies;
He loved, and he was loved again :—
  I won't waste time in proving,
There is no pleasure like the pain
  Of being loved, and loving.

Dame Fortune is a fickle gipsy,
And always blind, and often tipsy;
Sometimes, for years and years together,
She'll bless you with the sunniest weather,
Bestowing honor, pudding, pence,
You can't imagine why or whence;-
Then in a moment—Presto, Pass!—
Your joys are withered like the grass;
You find your constitution vanish,
Almost as quickly as the Spanish;
The murrain spoils your flocks and fleeces;
The dry-rot pulls your house to pieces;

Your garden raises only weeds;
Your agent steals your title-deeds;
Your banker's failure stuns the city;
Your father's will makes Sugden witty;
Your daughter, in her beauty's bloom,
Goes off to Gretna with the groom;
And you, good man, are left alone,
To battle with the gout and stone.

Ere long, Sir Isumbras began
To be a sad and thoughtful man:
They said the glance of an evil eye
Had been on the knight's prosperity
Less swift on the quarry his falcon went,
Less true was his hound on the wild deer's scent,
And thrice in the list he came to the earth,
By the luckless chance of a broken girth.
And Poverty soon in her rags was seen
At the board where Plenty erst had been;
And the guests smiled not as they smiled before,
And the song of the minstrel was heard no more;
And a base ingrate, who was his foe,
Because, a little month ago,
He had cut him down, with friendly ardor,
From a rusty hook in an Ogre's larder,
Invented an atrocious fable,
And ruined him quite at the Royal Table:
And she at last, the worshipped one,
For whom his valorous deeds were done,

The star of all his soul's reflections,
The rose of all his heart's affections,
Who had heard his vows and worn his jewels,
And made him fight so many duels—
She, too, when Fate's relentless wheel
Deprived him of the Privy Seal,
Bestowed her smiles upon another,
And gave his letters to her mother.

'Tis the last drop, as all men know,
That makes the bucket overflow,
And the last parcel of the pack
That bends in two the camel's back.
Fortune and Fame—he had seen them depart,
With a silent pride of a valiant heart:
Traitorous friends—he had passed them by,
With a haughty brow and a stifled sigh.
Boundless and black might roll the sea,
O'er which the course of his bark must be;
But he saw, through the storms that frowned above,
One guiding light and the light was Love.
Now all was dark; the doom was spoken!
His wealth all spent, and his heart half broken;
Poor youth! he had no earthly hope,
Except in laudanum, or a rope.

If e'er you happened, by a twist
Of Destiny's provoking wrist,
To find yourself one morning hurled
From all you had in all the world,—

Seeing your pretty limes and beeches
Supply the auction-mart with speeches,—
By base ingratitude disgusted
In him you most esteemed and trusted,
And cut, without the slightest reason,
By her who was so kind last season,—
You know how often meditation
Assures you, for your consolation,
That, if you had but been contented
To rent the house your father rented,
If, in Sir Paul you'd been inclined to
Suspect what no one else was blind to,
If, for that false girl, you had chosen
Either her sister or her cousin,
If any thing you had been doing
But just the very thing you're rueing,
You might have lived your day in clover,
Gay, rich, prized friend, and favored lover.
Thus was it with my Knight of knights;
While vanished all his vain delights,
The thought of being dupe and ass
Most galled the sick Sir Isumbras.

He ordered out his horse, and tried,
As the Leech advised, a gentle ride.
A pleasant path he took,
Where the turf, all bright with the April showers,
Was spangled with a thousand flowers,
Beside a murmuring brook.

Never before had he ridden that way;
And now, on a sunny first of May,
He chose the turning, you may guess,
Not for the laughing loveliness
Of turf, or flower, or stream; but only
Because it looked extremely lonely.

Yet but that Megrim hovering here
Had dimmed the eye and dulled the ear,
Jocund and joyous all around
Were every sight and every sound.
The ancient forest, whose calm rest
No axe did ever yet molest,
  Stretched far upon the right;
Here, deepening into trackless shades,
There, opening long and verdant glades,
  Unto the cheerful light:
Wide on the left, whene'er the screen
Of hedgerows left a space between
  To stand and gaze awhile,
O'er varied scenes the eye might rove,
Orchard and garden, mead and grove,
  Spread out for many a mile.
Around, in all the joy of spring,
The sinless birds were carolling;
  Low hummed the studious bees;
And softly, sadly, rose and fell
The echo of the ocean swell,
  In the capricious breeze.

But truly Sir Usumbras cared as much
For all that a happier heart might touch,
As Cottenham cares for a Highland reel,
When counsel opens a Scotch Appeal,
Or Hume for Pasta's glorious scenes,
When the House is voting the Ways and Means.

He had wandered, musing, scarce a mile,
In his melancholy mood,
When, peeping o'er a rustic stile,
He saw a little village smile,
Embowered in thick wood.
There were small cottages, arrayed
In the delicate jasmine's fragrant shade;
And gardens, whence the rose's bloom
Loaded the gale with rich perfume;
And there were happy hearts; for all
In that bright nook kept festival,
And welcomed in the merry May,
With banquet and with roundelay.

Sir Isumbras sate gazing there,
With folded arms, and mournful air;
He fancied—'twas an idle whim—
That the village looked like a home to him.

And now a gentle maiden came,
Leaving her sisters and their game,
And wandered up the vale;
Beauty so bright he had never seen
Saving her Majesty the Queen;—

But out on ugly doubts and fears!
Her eyes were very full of tears,
  Her cheeks were very pale.
None courted her stay of the joyous throng,
  As she passed from the group alone;
And he listened, which was vastly wrong,
And heard her singing a lively song,
  In a very dismal tone:

"Deep is the bliss of the belted knight,
  When he kisses at dawn the silken glove,
And goes, in his glittering armor dight,
  To shiver a lance for his Lady-love!"

That thrilling tone, so soft and clear—
Was it familiar to his ear?
And those delicious drooping eyes,
As blue and as pure as the summer skies—
Had he, indeed, in other days,
Been blessed in the light of their holy rays?
He knew not; but his knee he bent
  Before her in most knightly fashion,
And grew superbly eloquent
  About her beauty, and his passion.
He said that she was very fair,
  And that she warbled like a linnet;
And that he loved her, though he ne'er
  Had looked upon her till that minute.
He said, that all the Court possessed
  Of gay or grave, of fat or slender,

Poor things! were only fit, at best,
  To hold a candle to her splendor:
He vowed that when she once should take
  A little proper state upon her,
All lutes for her delight would wake,
  All lances shiver in her honor:
He grieved to mention that a Jew
  Had seized for debt his grand pavilion;
And he had little now, 'twas true,
  To offer, but a heart and pillion:
But what of that? In many a fight—
  Though he, who shouldn't say it, said it—
He still had borne him like a knight,
  And had his share of blows and credit:
And if she would but condescend
  To meet him at the Priest's to-morrow,
And be henceforth his guide, his friend,
  In every toil, in every sorrow,
They'd sail instanter from the Downs;
  His hands just now were quite at leisure;
And, if she fancied foreign crowns,
  He'd win them with the greatest pleasure.

"A year is gone"—the damsel sighed,
But blushed not, as she so replied—
"Since one I loved—alas! how well
He knew not, knows not—left our dell.
Time brings to his deserted cot
No tidings of his after lot;

But his weal or wo is still the theme
Of my daily thought and my nightly dream.
Poor Alice is not proud or coy;
But her heart is with her minstrel boy."

Away from his arms the damsel bounded,
And left him more and more confounded.
He mused of the present, he mused of the past,
And he felt that a spell was o'er him cast;
He shed hot tears, he knew not why,
And talked to himself and made reply,
Till a calm o'er his troubled senses crept.
And, as the daylight waned, he slept.
Poor gentleman!—I need not say,
Beneath an ancient oak he lay.

"He is welcome,"—o'er his bed,
Thus the bounteous Fairy said:
"He has conned the lesson now,
He has read the book of pain.
There are furrows on his brow,
I must make it smooth again.

"Lo, I knock the spurs away;
Lo, I loosen belt and brand;
Hark! I hear the courser neigh
For his stall in Fairy-land.

"Bring the cap, and bring the vest,
Buckle on his sandal shoon;
Fetch his memory from the chest
In the treasury of the Moon.

"I have taught him to be wise,
For a little maiden's sake;—
Lo! he opens his glad eyes,
Softly, slowly:—minstrel, wake!"

The sun has risen, and Wilfrid is come
To his early friends and his cottage home.
His hazel eyes and his locks of gold
Are just as they were in the time of old:
But a blessing has been on the soul within,
For that is won from its secret sin;
More loving now, and worthier love,
Of men below and of saints above.
He reins a steed with a lordly air,
Which makes his country cousins stare:
And he speaks in a strange and courtly phrase,
Though his voice is the voice of other days:
But where he has learned to talk and ride,
He will tell to none but his bonny bride.

(Written in 1830; but revised by the author and largely added to in 1837.)

THE LEGEND OF THE DRACHENFELS.

"DEATH be her doom! we must not spare,
Though the voice be sweet, though the face be fair,
When the looks deride and the lips blaspheme
The Serpent-God of our hallowed stream.

"Death be her doom! that the fearful King
May joy in the gift his votaries bring;
And smile on the valley, and smile on the rock,
To freshen the vine, and to fatten the flock.

"Death be her doom! ere the pitiless One
Leap from his rest at set of sun;
Seek from his crag his wonted prey,
And punish in wrath our long delay!"

It was a gray-haired Chief that said
  The words of fate, the words of fear;
A battered casque was on his head,
  And in his grasp a broken spear:
It was a captive maid that met,
  Sedate, serene, the stern command;
Around her neck her beads were set,
  An ivory cross was in her hand.

"Lead me away! I am weak and young,
Captive the fierce and the proud among;
But I will pray a humble prayer,
That the feeble to strike may be firm to bear.

"Lead me away! the voice may fail,
And the lips grow white, and the cheeks turn
pale;
Yet will ye know that nought but sin
Chafes or changes the soul within.

"Lead me away! oh, dear to mine eyes
Are the flowery fields, and the sunny skies;
But I cannot turn from the Cross divine
To bend my knee at an idol's shrine."

They clothe her in such rich array
As a bride prepares for her bridal day;
Around her forehead, that shines so bright,
They wreathe a wreath of roses white,
And set on her neck a golden chain—
Spoil of her sire in combat slain.

Over her head her doom is said;
And with folded arms, and measured tread,
In long procession, dark and slow,
Up the terrible hill they go,
Hymning their hymn, and crying their cry
To him, their Demon Deity.—
Mary, Mother! sain and save!
The maiden kneels at the Dragon's cave!

Alas! 'tis frightful to behold
That thing of Nature's softest mould,
In whose slight shape and delicate hue
Life's lovliness beams fresh and new,
Bound on the bleak hill's topmost height,
To die, and by such death, to-night!
But yester-eve, when the red sun
His race of grateful toil had run,
And over earth the moon's soft rays
Lit up the hour of prayer and praise,
She bowed within the pleasant shade
By her own fragrant jasmine made;
And while her clear and thrilling tone
Asked blessing from her Maker's throne,
Heard the notes echoed to her ear
From lips that were to her most dear.
Her sire, her kindred, round her knelt;
And the young Priestess knew and felt
That deeper love than that of men
Was in their natural temple then.
That love—is now its radiance chill?
Fear not; it guides, it guards her still!

The temper of our stoutest mail
In battle's fiery shock may fail;
The trustiest anchor may betray
Our vessel in the treacherous spray;
The dearest friend we ever knew
In our worst need may prove untrue:

But come what may of doubt or dread
About our lonely path or bed,
On tented field, or stormy wave,
In dungeon cell, or mountain cave,
In want, in pain, in death,—where'er
One meek heart prays, God's love is there!

The crowd departed: her wandering eye
Followed their steps, as they left her to die.
Down the steep and stern descent,
Strangely mingled, the Heathen went,–
Palsied dotard, and beardless boy,
Sharers to-night in their savage joy,—
Hoary priest, and warrior grim,
Shaking the lance, and chanting the hymn;
And ever and anxiously looking back,
To watch if yet, on his slimy track
He rolled him forth, that ghastly guest,
To taste of the banquet he loved the best.

The crowd departed; and alone
She kneeled upon the rugged stone.
Alas! it was a dismal pause,
When the wild rabble's fierce applause
  Died slowly on the answering air;
And, in the still and mute profound,
She started even at the sound
  Of the half-thought, half-spoken prayer
Her heart and lip had scarcely power
To feel or frame in that dark hour.

Fearful, yet blameless!—for her birth,
Had been of Nature's common earth,
And she was nursed, in happier hours,
By Nature's common suns and showers:
And when one moment whirls away
Whate'er we know or trust to-day,
And opens that eternal book
On which we long, and dread to look,
In that quick change of sphere and scope,—
  That rushing of the spirit's wings,
From all we have to all we hope,
  From mortal to immortal things,—
Though madly on the giddy brink
  Despair may jest, and Guilt dissemble,—
White Innocence awhile will shrink,
  And Piety be proud to tremble!

But quickly from her brow and cheek
  The flush of human terror faded;
And she aroused, the maiden meek,
  Her fainting spirit, self-upbraided;
And felt her secret soul renewed
In that her solemn solitude.
Unwonted strength to her was given
  To bear the rod, and drink the cup;
Her pulse beat calmer; and to heaven
  Her voice in firmer tone went up.
And as upon her gentle heart
  The dew of holy peace descended,

She saw her last sunlight depart,
With awe and hope so sweetly blended
Into a deep and tranquil sense
Of unpresuming confidence,
That if the blinded tribes, whose breath
Had doomed her to such dole and death,
Could but have caught one bright, brief glance
Of that ungrieving countenance,
And marked the light of glory shed
Already o'er her sinless head,
The tears, with which her eyes were full,
Tears not of anguish,—and the smile
Of new-born rapture, which the while,
As with a lustrous veil, arrayed
Her brow, her cheek, her lip, and made
Her beauty more than beautiful,—
Oh, would they not have longed to share
Her torture,—yea, her transport, there?

"Father, my sins are very great;
Thou readest them, whate'er they be:
But penitence is all too late;
And unprepared I come to thee,—
Uncleansed, unblest, unshriven!

"Yet thou, in whose all-searching sight
No human thing is undefiled,—
Thou, who art merciful in might,
Father, thou wilt forgive thy child,—
Father, thou hast forgiven!

"Thy will, not hers, be done to-day!—
If in this hour, and on this spot,
Her soul indeed must pass away,
Among fierce men who know thee not,—
Thine is the breath thou gavest!

"Or if thou wilt put forth thy hand
And shield her from the jaws of flame,
That she may live to teach the land
Whose people hath not heard thy name,—
Thine be the life thou savest!"

So spoke the blessed maid; and now
Crossing her hands upon her breast,
With quiet eye, and placid brow,
Awaited the destroying pest;
Not like a thing of sense and life
Soul-harrassed in such bitter strife,
But tranquil, as a shape of stone,
Upraised in ages long bygone,
To mark where, closed her toilsome race,
Some sainted sister sleeps in grace.

Such might she seem: about her grew
Sweet wild-flowers, sweet of scent and hue;
And she had placed, with pious care,
Her Crucifix before her there,
That her last look and thought might be
Of Christ, and of the Holy Tree.

And now, methinks, at what my lay
Of this poor maid hath yet to say,
Will Wit assume a scornful look,
And Wisdom con a grave rebuke.
I heed them not; full oft their lies
In such time-honored histories,
Hived through long ages in the store
Of the rude peasant's nursery lore,
A pathos of a deeper ruth,
A moral of a purer truth,
Than aught we study in the page
Of lofty bard or learned sage;
Therefore, my gentle Muse, prolong
In faith thy legendary song.

The day was gone, but it was not night:—
Whither so suddenly fled the light?
Nature seemed sick with a sore disease;
Over her hills and streams and trees
  Unnatural darkness fell;
The earth and the heaven, the river and shore,
In the lurid mist were seen no more;
And the voice of the mountain monster rose
As he lifted him up from his noon-tide repose,
First in a hiss, and then in a cry,
And then in a yell that shook the sky;—
The eagle from high fell down to die
  At the sound of that mighty yell:—
From his wide jaws broke, as in wrath he woke,
Scalding torrents of sulphurous smoke

And crackling coals, in mad ascent,
As from a red volcano went,
  And flames, like the flames of hell.
But his scream of fury waxed more shrill,
When, on the peak of the blasted Hill,
  He saw his victim bound.
Forth the Devourer, scale by scale,
Unveiled the folds of his steel-proof mail,
Stretching his throat, and stretching his tail,
And hither and thither rolling him o'er,
Till he covered four-score feet and four
  Of the wearied and wailing ground.
And at last he raised from his stony bed
The horrors of his speckled head;
Up, like a comet, the meteor went,
And seemed to shake the firmament,
  And batter heaven's own walls!
For many a long mile, well I ween,
The fires that shot from those eyes were seen;
The Burschen of Bonn, if Bonn had been,
  Would have shuddered in their halls.
Woe for the Virgin!—bootless here
Were gleaming shield, and whistling spear,
  Such battle to abide;
The mightiest engines that ever the trade
Of human homicide hath made,
Warwolf, balist, and catapult,
Would like a stripling's wand insult
  That adamantine hide.
Woe for the Virgin!—

Lo! what spell
Hath scattered the darkness, and silenced the yell,
And quenched those fiery showers?—
Why turns the Serpent from his prey?
The Cross hath barred his terrible way,
The Cross, among the flowers.
As an eagle pierced on his cloudy throne,
As a column sent from its base of stone,
Backward the stricken Monster dropped;
Never he stayed and never he stopped,
Till deep in the gushing tide he sank,
And buried lay beneath the stream,
Passing away like a loathsome dream.
Well may you guess how either bank
As with an earthquake shook;
The mountains rocked from brow to base;
The river boiled with a hideous din
As the burning mass fell heavily in;
And the wide, wide Rhine, for a moment's space,
Was scorched into a brook.
Night passed, ere the multitude dared to creep,
Huddled together, up the steep;
They came to the stone—in speechless awe
They fell on their face at the sight they saw:
The maiden was free from hurt or harm,—
But the iron had passed from her neck and arm,
And the glittering links of the broken chain
Lay scattered about like drops of rain!

And deem ye that the rescued child
  To her father-land would come,—
That the remnant of her kindred smiled
  Around her, in her home,
And that she lived in love of earth,
  Among earth's hopes and fears,
And gave God thanks for the daily birth
  Of blessings in after years?—
Holy and happy, she turned not away
From the task her Saviour set that day;—
What was her kindred, her home, to her?—
She had been heaven's own messenger!

Short time went by from that dread hour
Of manifested wrath and power,
Ere from the cliff a rising shrine
Looked down upon the rolling Rhine.
Duly the virgin Priestess there
Led day by day the hymn and prayer,
And the dark Heathen round her pressed
To know their Maker, and be blessed!

L'ENVOI.

TO THE COUNTESS VON C——, BONN.

I.

This is the Legend of the Drachenfels,—
  Sweet theme, most feebly sung:—and yet to me
My feeble song is grateful; for it tells
  Of far-off smiles and voices. Though it be
Unmeet, fair Lady, for thy breast or bower,
Yet thou wilt wear, for thou didst plant, the flower.

II.

It had been worthier of such birth and death,
  If it had bloomed where thou hadst watched its
    rise,
Fanned by the zephyr of thy fragrant breath,
  Warmed by the sunshine of thy gentle eyes;
And cherished by the love in whose pure shade
No evil thing can live, no good thing fade.

III.

It will be long ere thou wilt shed again
  Thy praise or censure on my childish lays,—

Thy praise, which makes me happy more than vain;
  Thy censure, kinder than another's praise.
Huge mountains frown between us; and the swell
Of the hoarse sea is mocking my farewell.

IV.

Yet not the less, dear Friend, thy guiding light
  Shines through the secret chambers of my thought;
Or when I waken, with revived delight,
  The lute young Fancy to my cradle brought,
Or when I visit, with a studious brow,
The less-loved task, to which I turn me now.

(Written in 1829; but revised by the author and largely added to in 1837.)

THE BRIDAL OF BELMONT.

A LEGEND OF THE RHINE.

WHERE foams and flows the glorious Rhine,
   Many a ruin wan and gray
O'erlooks the corn-field and the vine,
   Majestic in its dark decay.
Among their dim clouds, long ago,
They mocked the battles that raged below,
And greeted the guests in arms that came,
With hissing arrow, and scalding flame:
But there is not one of the homes of pride
That frown on the breast of the peaceful tide,
Whose leafy walls more proudly tower
Than these, the walls of Belmont Tower.

Where foams and flows the glorious Rhine,
   Many a fierce and fiery lord
Did carve the meat, and pour the wine,
   For all that revelled at his board.
Father and son, they were all alike,
Firm to endure, and fast to strike;

Little they loved but a Frau or a feast,
Nothing they feared but a prayer or a priest;
But there was not one in all the land
More trusty of heart, more stout of hand,
More valiant in field, or more courteous in bower,
Than Otto, the Lord of Belmont Tower.
His eyes were bright, his eyes were blue,
  As summer's sun, as summer's heaven;
His age was barely twenty-two;
  His height was just five feet eleven:
His hounds were of the purest strain,
  His hawks the best from every nation;
His courser's tail, his courser's mane,
  Was all the country's admiration:
His frowns were lightnings charged with fate;
  His smiles were shafts from Cupid's quiver;
He had a very old estate,
  And the best vineyards on the river.
So ancient dames, you need not doubt,
  Would wink and nod their pride and pleasure,
Whene'er the youthful Count led out
  Their eldest or their youngest treasure,
Take notes of what his Lordship said
  On shapes and colors, songs and dances,
And make their maidens white or red,
  According to their Lordship's fancies,
They whispered, too, from time to time,
  What might escape the Count's inspection;
That Linda's soul was all sublime;
  That Gertude's taste was quite perfection;

Or blamed some people's forward tricks,
  And very charitably hinted,
Their neighbor's neice was twenty-six,
  Their cousin's clever daughter squinted.

Are you rich, single, and "your Grace?"
I pity your unhappy case;
Before you launch your first new carriage,
The women have arranged your marriage;
Where'er your weary wit may lead you,
They pet you, praise you, fret you, feed you;
Consult your taste in wreaths and laces,
And make you make their books at Races;
Your little pony, Tam O'Shanter,
Is found to have the sweetest canter;
Your curricle is quite reviving,
And Jane's so bold when you are driving!
One recollects your father's habits,
And knows the warren, and the rabbits!
The place is really princely—only
They're sure you'll find it vastly lonely.
Another, in more tender phrases,
Records your sainted mother's praises;
Pronounces her the best of creatures,
And finds in you her tones and features.

You go to Cheltenham, for the waters,
And meet the Countess and her daughters;
You take a cottage at Geneva—
Lo! Lady Anne and Lady Eva.

After a struggle of a session,
You just surrender at discretion,
And live to curse the frauds of mothers,
And envy all your younger brothers.

Count Otto bowed, Count Otto smiled,
When My Lady praised her darling child;
Count Otto smiled, Count Otto bowed,
When the child those praises disavowed;
But out on the cold one! he cared not a rush
For the motherly pride, or the maidenly blush.
As a knight should gaze Count Otto gazed,
Where Bertha in all her beauty blazed;
As a knight should hear Count Otto heard,
When Liba sang like a forest bird;
But he thought, I trow, about as long
Of Bertha's beauty and Liba's song,
As the sun may think of the clouds that play
O'er his radiant path on a summer day.

Many a maid had dreams of state,
As the Count rode up to her father's gate;
Many a maid shed tears of pain,
As the Count rode back to his Tower again;
But little he cared, as it should seem,
For the sad, sad tear, or the fond, fond dream—
Alone he lived—alone, and free
As the owl that dwells in the hollow tree;
And belles and barons said and swore,
There never was knight so shy before!

It was almost the first of May
The sun all smiles had passed away;
  The moon was beautifully bright;
Earth, heaven, as usual in such cases,
Looked up and down with happy faces;
  In short, it was a charming night.
And all alone, at twelve o'clock,
The young Count clambered down the rock,
Unfurled the sail, unchained the oar,
And pushed the shallop from the shore.
The holiness that sweet time flings
Upon all human thoughts and things,
When Sorrow checks her idle sighs,
And care shuts fast her wearied eyes;
The splendor of the hues that played
Fantastical o'er hill and glade,
As verdant slope and barren cliff
Seemed darting by the tiny skiff;
The flowers, whose faint tips, here and there,
Breathed out such fragrance, you might swear
That every soundless gale that fanned
The tide came fresh from fairy land;
The music of the mountain rill,
Leaping in glee from hill to hill,
To which some wild bird, now and then,
Made answer from her darksome glen—
All this to him had rarer pleasure
Than jester's wit or minstrel's measure;
And, if you ever loved romancing,
Or felt extremely tired of dancing,

You'll hardly wonder that Count Otto
  Left, for the scene my muse is painting,
The Lady Hildebrand's ridotto,
  Where all the Rhenish world was fainting.

What melody glides o'er the star-lit stream?
  "Lurley! Lurley!"
Angels of grace! does the young Count dream?
  "Lurley! Lurley!"
Or is the scene indeed so fair
That a nymph of the sea or a nymph of the air
Has left the home of her own delight,
To sing to our roses and rocks to-night?
  "Lurley! Lurley!"
Words there are none; but the waves prolong
The notes of that mysterious song:
He listens, he listens, and all around
Ripple the echoes of that sweet sound—
  "Lurley! Lurley!"
No form appears on the river side;
No boat is borne on the wandering tide;
And the tones ring on, with naught to show
Or whence they come or whither they go—
  "Lurley! Lurley!"
As fades one murmur on the ear,
There comes another, just as clear;
And the present is like to the parted strain
As link to link of a golden chain:
  Lurley! Lurley!"

Whether the voice be sad or gay,
'T were very hard for the Count to say ;
But pale are his cheeks and pained his brow,
And the boat drifts on he recks not how ;
His pulse is quick and his heart is wild,
And he weeps, he weeps, like a little child.

O mighty music! they who know
The witchery of thy wondrous bow,
Forget, when thy strange spells have bound them,
The visible world that lies around them.
When Lady Mary sings Rosini,
Or stares at spectral Paganini,
To Lady Mary does it matter
Who laugh, who love, who frown, who flatter?
Oh no ; she cannot heed or hear
Reason or rhyme from prince or peer:
In vain for her Sir Charles denounces
The horror of the last new flounces;
In vain her friend the Member raves
Of ballot, bullion, sugars, slaves ;
Predicts the nation's future glories,
And chants the requiem of the Tories;
And if some fond and foolish lisper
Recites, in passion's softest whisper,
The raptures which young love imparts
To mutual minds and kindred hearts,—
Poor boy,—she minds him just as much
As if 'twere logic, or High Dutch.

As little did the young Knight care,—
While still he listened to the air
Breathed by some melodist unseen,
Much wondering what it all might mean,—
For those odd changes of the sky,
To dark from bright, to moist from dry,
Which furnish to the British nation
Three quarters of its conversation.
Meantime a gust, a drop, a flash
Had warned, perhaps, a youth less rash,
To shun a storm of fiercer fury,
Than ever stunned the gods of Drury.

Hid was the bright heaven's loveliness
   Beneath a sudden cloud,
As a bride might doff her bridal dress
   To don her funeral shroud;
And over flood, and over fell,
   With a wild and wicked shout,
From the secret cell, where in chains they dwell,
   The joyous winds rushed out;
And the tall hills through, the thunder flew,
   And down the fierce hail came;
And from peak to peak the lightning threw
   Its shafts of liquid flame.
The boat went down; without delay,
The luckless boatman swooned away;
And when, as a clear Spring morning rose
He woke in wonder from repose,

The river was calm as the river could be,
And the thrush was awake on the gladsome tree,
And there he lay, in a sunny cave,
On the margin of the tranquil wave,
Half deaf with that infernal din,
And wet, poor fellow, to the skin.
He looked to the left and he looked to the right—
Why hastened he not, the noble knight,
To dry his aged nurse's tears,
To calm the hoary butler's fears,
To listen to the prudent speeches
Of half a dozen loquacious leeches—
To swallow cordials circumspectly,
And change his dripping cloak directly ?
With foot outstretched, with hand upraised,
In vast surprise he gazed, and gazed :
Within a deep and damp recess
A maiden lay in her loveliness !
Lived she ?—in sooth 't were hard to tell,
Sleep counterfeited Death so well.
A shelf of the rock was all her bed;
A ceiling of crystal was o'er her head ;
Silken veil nor satin vest,
Shrouded her form in its silent rest ;
Only her long, long golden hair
About her lay like a thin robe there ;
Up to her couch the young knight crept :
How very sound the maiden slept !
Fearful and faint the young knight sighed :
The echoes of the cave replied.

He leaned to look upon her face;
He clasped her hand in a wild embrace;
Never was form of such fine mould—
But the hands and the face were as white and cold
As they of the Parian stone were made,
To which, in great Minerva's shade,
The Athenian sculptor's toilsome knife
Gave all of loveliness but life.
On her fair neck there seemed no stain,
Where the pure blood coursed thro' the delicate vein,
And her breath, if breath indeed it were,
Flowed in a current so soft and rare,
It would scarcely have stirred the young moth's wing
On the path of his noonday wandering;
Never on earth a creature trod,
Half so lovely, or half so odd.

Count Otto stares till his eyelids ache,
And wonders when she 'll please to wake;
While Fancy whispers strange suggestions,
And Wonder prompts a score of questions.
Is she a nymph of another sphere?
How came she hither?—what does she here?
Or if the morning of her birth
Be registered on this our earth,
Why hath she fled from her father's halls?
And where hath she left her cloaks and shawls?
There was no time for Reason's lectures,
There was no time for Wit's conjectures;
He threw his arm, with timid haste,
Around the maiden's slender waist,

And raised her up in a modest way,
From the cold, bare rock on which she lay.
He was but a mile from his castle gate,
And the lady was scarcely five stone weight;
He stopped, in less than half an hour,
With his beauteous burden, at Belmont Tower.

Gayly, I ween, was the chamber dressed,
As the Count gave order for his guest;
But scarcely on the couch, 'tis said,
That gentle guest was fairly laid,
When she opened at once her great blue eyes,
And, after a glance of brief surprise,
Ere she had spoken, and ere she had heard
Of wisdom or wit a single word,
She laughed so long, and laughed so loud,
That Dame Ulrica often vowed
A dirge is a merrier thing by half
Than such a senseless, soulless laugh.
Around the tower the elfin crew
Seemed shouting in mirthful concert too;
And echoed roof, and trembled rafter,
With that unsentimental laughter.

As soon as that droll tumult passed,
The maiden's tongue, unchained at last,
Asserted all its female right,
And talked and talked with all its might.
Oh, how her low and liquid voice
Made the rapt hearer's soul rejoice!

'T was full of those clear tones that start
From innocent childhood's happy heart,
Ere passion and sin disturb the well
In which their mirth and music dwell.
But man nor master could make out
What the eloquent maiden talked about;
The things she uttered like did seem
To the babbling waves of a limpid stream;
For the words of her speech, if words they might be,
Were the words of a speech of a far countrie;
And when she had said them o'er and o'er,
Count Otto understood no more
Than you or I of the slang that falls
From dukes and dupes at Tattersall's,
Of Hebrew from a bearded Jew,
Or metaphysics from a Blue.

Count Otto swore, (Count Otto's reading
Might well have taught him better breeding,)
That whether the maiden should fume or fret,
The maiden should not leave him yet;
And so he took prodigious pains
To make her happy in her chains;
From Paris came a pair of cooks,
From Gottingen a load of books;
From Venice stores of gorgeous suits,
From Florence minstrels and their lutes;
The youth himself had special pride
In breaking horses for his bride;
And his old tutor, Doctor Hermann,
Was brought from Bonn to teach her German.

He who with curious step hath strayed
Alone through some suburban shade,
To rural Chelsea sauntering down,
Or wandering over Camden Town,
The sacred mansions oft has seen,
Whose walls are white, whose gates are green,
Where ladies with respected names,
Miss Black, Miss Brown, Miss Jenks, Miss James,
For fifty pounds a year or so
Teach beauty all it ought to know,—
How long have been the reigns and lives
Of British monarchs and their wives,—
How fast the twinkling planets run,
From age to age about the sun,—
The depths of lakes, the heights of hills,
The rule of three, the last quadrilles,
Italian airs, Parisian phrases,
The class and sex of shells and dasies,
The rules of grammar and of grace,
Right sentiments, and thorough-bass.
There quick the young idea shoots,
And bears its blossoms and its fruits.
The rosy nymph, who nothing knows
  But just to scream a noisy ballad,
To mend her little brother's hose,
  To make a cake, or mix a salad,
Tormented for a year or two,
  (So fast the female wit advances)
Shall grow superlatively blue,
  And print a volume of romances.

But ne'er did any forward child,
In any such sequestered college,
Trip faster than my maiden wild
Through every path of useful knowledge.

In May o'er grassy hill and vale
Like some young fawn's her footsteps bounded;
In May upon the morning gale
Like some blithe bird's her carols sounded:
June came;—she practised pirouettes
That might have puzzled Bigottini,
And decked her simple canzonets
With shakes that would have charmed Rossini.
In spring to her the A, B, C,
Appeared a mystery quite as murky
As galvanism to Owhyhee,
Or annual Parliaments to Turkey;
But when upon the flood and fell
Brown autumn's earliest storms were low'ring,
She was quite competent to spell
Through all the books of Doctor Bowring.

No cheerful friend, no quiet guest,
Doth Wisdom come to human breast;
She brings the day-beam, but in sooth
She brings its trouble with its truth.
With every cloud that flits and flies
Some dear delusion fades and dies;
With every flash of perfect light
Some loveless prospect blasts the sight.

Shut up the page ; for in its lore
Are fears and doubts unfelt before :
Fling down the wreath ; for sorrow weaves
Amid the laurel cypress leaves.

Moons waxed and waned ; and you might trace
  In the captive maiden gradual change ;
Ever and ever of form and face
  Some charm seemed fresh and new and strange :
Over her cold and colorless cheek
  The blush of the rose began to glow,
And her quickened pulse began to speak
  Of human bliss and human woe ;
Her features kept their beauty still,
  But a graver shade was o'er them thrown ;
Her voice had yet its clear soft thrill,
  But its echo took a sadder tone.

Oft, till the Count came up from wine,
  She sat alone by the lattice high,
Tracing the course of the rolling Rhine
  With a moody brow and a wistful eye ;
Still, as the menials oft averred,
  Talking and talking, low and long,
In that droll language which they heard,
  At her first coming, from her tongue.
None but the Pope of Rome, they deemed,
  Could construe what the damsel said ;
But this they knew, by turns she seemed
  To soothe, to threaten, to upbraid.

And oft on a crag at dawn she stood,
  Her golden harp in her pretty hand,
And sang such songs to the gurgling flood
  As an exile sings to his native land;
Till, if a listener dared intrude,
  She hastened back to the postern-gate,
Blushing, as if her solitude
  Were as dear and as wrong as a *tête-à-tête*.

'Twas wondrous all; but most of all,
That, held in strict though gentle thrall,
She seemed so slow to take upon her
The style and state of threatened honor.
For often, when on bended knee
Count Otto pressed his amorous plea,
And begged, before his heart should break,
She'd be a Countess for his sake,
Without the slightest show of flurry,
She chid his heat, and checked his hurry:
He might allow her time, she said,
To learn the life his Lordship led;
Such hawking, hunting, dining, drinking,—
At times she felt her poor heart sinking!
At home, in bed the livelong day,
She lived in such a different way;
So calm, so cool,—her father's daughter
Was ne'er a minute in hot water.

Then their acquaintance, she must state,
Was of a very recent date;

They met in May, he should remember,
And now were hardly in December;
Such eyes as hers, she had a notion,
Were worth at least a year's devotion.
Her kindred had their fancies too
Of what young ladies ought to do:
All sorts of mischief might befall,
If rashly in her father's hall
Before twelve months of courtship ended
She showed her face with her intended.—
But where that father's hall?—vain, vain;
 She turned her eyes in silence down;
And if you dared to ask again,
 Her only answer was a frown.
Some people have a knack, we know,
Of saying things mal-à-propos,
And making all the world reflect
On what it hates to recollect.
They talk to misers of their heir,
To women of the days that were,
To ruined gamblers of the box,
To thin defaulters of the stocks,
To poets of the wrong Review,
And to the French of Waterloo.
The Count was not of these; he never
Was half so clumsy, half so clever;
And when he found the girl would rather
Say nothing more about her father,
He changed the subject—told a fable—
Believed that dinner was on table—

Or hinted, with an air of sorrow,
The certainty of rain to morrow.

Meantime the world began to prate
Of young Count Otto's purposed marriage;
Discussed the jewels and the plate,
Described the dresses and the carriage.
The lady's rank, the lady's name,
As usual in such curious cases,
Were asked by many a noble dame,
With most expressive tones and faces;
The grave and gay, the old and young,
Looked very arch, or very serious;
Some whispered something that was wrong,
Some murmured much that was mysterious.

One aunt, a strict old maiden, thought,—
And could not bear the thought to smother,—
Young persons positively ought
To have a father and a mother;
And wondered, with becoming scorn,
How far presumption might be carried,
When hussies who had ne'er been born
Began to think of being married:
Another, fair, and kind as fair,
Was heard by many to protest
It was her daily wish and prayer
That she might see her nephew blest;
And though, as matters stood, of course
'Twas quite impossible to call

On somebody, whom she perforce
  Considered nobody at all,
When once the Church had done its part,
  And ratified the Count's selection,
She'd clasp the Countess to her heart,
  Impromptu, with profound affection.

The winter storms went darkly by,
And, from a blue and cloudless sky,
Again the sun looked cheerfully
  Upon the rolling Rhine;
And spring brought back to the budding flowers
Its genial light and freshening showers,
And music to the shady bowers,
  And verdure to the vine.

And now it is the first of May;
For twenty miles round all is gay;
Cottage and castle keep holiday;
  For how should sorrow lower
On brow of rustic or of knight,
When heaven itself looks all so bright,
Where Otto's wedding feast is dight
  In the hall of Belmont Tower?

For the maiden's hair the wreath is wrought;
For the maiden's hand the ring is bought;
Be she a Fiend, or be she a Fay,
She shall be Otto's bride to-day.
And he,—for he at last discovers
That "no" is a word unfit for lovers,—

Has promised, as soon as the priest has done
The terrible rite that makes them one,
To step with her to the carriage and four
That waits e'en now at the castle-door,
And post to visit—"although," saith she,
"A very odd road our road may be"—
Her father, her mother, and two or three dozens
Of highly respectable aunts and cousins:
And he has sanctioned his consent,
Lest he should happen to repent,
By a score or more of the oaths that slip,
As matters of course, from a bridegroom's lip.

Stately matron and warrior tall
Come to the joyous festival;
Gladly Otto welcomes all,
  As through the gate they throng;
He fills to the brim the wassail cup;
In the bright wine pleasure sparkles up,
  And draughts and tales grow long;
But grizzly knights are still and mute,
And dames set down the untasted fruit,
When the bride awakes her golden lute,
  And charms them all with song.

  "The dawn is past, the dusk comes fast,
    No longer may I roam;
  Full soon, full soon, the young May moon
    Will guide the truant home:

Hasten we, hasten, groom and bride;
  How merry we shall be!
Now open, father, open wide,
  Let in my lord with me.

"Though treasures old of silver and gold
  Lie in thy secret store,
I bring thee to-night, to charm thy sight,
  Gifts thou wilt value more;
Knightly valor, and lordly pride,
  Leal heart, and spirit free;—
Now open, father, open wide,
  Let in my lord with me.

"I hear, I hear, with joy and fear,
  The old familiar tone;
I hear him call to his ancient hall
  His favorite, his own;
How will he chafe and how will he chide!
  For a fretful mood hath he;—
Now open, father, open wide,
  Let in my lord with me!"

The nurses to the children say
That, as the maiden sang that day,
The Rhine to the heights of the beetling tower
Sent up a cry of fiercer power,
And again the maiden's cheek was grown
As white as ever was marble stone,
And the bridesmaid her hand could hardly hold,
Its fingers were so icy cold.

Rose Count Otto from the feast,
As entered the hall the hoary priest.
A stalwart warrior, well I ween,
That hoary priest in his youth had been;
But the might of his manhood he had given
To penance and prayer, the Church and Heaven.

For he had travelled o'er land and wave;
He had kneeled on many a martyr's grave;
He had prayed in the meek St. Jerome's cell,
And had tasted St. Anthony's blessed well.
And reliques round his neck had he,
Each worth a haughty kingdom's fee—
Scrapings of bones, and points of spears,
And vials of authentic tears–
From a prophet's coffin a hallowed nail,
And a precious shred of our Lady's veil;
And therefore at his awful tread,
The powers of darkness shrank with dread;
And Satan felt that no disguise
Could hide him from those chastened eyes.
He looked on the bridegroom, he looked on the bride,
The young Count smiled, but the old priest sighed.

" Fields with the father I have won;
I am come in my cowl to bless the son;
Count Otto, ere thou bend thy knee,
What shall the hire of my service be?"

"Greedy hawk must gorge his prey,
Pious priest must grasp his pay;

Name the guerdon, and so to the task;
Thine it is, ere thy lips can ask."

He frowned as he answered—"Gold and gem,
Count Otto, little I reck of them;
But your bride has skill of the lute, they say:
Let her sing me the song I shall name to-day."

Loud laughed the Count: "And if she refuse
The ditty, Sir Priest, thy whim shall choose,
Row back to the house of old St. Goar;
I never bid priest to a bridal more."

Beside the maiden he took his stand,
He gave the lute to her trembling hand;
She gazed around with a troubled eye;
The guests all shuddered, and knew not why;
It seemed to them as if a gloom
Had shrouded all the banquet room,
Though over its boards, and over its beams,
Sunlight was glowing in merry streams.

The stern priest throws an angry glance
On that pale creature's countenance;
Unconsciously her white hand flings
Its soft touch o'er the answering strings;
The good man starts with a sudden thrill,
And half relents from his purposed will;
But he signs the cross on his aching brow
And arms his soul for its warfare now.

"Mortal maid or goblin fairy,
Sing me, I pray thee, an Ave-Mary!"

Suddenly the maiden bent
O'er the gorgeous instrument;
But of song, the listeners heard
Only one wild, mournful word—
"Lurley! Lurley!"
And when the sound, in the liquid air,
Of that brief hymn had faded,
Nothing was left of the nymph who there
For a year had masqueraded;
But the harp in the midst of the wide hall set,
Where her last strange word was spoken!
The golden frame with tears was wet,
And all the strings were broken!

(Written in 1831; but revised by the Author and largely added to in 1837. In the original version the song of the bride stood thus:—

"A voice ye hear not, in mine ear is crying;—
What does the sad voice say?
'Dost thou not heed thy weary father's sighing?
Return, return to-day!
Twelve moons have faded now:
My daughter, where art thou?'

"Peace! in the silent evening we will meet thee,
Gray ruler of the tide!
Must not the lover with the loved one greet thee?
The bridegroom with his bride?
Deck the dim couch aright,
The bridal couch, to-night.")

THE LEGEND OF THE TEUFEL-HAUS.

The way was lone, and the hour was late,
And Sir Rudolph was far from his castle gate.
The night came down, by slow degrees,
On the river stream, and the forest-trees;
And by the heat of the heavy air,
And by the lightning's distant glare,
And by the rustling of the woods,
And by the roaring of the floods,
In half an hour, a man might say,
The Spirit of Storm would ride that way.
But little he cared, that stripling pale,
For the sinking sun, or the rising gale;
For he, as he rode, was dreaming now,
Poor youth, of a woman's broken vow,
Of the cup dashed down, ere the wine was tasted,
Of eloquent speeches sadly wasted,
Of a gallant heart all burnt to ashes,
And the Baron of Katzberg's long mustaches.
So the earth below, and the heaven above,
He saw them not;—those dreams of love,
As some have found, and some will find,
Make men extremely deaf and blind.

At last he opened his great blue eyes,
And looking about in vast surprise,
Found that his hunter had turned his back,
An hour ago, on the beaten track,
And now was threading a forest hoar,
Where steed had never stepped before.

"By Cæsar's head," Sir Rudolph said,
"It were a sorry joke,
If I to-night should make my bed
On the turf, beneath an oak!
Poor Roland reeks from head to hoof;—
Now, for thy sake, good roan,
I would we were beneath a roof,
Were it the foul fiend's own!"

Ere the tongue could rest, ere the lips could close,
The sound of a listener's laughter rose.
It was not the scream of a merry boy
When harlequin waves his wand of joy;
Nor the shout from a serious curate, won
By a bending bishop's annual pun;
Nor the roar of a Yorkshire clown;—oh, no!
It was a gentle laugh, and low;
Half uttered, perhaps, and stifled half,
A good old-gentlemanly laugh;
Such as my uncle Peter's are,
When he tells you his tales of Dr. Parr.
The rider looked to the left and the right,
With something of marvel, and more of fright:

But brighter gleamed his anxious eye,
When a light shone out from a hill hard by.
Thither he spurred, as gay and glad
As Mrs. Macquill's delighted lad,
When he turns away from the Pleas of the Crown,
Or flings, with a yawn, old Saunders down,
And flies, at last, from all the mysteries
Of Plaintiffs' and Defendants' histories,
To make himself sublimely neat,
For Mrs. Camac's in Mansfield Street.
At a lofty gate Sir Rudolph halted;
Down from his seat Sir Rudolph vaulted:
And he blew a blast with might and main,
On the bugle that hung by an iron chain
The sound called up a score of sounds;—
The screeching of owls, and the baying of hounds,
The hollow toll of the turret bell,
The call of the watchful sentinel,
And a groan at last, like a peal of thunder,
As the huge old portals rolled asunder,
And gravely from the castle hall
Paced forth the white-robed seneschal.
He stayed not to ask of what degree
So fair and famished a knight might be;
But knowing that all untimely question
Ruffles the temper, and mars the digestion,
He laid his hand upon the crupper,
And said,—"You're just in time for supper!"
They led him to the smoking board,
And placed him next to the castle's lord.

He looked around with a hurried glance:
You may ride from the border to fair Penzance,
And nowhere, but at Epsom Races,
Find such a group of ruffian faces
As thronged that chamber: some were talking
Of feats of hunting and of hawking,
And some were drunk, and some were dreaming,
And some found pleasure in blaspheming.
He thought, as he gazed on the fearful crew,
That the lamps that burned on the walls burned blue.
They brought him a pasty of mighty size,
To cheer his heart, and to charm his eyes;
They brought the wine, so rich and old,
And filled to the brim the cup of gold;
The knight looked down, and the knight looked up,
But he carved not the meat, and he drained not the cup.

"Ho, ho," said his host with angry brow,
"I wot our guest is fine;
Our fare is far too coarse, I trow,
For such nice taste as thine:
Yet trust me I have cooked the food,
And I have filled the can,
Since I have lived in this old wood,
For many a nobler man."—
"The savory buck and the ancient cask
To a weary man are sweet;
But ere he taste, it is fit he ask
For a blessing on bowl and meat.

Let me but pray for a minute's space,
And bid me pledge ye then;
I swear to ye, by our Lady's grace,
I shall eat and drink like ten!"

The lord of the castle in wrath arose,
He frowned like a fiery dragon;
Indignantly he blew his nose,
And overturned the flagon.
And, "Away," quoth he, "with the canting priest,
Who comes uncalled to a midnight feast,
And breathes through a helmet his holy benison,
To sour my hock, and spoil my venison!"

That moment all the lights went out;
And they dragged him forth, that rabble rout,
With oath, and threat, and foul scurrility,
And every sort of incivility.
They barred the gates; and the peal of laughter,
Sudden and shrill, that followed after,
Died off into a dismal tone,
Like a parting spirit's painful moan.
"I wish," said Rudolph, as he stood
On foot in the deep and silent wood;
"I wish, good Roland, rack and stable
May be kinder to-night than their master's table!"
By this the storm had fleeted by;
And the moon with a quiet smile looked out
From the glowing arch of a cloudless sky,
Flinging her silvery beams about

On rock, tree, wave, and gladdening all
  With just as miscellaneous bounty,
As Isabel's, whose sweet smiles fall
  In half an hour on half the county.
Less wild Sir Rudolph's pathway seemed,
  As he turned from that discourteous tower;
Small spots of verdure gayly gleamed
  On either side; and many a flower,
Lily, and violet, and heart's-ease,
  Grew by the way, a fragrant border;
And the tangled boughs of the hoary trees
  Were twined in picturesque disorder:
And there came from the grove, and there came from the hill
  The loveliest sounds he had ever heard,
The cheerful voice of the dancing rill,
  And the sad, sad song of the lonely bird.

And at last he stared with wondering eyes,
  As well he might, on a huge pavilion:
'Twas clothed with stuffs of a hundred dyes,
  Blue, purple, orange, pink, vermilion;
And there were quaint devices traced
  All round in the Saracenic manner;
And the top which gleamed like gold, was graced
  With the drooping folds of a silken banner;
And on the poles, in silent pride,
  There sat small doves of white enamel;
And the veil from the entrance was drawn aside,
  And flung on the humps of a silver camel.

In short it was the sweetest thing
  For a weary youth in a wood to light on;
And finer far than what a king
  Built up, to prove his taste, at Brighton.
  The gilded gate was all unbarred;
And, close beside it, for a guard,
There lay two dwarfs with monstrous noses,
Both fast asleep upon some roses.
Sir Rudolph entered; rich and bright
Was all that met his ravished sight;
Soft tapestries from far countries brought,
Rare cabinets with gems inwrought,
White vases of the finest mould,
And mirrors set in burnished gold.
Upon a couch a grayhound slumbered;
And a small table was encumber'd
With paintings, and an ivory lute,
And sweetmeats, and delicious fruit.
Sir Rudolph lost no time in praising;
For he, I should have said, was gazing,
In attitude extremely tragic,
Upon a sight of stranger magic;
A sight, which, seen at such a season,
Might well astonish Mistress Reason,
And scare Dame Wisdom from her fences
Of rules and maxims, moods and tenses.
Beneath a crimson canopy
  A lady, passing fair, was lying;
Deep sleep was on her gentle eye,
  And in her slumber she was sighing

Bewitching sighs, such sighs as say
  Beneath the moonlight, to a lover,
Things which the coward tongue by day
  Would not, for all the world, discover:
She lay like a shape of sculptured stone,
So pale, so tranquil:—she had thrown,
  For the warm evening's sultriness,
The broidered coverlet aside;
And nothing was there to deck or hide
  The glory of her loveliness,
But a scarf of gauze so light and thin
You might see beneath the dazzling skin,
And watch the purple streamlets go
Through the valleys of white and stainless snow,
Or here and there a wayward tress
Which wandered out with vast assurance
From the pearls that kept the rest in durance,
And fluttered about, as if 'twould try
To lure a zephyr from the sky.

"Bertha!"—large drops of anguish came
On Rudolph's brow, as he breathed that name,—
"Oh fair and false one, wake, and fear;
I the betrayed, the scorned, am here."
The eye moved not from its dull eclipse,
The voice came not from the fast-shut lips;
No matter! well that gazer knew
The tone of bliss, and the eyes of blue.
  Sir Rudolph hid his burning face
With both his hands for a minute's space,

And all his frame in awful fashion
Was shaken by some sudden passion.
What guilty fancies o'er him ran?—
Oh, Pity will be slow to guess them;
And never, save to the holy man,
Did good Sir Rudolph e'er confess them,
But soon his spirit you might deem
Came forth from the shade of the fearful dream;
His cheek, though pale, was calm again,
And he spoke in peace, though he spoke in pain:
"Not mine! not mine! now, Mary, mother,
Aid me the sinful hope to smother!
Not mine, not mine!—I have loved thee long;
Thou hast quitted me with grief and wrong.
But pure the heart of a knight should be,—
Sleep on, sleep on, thou art safe for me.
Yet shalt thou know by a certain sign,
Whose lips have been so near to thine,
Whose eyes have looked upon thy sleep,
And turned away, and longed to weep,
Whose heart,—mourn,—madden as it will,—
Has spared thee, and adored thee, still!"
His purple mantle, rich and wide,
From his neck the trembling youth untied,
And flung it o'er those dangerous charms,
The swelling neck, and the rounded arms.
Once more he looked, once more he sighed;
And away, away, from the perilous tent,
Swift as the rush of an eagle's wing,
Or the flight of a shaft from Tartar string,
Into the wood Sir Rudolph went:

Not with more joy the school-boys run
To the gay green fields, when their task is done;
Not with more haste the members fly,
When Hume has caught the Speaker's eye.
At last the daylight came; and then
A score or two of serving men,
Supposing that some sad disaster
Had happened to their lord and master,
Went out into the wood, and found him,
Unhorsed, and with no mantle round him.
Ere he could tell his tale romantic,
The leech pronounced him clearly frantic,
So ordered him at once to bed,
And clapped a blister on his head.
Within the sound of the castle-clock
There stands a huge and rugged rock,
And I have heard the peasants say,
That the grieving groom at noon that day
Found gallant Roland, cold and stiff,
At the base of the black and beetling cliff.
Beside the rock there is an oak,
Tall, blasted by the thunder-stroke,
And I have heard the peasants say,
That there Sir Rudolph's mantle lay,
And coiled in many a deadly wreath
A venomous serpent slept beneath.

(1830)

THE RED FISHERMAN.

OR

THE DEVIL'S DECOY.

"O flesh, flesh, how art thou fishified!"
Romeo and Juliet.

THE abbot arose, and closed his book,
And donned his sandal shoon,
And wandered forth, alone, to look
Upon the summer moon:
A starlight sky was o'er his head,
A quiet breeze around;
And the flowers a thrilling fragrance shed,
And the waves a soothing sound:
It was not an hour, nor a scene, for aught
But love and calm delight;
Yet the holy man had a cloud of thought
On his wrinkled brow that night.
He gazed on the river that gurgled by,
But he thought not of the reeds:
He clasped his gilded rosary,
But he did not tell the beads;
If he looked to the heaven, 'twas not to invoke
The Spirit that dwelleth there;
If he opened his lips, the words they spoke
Had never the tone of prayer.

A pious priest might the abbot seem,
He had swayed the crosier well;
But what was the theme of the abbot's dream,
The abbot were loth to tell.

Companionless, for a mile or more,
He traced the windings of the shore.
Oh, beauteous is that river still,
As it winds by many a sloping hill,
And many a dim o'erarching grove,
And many a flat and sunny cove,
And terraced lawns, whose bright arcades
The honeysuckle sweetly shades,
And rocks, whose very crags seemed bowers,
So gay they are with grass and flowers!

But the abbot was thinking of scenery,
About as much in sooth,
As a lover thinks of constancy,
Or an advocate of truth.
He did not mark how the skies in wrath
Grew dark above his head;
He did not mark how the mossy path
Grew damp beneath his tread;
And nearer he came, and still more near,
To a pool, in whose recess
The water had slept for many a year,
Unchanged and motionless;
From the river stream it spread away
The space of a half a rood;
The surface had the hue of clay
And the scent of human blood;

The trees and the herbs that round it grew
  Were venomous and foul;
And the birds that through the bushes flew
  Were the vulture and the owl;
The water was as dark and rank
  As ever a Company pumped;
And the perch, that was netted and laid on the bank,
  Grew rotten while it jumped:
And bold was he who thither came
  At midnight, man or boy;
For the place was cursed with an evil name,
  And that name was "The Devil's Decoy!"

The abbot was weary as abbot could be,
And he sat down to rest on the stump of a tree:
When suddenly rose a dismal tone—
Was it a song, or was it a moan?
    O ho! O ho!
    Above, below!
Lightly and brightly they glide and go;
The hungry and keen on the top are leaping,
The lazy and fat in the depths are sleeping;
Fishing is fine when the pool is muddy,
Broiling is rich when the coals are ruddy!"
In a monstrous fright, by the murky light,
He looked to the left and he looked to the right,
And what was the vision close before him,
That flung such a sudden stupor o'er him?
'Twas a sight to make the hair uprise,
  And the life-blood colder run:
The startled priest struck both his thighs,
  And the abbey clock struck one!

All alone, by the side of the pool,
A tall man sat on a three-legged stool,
Kicking his heels on the dewy sod,
And putting in order his reel and rod;
Red were the rags his shoulders wore,
And a high red cap on his head he bore;
His arms and his legs were long and bare ,
And two or three locks of long red hair
Were tossing about his scraggy neck,
Like a tattered flag o'er a splitting wreck.
It might be Time, or it might be trouble,
Had bent that stout back nearly double—
Sunk in their deep and hollow sockets
That blazing couple of Congreve rockets,
And shrunk and shrivelled that tawny skin,
Till it hardly covered the bones within.
The line the abbot saw him throw
Had been fashioned and formed long ages ago,
And the hands that worked his foreign vest
Long ages ago had gone to their rest:
You would have sworn, as you looked on them,
He had fished in the flood with Ham and Shem!

There was turning of keys, and creaking of locks,
As he took forth a bait from his iron box.
Minnow or gentle, worm or fly—
It seemed not such to the abbot's eye;
Gayly it glittered with jewel and gem,
And its shape was the shape of a diadem.
It was fastened a gleaming hook about,
By a chain within and a chain without;

The fisherman gave it a kick and a spin,
And the water fizzed as it tumbled in!

From the bowels of the earth,
Strange and varied sounds had birth—
Now the battle's bursting peal,
Neigh of steed, and clang of steel;
Now an old man's hollow groan
Echoed from the dungeon stone;
Now the weak and wailing cry
Of a stripling's agony!

Cold by this was the midnight air;
But the abbot's blood ran colder,
When he saw a gasping knight lie there,
With a gash beneath his clotted hair,
And a hump upon his shoulder.
And the loyal churchman strove in vain
To mutter a Pater Noster;
For he who writhed in mortal pain
Was camped that night on Bosworth plain—
The cruel Duke of Gloster!

There was turning of keys, and creaking of locks,
As he took forth a bait from his iron box.
It was a haunch of princely size,
Filling with fragrance earth and skies.
The corpulent abbot knew full well
The swelling form, and the steaming smell;
Never a monk that wore a hood
Could better have guessed the very wood

Where the noble hart had stood at bay,
Weary and wounded, at close of day.

Sounded then the noisy glee
Of a revelling company—
Sprightly story, wicked jest,
Rated servant, greeted guest,
Flow of wine, and flight of cork,
Stroke of knife, and thrust of fork:
But, where'er the board was spread,
Grace, I ween, was never said!

Pulling and tugging the fisherman sat;
And the priest was ready to vomit,
When he hauled out a gentleman, fine and fat,
With a belly as big as a brimming vat,
And a nose as red as a comet.
"A capital stew," the fisherman said,
"With cinnamon and sherry!"
And the abbot turned away his head,
For his brother was lying before him dead,
The mayor of St. Edmond's Bury!

There was turning of keys, and creaking of locks,
As he took forth a bait from his iron box:
It was a bundle of beautiful things—
A peacock's tail, and a butterfly's wings,
A scarlet slipper, an auburn curl,
A mantle of silk, and a bracelet of pearl,
And a packet of letters, from whose sweet fold
Such a stream of delicate odors rolled,

That the abbot fell on his face, and fainted,
And deemed his spirit was half-way sainted.

Sounds seemed dropping from the skies,
Stifled whispers, smothered sighs,
And the breath of vernal gales,
And the voice of nightingales:
But the nightingales were mute,
Envious, when an unseen lute
Shaped the music of its chords
Into passion's thrilling words:

"Smile, lady, smile!—I will not set
Upon my brow the coronet,
Till thou wilt gather roses white
To wear around its gems of light.
Smile, lady, smile!—I will not see
Rivers and Hastings bend the knee,
Till those bewitching lips of thine
Will bid me rise in bliss from mine.
Smile, lady, smile!—for who would win
A loveless throne through guilt and sin?
Or who would reign o'er vale and hill,
If woman's heart were rebel still?"

One jerk, and there a lady lay,
A lady wondrous fair;
But the rose of her lip had faded away,
And her cheek was as white and as cold as clay,
And torn was her raven hair.
"Ah ha!" said the fisher, in merry guise,

"Her gallant was hooked before;"
And the abbot heaved some piteous sighs,
For oft he had blessed those deep blue eyes,
The eyes of Mistress Shore!

There was turning of keys, and creaking of locks,
As he took forth a bait from his iron box.
Many the cunning sportsman tried,
Many he flung with a frown aside;
A minstrel's harp, and a miser's chest,
A hermit's cowl, and a baron's crest,
Jewels of lustre, robes of price,
Tomes of heresy, loaded dice,
And golden cups of the brightest wine
That ever was pressed from the Burgundy vine;
There was a perfume of sulphur and nitre,
As he came at last to a bishop's mitre!
From top to toe the abbot shook,
As the fisherman armed his golden hook;
And awfully were his features wrought
By some dark dream or wakened thought.
Look how the fearful felon gazes
On the scaffold his country's vengeance raises,
When the lips are cracked and the jaws are dry
With the thirst which only in death shall die:
Mark the mariner's frenzied frown
As the swaling wherry settles down,
When peril has numbed the sense and will,
Though the hand and the foot may struggle still:
Wilder far was the abbot's glance,
Deeper far was the abbot's trance:

Fixed as a monument, still as air,
He bent no knee, and he breathed no prayer;
But he signed—he knew not why or how—
The sign of the Cross on his clammy brow.

There was turning of keys, and creaking of locks,
As he stalked away with his iron box.
        "O ho! O ho!
        The cock doth crow;
It is time for the fisher to rise and go.
Fair luck to the abbot, fair luck to the shrine!
He hath gnawed in twain my choicest line;
Let him swim to the north, let him swim to the south,
The abbot will carry my hook in his mouth!"

The abbot had preached for many years,
  With as clear articulation
As ever was heard in the House of Peers
  Against Emancipation;
His words had made battalions quake,
  Had roused the zeal of martyrs;
He kept the court an hour awake,
  And the king himself three quarters:
But ever, from that hour, 'tis said,
  He stammered and he stuttered,
As if an axe went through his head
  With every word he uttered.
He stuttered o'er blessing, he stuttered o'er ban,
  He stuttered, drunk or dry;
And none but he and the fisherman
  Could tell the reason why!

(1827.)

POEMS OF LOVE AND FANCY.

LIDIAN'S LOVE.

The gayest gallants of the Court
Oft fell in love, on mere report,
With eyes they had not seen;
And knelt, and rhymed, and sighed, and frowned,
In talismanic fetters bound,
With flowers and sunshine all around—
And five-score leagues between.—*MS. Poem.*

I.

Sir Lidian had attained his sixteenth year;
The golden age of life, wherein are met
Boyhood's last hope and Manhood's earliest fear
In mingled bliss and beauty;—you forget
Your cradle's laughter, and your school-room's tear,
Your maiden medal, and your first gazette;
But never, never, the bright dreams that blind you
When sixteen years are newly left behind you.

II.

The daily longings to be very great,
The nightly studies to be very killing,
The blessed recklessness of human hate,
The sonnet-singing, and the sigh-distilling,
The chase of folly, and the scorn of fate,
Friendship's fresh throb, and Passion's April thrill-
ing
For some high lady, whom your elder brother
Declares is old enough to be your mother.

III.

Sir Lidian had attained his sixteenth year,
  And was the loveliest stripling in the land:
His small soft features and his color clear
  Were like a budding girl's; his delicate hand
Seemed fitter for the distaff than the spear;
  Locks of bright brown his spotless forehead fanned;
And he had eyes as blue as summer's heaven,
And stood a little more than five feet seven.

IV.

No gallant flung a lance so fleet and true
  From the trained courser through the golden ring,
No joyous harper at the banquet threw
  A lighter touch across the sounding string;
Yet on his cheek there was the hectic hue
  And in his eye the fitful wandering
Which chill our praise to pity, that a bloom
So fresh and fair is destined to the tomb!

V.

And though he danced and played, as I have hinted,
  In dance and song he took but little pleasure;
He looked contented though his partner squinted,
  And seldom frowned when minstrels marred the measure;
When the rich sky by evening's glow was tinted,
  More glad was he to wander at his leisure,
Despising fogs, apostrophizing fountains,
Wasting the time, and worshipping the mountains.

VI.

And yet he had not loved!—his early fancies
Of love, first love, the transport and the pain,
Had been extracted from the best romances,
And were, perhaps, of too sublime a strain;
So when he woke from those delicious trances,
He shut his eyes and chose to sleep again,
Shunning realities for shades, and fleeing
From all he saw to all he dreamed of seeing.

VII.

In starlit dells and zephyr-haunted bowers,
Moistened by rivulets whose milky foam
Murmured the sweetest music, where warm showers
That trickled fresh from Heaven's eternal dome
Watered bright jewels that spring up like flowers,—
In such a scene his fancy found a home,
A Paradise of Fancy's fabrication,
Peopled by Houris of the heart's creation;

VIII.

Who never thrummed upon the virginals,
Nor tripped by rule, nor fortunately fainted,
Nor practised paying compliments and calls,
Looking satirical, or looking sainted,
Nor shrieked at tournaments, nor blushed at balls,
Nor lisped, nor sighed, nor drooped, nor punned,
nor painted;
Nor wrote a book, nor traded in caresses,
Nor made remarks on other people's dresses.

IX.

These were his raptures;—these have all been mine;
  I could have worshipped once a constellation,
Filled the fine air with habitants divine,
  Found in the sea all sorts of inspiration;
Gone out at noon-day with a Nymph to dine,
  Held with an Echo charming conversation,
Commenced intriguing with a star, and kissed,
Like old Ixion, a coquettish mist.

X.

Now all is over! passion is congealing,
  The glory of the soul is pale and dim;
I gaze all night upon a whitewashed ceiling,
  And get no glimpses of the seraphim;
Nothing is left of high and bright revealing
  But a weak longing and a wayward whim;
And when Imagination takes the air,
She never wanders beyond Grosvenor Square.

XI.

Not that I've been more wicked in my day
  Than some, perhaps, who call themselves my betters;
I liked to prattle better than to pray,
  And thought that freedom was as sweet as fetters;
Yet when my lip and lute are turned to clay,
  The honest friend who prints my Life and Letters
Will find few stories of satanic arts,
Of broken promises or broken hearts.

XII.

But I have moved too long in cold society,
Where it's the fashion not to care a rush;
Where girls are always thinking of propriety,
And men are laughed at if they chance to blush;
And thus I've caught the sickness of sobriety,
Forbidden sighs to sound, and tears to gush;
Become a great philosopher, and curled
Around my heart the poisons of the world.

XIII.

And I have learned at last the hideous trick
Of laughing at whate'er is great or holy;
At horrid tales that turn a soldier sick,
At griefs that make a Cynic melancholy;
At Mr. Lawless, and at Mr. Bric,
At Mr. Milman, and at Mr. Croly;
At Talma and at Young, Macbeth and Cinna,—
Even at you, adorable Corinna!

XIV.

To me all light is darkness;—love is lust,
Painting soiled canvas, poetry soiled paper;
The fairest loveliness a pinch of dust,
The proudest majesty a breath of vapor;
I have no sympathy, no tear, no trust,
No morning musing and no midnight taper
For daring manhood, or for dreaming youth,
Or maiden purity, or matron truth.

XV.

But sweet Sir Lidian was far more refined;
He shrank betimes from life and life's defiling;
His step was on the earth, but oh! his mind
Made for itself a heaven! the fool's reviling
He did not seek, or shun; and thus, enshrined
In glad and innocent thoughts, he went on smiling,
Alone in crowds, unhearing and unheeding,
Fond of the fields, and very fond of reading.

XVI.

When lords and ladies went to hunt together,
The milkmaid, as he passed, kicked down her pan;
When witty courtiers criticised the weather,
The Countess swore he was a learned man;
For him the proudest bowed beneath a feather,
For him the coldest blushed behind a fan;
And titled dames gave fêtes upon the water,
To introduce him to their angel daughter.

XVII.

But happy, happy Lidian! for he never
Watched the caprices of a pretty face;
Nor longed, as I have longed, with vain endeavor
To tear that plaguy wall of Mechlin lace;
His apathy seemed like to last forever;
When suddenly an incident took place
Which broke the talisman, and burst the bubble,
And gave his friends considerable trouble.

XVIII.

He laid a bet upon his falcon's flight,
  Rode home, as usually he did, a winner;
And sent a dozen pages to invite
  Ten dozen Barons to a peacock dinner:
They came, they ate, they talked through half the
      night;
  And the gay crowd grew naturally thinner,
And old Sir Guy, a story-teller stanch,
Began the story of the Lady Blanch.

XIX.

How she was born just twenty years before;
  And how her father was a Maltese Knight,
Sir Raymond styled, and skilled in knightly lore,
  And true in love, and terrible in fight;
And how her mother, Lady Leonore,
  Had perished when her offspring saw the light;
And how, because there was no other heir,
She was brought up with most uncommon care.

XX.

How she was never, when she was a child,
  Restrained in any innocent vagary;
And how she grew up beautiful and wild,
  And sang as sweetly as a caged canary;
And how all artlessly she wept and smiled;
  And how she danced cotilons like a fairy;
And how she proved what metal she was made of,
By mounting mares her groom was quite afraid of.

XXI.

How Bishop Bembo mended her cacology,
  And gave her all the graces of the Attics;
How Father Joseph taught her physiology,
  And Father Jerome taught her mathematics;
And how she picked up something of astrology
  From two white-haired, long-bearded Asiatics;
And how she had a genius for gastronomy,
And private—not political—economy;

XXII.

And how, as soon as she dismissed her tutor,
  And sat at tiltings for the men's inspection,
She was besieged by many an anxious suitor
  With sighs and sonnets, rhetoric and affection;
And how Sir Raymond stood completely neuter;
  And how she gave to all the same rejection,
For being serious, or for being funny,
For want of genius, or for want of money;

XXIII.

And how the father of this matchless daughter,
  Who for long years had been a great dragooner,
Found Fate as fickle as old Horace thought her,
  Which many soldiers find a great deal sooner;
How he was grounded in some shallow water,
  And taken prisoner by a pirate schooner;
And how the Bey of Tunis made a slave of him,
And swore one day the sea should be the grave of
    him.

XXIV.

And how poor Blanch, when that sad tale was told
her,
Speechless and senseless, fell upon her face;
And how 'twas all two knights could do to hold her;
And how, at last, she took her writing-case,
And wrote, before she was a minute older,
To pray that she might fill her father's place,
Suggesting that a maiden, young and handsome,
Was more than worth an ugly old man's ransom;

XXV.

And how the Bey behaved himself correctly,
Knowing such beauty was not for a Bey;
And how he shipped her, very circumspectly,
A present for the Sultan's own serai;
And how the Sultan fell in love directly;
And how he begged her, one fine summer's day,
To calm her passion, and assuage her grief,
And share his throne, his bed, and his belief.

XXVI.

And how she told him his proposals shocked her,
Crescent and crown heroically spurning;
And how she reasoned with a Turkish Doctor;
And how the Muftis marvelled at her learning;
And how the Vizier in a dungeon locked her;
And how three Pachas recommended burning;
And how, in spite of all their inhumanity,
She kept her character, and Christianity.

XXVII.

How she escaped by preaching to her jailer;
  How Selim tore his beard and wore his willow;
How she put on the trousers of a sailor;
  How Zephyr kindly helped her o'er the billow;
How all her friends were very glad to hail her;
  How she was married now to Don Pedrillo;
And how she showed, by every look and action,
She loved her lord and master to distraction.

XXVIII.

Such was the tale;—a tale to make men weep,
  Yet half the guests were laughing in their sleeve;
Some fell a fighting, others fell asleep,
  The wild took bumpers, and the wise took leave;
But oh, the trance, so passionate and deep,
  In which Sir Lidian sate!—you might believe
From his short breathing, and his gushing tears,
His very soul was listening, not his ears.

XXIX.

Oh, what a treasure all such listeners are!
  He longed to praise, but held his tongue to wonder,
Rapt as a cornet ere his maiden war,
  Dumb as a schoolboy when he doubts a blunder,
Pale as a culprit at the fatal bar,
  Faint as a lady in a storm of thunder,
And wild of heart, as I sometimes have been,
When you were singing, silver-toned Adine!—

XXX.

Queen of enchanting sounds, at whose sweet will
The spirit sinks and rises, glows and shivers,
Your voice is now for dearer friends; but still
In my lone heart its every echo quivers,
A viewless melody!—no purer thrill
Do fairies wake from their own groves and rivers,
When they would fling on minstrels' dreams by night
Some bounteous vision of intense delight.

XXXI.

You've very often asked me for a song;
I've very often promised to bestow it;
But when my admiration is most strong,
I'm frequently the least disposed to show it;
However, here I swear that I have long
Sighed to be styled your four-and-twentieth poet,
And that your voice is richer far to me,
Than a fat client's, five years hence, will be.—

XXXII.

But all this time Sir Guy was in his glory;
He was not used to be respected so;
For though he once was matchless at a story,
Age chills the tongue, and checks the humor's
flow;
His talk grew tedious as his hairs grew hoary;
And coxcombs stopped his—"Fifty years ago"—
With questions of their hawking, hunting, baiting,
Or—"Fair Sir Guy, the hypocras is waiting."

XXXIII.

Hence, when he saw in what a mute abstraction
  His youthful host to his romance attended,
He took unusual pains with every fraction,
  Kept his dénouement artfully suspended,
Grew quite theatrical in tone and action,
  And went away as soon as he had ended,
Supported to his palfrey by a vassal,
Half drunk with vanity, and half with wassail.

XXXIV.

The guests are gone! within that lofty hall
  No boastful baron curls his wet mustaches;
The wreaths of flowers are withered on the wall,
  The logs upon the earth are dust and ashes;
Where late some lover pledged his amorous thrall,
  The wine-cup stands inverted; and the flashes
From torch and taper o'er the bright floor thrown
Fall faint and rare!—Sir Lidian is alone.

XXXV.

Alone?—Oh no! the lady and her grieving
  Too truly, deeply, on his soul are wrought;
She has become to him his heart's conceiving,
  The very essence of the love he sought,
A present hope, a passionate believing,
  A sleepless vision, an embodied thought;
Not fancy quite, nor quite materiality,
Too clear for dream, too lovely for reality.

XXXVI.

Hark! the wind whistles through the grove of firs;—
  The Lady Blanch beneath their shade reposes:
Lo! the dark tapestry in the torch-light stirs;—
  The Lady Blanch beneath the curtain dozes:
He gazes on his pictured ancestors,
  And even there, the ancient lips and noses
Recall, with most astonishing activity,
The Lady Blanch, her charms and her captivity.

XXXVII.

And now she looks into his slumb'rous eyes,
  And now she trifles with his flowing tresses;
He speaks to her,—anon her lip replies;
  He kneels to her,—she shrinks from his caresses;
Coining all eloquence of smiles and sighs,
  Wearing by turns a thousand forms and dresses,
Beauteous in all!—alone?—in bliss or pain,
Sir Lidian ne'er will be alone again!

XXXVIII.

Poor youth! the chamber now was wrapt in gloom,
  The servants all had gone to rest; but still he
Wandered in silence up and down the room,
  Forgetting that the morning would be chilly,
Tossing about his mantle and his plume,
  And looking very sad and very silly;
At last he snatched his harp, and stopped his tread,
And warbled thus before he went to bed:—

"O Love! O beauteous Love!
Thy home is made for all sweet things,
A dwelling for thine own soft dove
And souls as spotless as her wings;
There summer ceases never:
The trees are rich with luscious fruits,
The bowers are full of joyous throngs,
And gales that come from Heaven's own lutes
And rivulets whose streams are songs
Go murmuring on forever!

"O Love! O wretched Love!
Thy home is made for bitter care;
And sounds are in thy myrtle grove
Of late repentance, long despair,
Of feigning and forsaking:
Thy banquet is the doubt and fear
That come, we know not whence or why,
The smile that hardly masks a tear,
The laughter that is half a sigh,
The heart that jests in breaking!

"O Love! O faithless Love!
Thy home is like the roving star
Which seems so fair, so far above
The world where woes and sorrows are;
But could we wander thither,

There's nothing but another earth,
  As dark and restless as our own,
Where misery is child of mirth,
  And every heart is born to groan,
    And every flower to wither!"

(1826.)

MY FIRST FOLLY.

STANZAS WRITTEN AT MIDNIGHT.

Pretty coquette! the ceaseless play
  Of thine unstudied wit,
And thy dark eye's remembered ray,
  By buoyant fancy lit,
And thy young forehead's clear expanse,
Where the locks slept as through the dance,
  Dreamlike, I saw thee flit,—
Are far too warm, and far too fair
To mix with aught of earthly care,
But the vision shall come when my day is done,
A frail, and a fair, and a fleeting one!

And if the many boldly gaze
  On that bright brow of thine,
And if thine eye's undying rays
  On countless coxcombs shine,
And if thy wit flings out its mirth,
Which echoes more of air than earth,
  For other ears than mine,—
I heed not this, ye are fickle things,
And I like your very wanderings;
I gaze, and if thousand's share the bliss,
Pretty capricious! I heed not this.

In sooth I am a wayward youth,
  As fickle as the sea,
And very apt to speak the truth,
  Unpleasing though it be;
I am no lover, yet as long
As I have heart for jest or song,
  An image, sweet, of thee,
Locked in my heart's remotest treasures,
Shall ever be one of its hoarded pleasures;
This from the scoffer thou has won,
And more than this he gives to none.

(December 20, 1821.)

A SHOOTING STAR.

"An ignis fatuus gleam of love."—*Byron.*

A SHOOTING Star!—the dim blue night
  Gleamed where the wanderer went,
For it flung a stream of gushing light
  Around its bright ascent.
I saw it fade!—in cold and cloud
  The young light fleeted by,
And the shrill night-wind whistled loud,
As darkness spread her solemn shroud
  Over the midnight sky.

Thou Maiden of the secret spell,
Star of the soul, farewell, farewell!
E'en such has been thy lovely light,
So calmly keen, so coldly bright;
A meteor, seen and worshipped only
To leave a lonely heart more lonely.
The Star hath set!—the spell is broken;
And thou hast left behind no token—
No token, lovely one, to me,
Of what thou art, or art to be;
Except one dear and cherished thought
In Memory's sunless caverns wrought,

One moonlight vision, one sweet shade,
Quick to appear, and slow to fade,
A warm and silent recollection,
The fancy's dream, the heart's affection.

Bright be thy lot in other years!—
  Fill high the cup of wine;
In all the pain of hopes and fears
I will not bathe with any tears
  That laughing love of thine.
Yet often in my waking slumbers
Thy voice shall speak its magic numbers,
And I shall think on that dark brow
On which my fancy gazes now,
And sit in revery lone and long
To muse on that Italian song.

And thou, perhaps, in happier times,
And fairer scenes, and warmer climes,
Wilt think of one who would not dim
With aught of care that wit and whim,—
Of one who oft, in other years,
  Fills high the cup of wine,
Because, in all his hopes and fears,
He will not bathe with any tears
  That laughing love of thine!

(March 15, 1822.)

STANZAS

WRITTEN FOR A FRIEND.

Bliss to those that love thee!
  Bliss to those thou lovest!
May Heaven smile above thee
  Wheresoe'er thou rovest!
May no storm come nigh thee
  On the tumbling ocean!
May the green wave ripple by thee
  With a lulling motion!

The wild voice of thy laughter
  Hath fleeted from before me!
But an echo lingers after,
  Flinging magic o'er me!
Thy fair smile is not beaming
  Its young mirth around me,
But I dote upon it, dreaming,
  When the spell hath bound me.

I cannot see or hear thee,
  Dearest of Earth's daughters;
But my soul is ever near thee,
  On the quiet waters.

Bliss to those that love thee!
  Bliss to those thou lovest!
And may Heaven smile above thee
  Wheresoe'er thou rovest!

(1822.)

L'INCONNUE.

MANY a beaming brow I've known,
  And many a dazzling eye,
And I've listened to many a melting tone
  In magic fleeting by;
And mine was never a heart of stone,
And yet my heart hath given to none
  The tribute of a sigh;
For Fancy's wild and witching mirth
Was dearer than aught I found on earth,
And the fairest forms I ever knew
Were far less fair than—L'Inconnue!

Many an eye that once was bright
  Is dark to-day in gloom;
Many a voice that once was light
  Is silent in the tomb;
Many a flower that once was dight
In Beauty's most entrancing might
  Hath faded in its bloom;
But she is still as fair and gay
As if she had sprung to life to-day;
A ceaseless tone and a deathless hue
Wild Fancy hath given to—L'Inconnue.

Many an eye of piercing jet
  Hath only gleamed to grieve me;
Many a fairy form I've met,
  But none have wept to leave me;
When all forsake and all forget,
One pleasant dream shall haunt me yet,
  One hope shall not deceive me;
For oh! when all beside is past,
Fancy is found our friend at last,
And the faith is firm and the love is true
Which are vowed by the lips of—L'Inconnue!

PEACE BE THINE.

WHEN Sorrow moves with silent tread
  Around some mortal's buried dust,
And muses on the mouldering dead
  Who sleep beneath their crumbling bust,
Though all unheard and all unknown
The name on that sepulchral stone,
  She looks on its recording line,
  And whispers kindly, "Peace be thine!"

O Lady! me thou knowest not,
  And what I am, or am to be;
The pain and pleasure of my lot
  Are naught, and must be naught, to thee;
Thou seest not my hopes and fears;
Yet thou perhaps, in other years,
  Wilt look on this recording line,
  And whisper kindly, "Peace be thine!"

TO ——

I.

I.

We met but in one giddy dance,
  Good-night joined hands with greeting;
And twenty thousand things may chance
  Before our second meeting:
For oh! I have been often told
  That all the world grows older,
And hearts and hopes to-day so cold,
  To-morrow must be colder.

II.

If I have never touched the string
  Beneath your chamber, dear one,
And never said one civil thing
  When you were by to hear one,—
If I have made no rhymes about
  Those looks which conquer Stoics,
And heard those angel tones, without
  One fit of fair heroics,—

III.

Yet do not, though the world's cold school
  Some bitter truths has taught me,

Oh, do not deem me quite the fool
  Which wiser friends have thought me!
There is one charm I still could feel,
  If no one laughed at feeling;
One dream my lute could still reveal,—
  If it were worth revealing.

IV.

But Folly little cares what name
  Of friend or foe she handles,
When merriment directs the game,
  And midnight dims the candles;
I know that Folly's breath is weak
  And would not stir a feather;
But yet I would not have her speak
  Your name and mine together.

V.

Oh no! this life is dark and bright,
  Half rapture and half sorrow;
My heart is very full to-night,
  My cup shall be to-morrow:
But they shall never know from me,
  On any one condition,
Whose health made bright my Burgundy,
  Whose beauty was my vision!

TO ——.

II.

I.

As o'er the deep the seaman roves
  With cloud and storm above him,
Far, far from all the smiles he loves,
  And all the hearts that love him,
'Tis sweet to find some friendly mast
  O'er that same ocean sailing,
And listen in the hollow blast
  To hear the pilot's hailing.

II.

On rolls the sea! and brief the bliss,
  And farewell follows greeting;
On rolls the sea! one hour is his
  For parting and for meeting;
And who shall tell, on sea or shore,
  In sorrow or in laughter,
If he shall see that vessel more,
  Or hear that voice hereafter?

III.

And thus, as on through shine and shower
  My fickle shallop dances,

And trembles at all storms that lower,
  And courts all summer glances,
'Tis very sweet, when thoughts oppress
  And follies fail to cheer me,
To find some looks of loveliness,
  Some tones of kindness, near me.

IV.

And yet I feel, while hearts are gay,
  And smiles are bright around me,
That those who greet me on my way
  Must leave me as they found me,
To rove again, as erst I roved,
  Through winter and rough weather,
And think of all the friends I loved,
  But loved and lost together:

V.

And scenes and smiles, so pure and glad,
  Are found and worshipped only
To make our sadness seem more sad,
  Our loneliness more lonely;—
It matters not! a pleasant dream
  At best can be but dreaming;
And if the true may never beam,
  Oh! who would slight the seeming?

VI.

And o'er the world my foot may roam,
  Through foreign griefs and pleasures,

And other climes may be my home,
  And other hearts my treasures;
But in the mist of memory
  Shall time and space be cheated,
And those kind looks revived shall be,
  And those soft tones repeated!

VII.

Believe,—if e'er this rhyme recall
  One thought of him who frames it,—
Believe him one who brings his all
  Where Love or Friendship claims it;
Though cold the surface of his heart,
  There's warmth beneath the embers;
For all it hopes, it would not part
  With aught that it remembers!

TO ——.

III.

"Bientôt je vis rassembler autour de moi tous les objets qui m'avoient donné de l'émotion dans ma jeunesse."—*Rousseau.*

I.

O Lady, when I mutely gaze
  On eyes, whose chastened splendor
Forbids the flatterer's wanton praise,
  And makes the Cynic tender,
Believe not that my gaze that night
  Has nothing, Lady, in it,
Beyond one vision of delight,
  The rapture of one minute.

II.

And, Lady, when my ear has heard
  That voice, whose natural gladness
Has caught from Heaven, like some sweet bird,
  Its tone of sainted sadness,
Believe not that those uttered words
  In the far winds have fleeted,
Like echoes from my own poor chords,
  Uncherished, unrepeated.

III.

Within the soul, where Memory shrouds
  Whate'er has bloomed and faded,
And consecrates the very clouds
  By which her cells are shaded,
Re-echoed from unnoticed strings,
  Traced by an unseen finger,
Amid all holy thoughts and things
  Those smiles, those words, will linger!

IV.

The present is a narrow cave
  With gloomy walls to bound it;
The future is a pathless wave
  With darkness all around it;
But I did fill the shadowy past,
  As Life was loitering through it,
With many a shape, which beams at last
  As bright as Boyhood knew it.

V.

Those shapes are viewless to the eye,
  But still the heart enjoys them;
And Fancy can their hues supply
  As fast as Time destroys them;
Until the past, with all its dreams
  Of love, and light, and glory,
Is fairer than the future seems
  In fabling Mecca's story.

VI.

And though I weep, as I repair
  Some bitter recollection
Of bootless labor, baffled prayer,
  Scorned passion, crushed affection,
Yet I would never give away
  One tear of such rare sorrow
For all I have of bliss to-day,
  Or all I hope to-morrow.

VII.

Lady, if I would e'er renew,
  When Care's cold night has bound me,
The brightest morn that ever threw
  Its youthful radiance round me,
Or deck with bloom, when Hope is bare,
  And Pleasure's wreaths are serest,
Of all dead flowers, so dear and fair,
  The fairest, and the dearest,—

VIII.

If, when my lute in other days
  Is silent or unheeded,
I would revive one voice, whose praise
  Was all the fame it needed,—
If, when false Friendship has betrayed
  Or fickle Love deceived me,
My heart would cling to one soft shade
  Which could not so have grieved me,—

IX.

In bower or banquet, heath or hill,
  The form I seek will glisten;
Again the liquid voice will thrill,
  The fair face bend to listen:
But whatsoe'er the hour or place,
  No bribe or prayer shall win me
To say whose voice, or form, or face,
  That spell awoke within me!

THE PORTRAIT.

Oh yes! these lips are very fair,
  Half lifted to the sky,
As if they breathed an angel's prayer
  Mixed with a mortal's sigh;
But theirs is not the song that flings
O'er evening's still imaginings
  Its cherished witchery;
No, these are not the lips whose tone
Sad Memory has made her own.

And these long curls of dazzling brown
  In many a fairy wreath
Float brightly, beautifully, down
  Upon the brow beneath;
But these are not the locks of jet
For which I sought the violet
  On that remembered heath;
No, these are not the locks that gleam
Around me in my moonlight dream.

And these blue eyes—a very saint
  Might envy their pure rays—
Are such as limners learn to paint,
  And poets long to praise;

But theirs is not the speaking glance
On which, in all its young romance,
  My spirit loves to gaze;
No, these are not the eyes that shine,
Like never-setting stars, on mine.

By those sweet songs I hear to-night,
  Those black locks on the brow,
And those dark eyes, whose living light
  Is beaming o'er me now,
I worship naught but what thou art!
Let all that was—decay—depart,
  I care not when or how;
And fairer far these hues may be,—
They seem not half so fair to me!

(1825.)

TO ——.

I.

STILL is the earth, and still the sky;
The midnight moon is fleeting by;
And all the world is wrapt in sleep,
But the hearts that love, and the eyes that weep.

II.

And now is the time to kiss the flowers
Which shun the sunbeam's busy hours;
For the book is shut, and the mind is free
To gaze on them, and to think of thee.

III.

Withered they are and pale in sooth;
So are the radiant hopes of youth;
But Love can give with a single breath
Bloom to languor, and life to death.

IV.

Though I must greet thee with a tone
As calm to-morrow as thine own,
Oh! Fancy's vision, Passion's vow,
May be told in stillness and darkness now!

V.

For the veil from the soul is rent away
Which it wore in the glare of gaudy day;
And more, much more, the heart may feel
Than the pen may write or the lip reveal.

VI.

Why can I not forego—forget
That ever I loved thee—that ever we met?
There is not a single link or sign
To blend my lot in the world with thine;

VII.

I know not the scenes where thou hast roved,
I see not the faces which thou hast loved,—
Thou art to me as a pleasant dream
Of a boat that sails on a distant stream.

VIII.

Thou smilest! I am glad the while,
But I share not the joy that bids thee smile;
Thou grievest! when thy grief is deepest,
I weep, but I know not for whom thou weepest.

IX.

I would change life's spring for his roughest weather
If we might bear the storm together;
And give my hopes for half thy fears,
And sell my smiles for half thy tears.

X.

Give me one common bliss or woe,
One common friend, one common foe,
On the earth below, or the clouds above,
One thing we both may loathe, or love.

XI.

It may not be ; but yet—but yet
O deem not I can e'er forget !
For fondness such as mine supplies
The sympathy which Fate denies :

XII.

And all my feelings, well thou knowest,
Go with thee, Lady, where'er thou goest ;
And my wayward spirit bows to thee,
Its first and last idolatry !

TO ———.

I.

In such a time as this, when every heart is light,
And greetings sound more welcome, and faces smile
more bright,
O how wearily—how wearily my spirit wanders back
Among the faded joys that lie on Memory's ruined
track!
Where art thou, best and fairest? I call to thee in
vain;
And thou art lone and distant far, in sickness and in
pain!

II.

Beloved one, if anguish would fall where fall it may,
If sorrow could be won by gifts to barter prey for
prey,
There is an arm would wither, so thine revived might
be,
A lip which would be still and mute, to make thy
music free,
An eye which would forget to wake, to bid thy morn-
ing shine,
A heart whose very strings would break, to steal one
pang from thine.

III.

If this be all too wild a wish, it were a humbler prayer
That I might sit beside thy couch, watching and weeping there;
Alas, that grief should sever the hearts it most endears,—
That friends who have been joined in smiles, are parted in their tears,—
That when there's danger in the path, or poison in the bowl,
Unloving hands must minister, unloving lips console!

IV.

Yet in the twilight hour, when all our hopes seem true,
And Fancy's wild imaginings take living form and hue,
I linger, and thou chidest not, beside thy lonely bed,
And do thy biddings, dearest, with slow and noiseless tread,
And tremble all the while at the feeblest wind that blows,
As if indeed its idle breath were breaking thy repose.

V.

To kiss thine eyelids, when they droop with heaviness and pain,
To pour sad tears upon thy hand, the heart's most precious rain,

To mark the changing color as it flits across thy cheek,
To feel thy very wishes ere the feverish lip can speak,
To listen for the weakest word, watch for the lightest token,
Oh bliss, that such a dream should be! oh pain, that it is broken!

VI.

Farewell, my best beloved; beloved, fare thee well!
I may not mourn where thou dost weep, nor be where thou dost dwell;
But when the friend I trusted all coldly turns away,
When the warmest feelings wither, and the dearest hopes decay,
To thee—to thee—thou knowest, whate'er my lot may be,
For comfort and for happiness, my spirit turns to thee.

THE PARTING.

"Alla prigione antica
Quell' augellin ritorna
Ancorchè mano amica
Gli abbia disciolto il piè."

Metastasio.

I.

Farewell;—I will not now
The wasted theme renew;
No cloud upon my cheek or brow
Shall wake one pang for you;
But here, unseen, unheard,
Ere evening's shadows fly,
I will but say that one weak word,
And pass unwelcomed by.

II.

Farewell;—but it is strange,
As round your towers I roam,
To think how desolate a change
Has come o'er heart and home;
Where stranger minstrels throng,
Where harsher harps are cherished,
The very memory of my song
Is, like its echo, perished.

III.

The bird your gold has brought
  From its own orient bowers,
Where every wandering wind is fraught
  With the sweet breath of flowers,
Will never murmur more
  A note so clear and high
As that which he was wont to pour
  Beneath his native sky.

IV.

Yet 'twere a cruel thing,
  If Pity's tears and sighs
Could give the breezes to his wing,
  The daylight to his eyes;
His vision is the night,
  His home the prison, now,
He could not look upon the light,
  Nor sleep upon the bough.

V.

Lady, when first your mirth
  Flung magic o'er my way,
Mine was the gayest soul on earth
  When all the earth was gay;
My songs were full of joy,—
  You might have let them flow;
My heart was every woman's toy,—
  You might have left it so!

VI.

But now to send me back
  To faded hopes and fears,
To bid me seek again the track
  My foot has left for years,
To cancel what must be,
  To alter what has been,—
Ah! this indeed is mockery
  Fit for a Fairy Queen!

VII.

The lip that was so gay
  More dark and still hath grown;
The listless lute of yesterday
  Hath learned a sadder tone;
And uttered is the thought,
  And written is the vow;—
You might have left this charm unwrought,—
  You must not rend it now!

VIII.

When first upon my lance
  I saw the fair sun shine,
I courted not that fairer glance,—
  And yet it turned to mine;
When music's rich delight
  From lips so lovely came,
I looked not on those lips that night,—
  And yet they breathed my name!

IX.

When our last words were broken
  By passion's bitter tears,
I asked not the recording token
  Which I must love for years;
And when between us lay
  Long tracks of sand and sea,
The carrier pigeon went his way
  Unbegged, unbought, by me.

X.

Farewell!—when I was bound
  In every Beauty's thrall,
I could have lightly whispered round
  That little word to all;
And now that I am cold,
  And deemed the slave of none,
I marvel how my lips have told
  That little word to one.

XI.

Farewell!—since bliss so rare
  Hath beamed but to betray,
It will be long ere I shall wear
  The smile I wore to-day;
And since I weep not here
  To call you false and vain,
I think I shall not shed one tear
  For all this world again!

THE LAST.

Πανύστατον δὴ, κ'οὔποτ' αὖθις ὑστέρον.

Soph. *Ajax.*

I.

It is the lute, the same poor lute;—
  Why do you turn away?
To-morrow let its chords be mute,
  But they must sound to-day.
The bark is manned, the seamen throng
  Around the creaking mast:
Lady, you heard my first love song,—
    Hear now my last!

II.

Sigh not!—I knew the star must set,
  I knew the rose must fade;
And if I never can forget,
  I never will upbraid;
I would not have you aught but glad,
  Where'er my lot is cast;
And if my sad words make you sad,
    They are the last!

III.

No more, no more, oh! never more
  Will look or tone of mine
Bring clouds that ivory forehead o'er,
  Or dim that dark eye's shine;
Look out, dear Lady, from your tower;
  The wave rolls deep and vast:
Oh, would to God this bitter hour
    Might be my last!

IV.

I think that you will love me still,
  Though far our fates may be;
And that your heart will fondly thrill
  When strangers ask of me;
My praise will be your proudest theme
  When these dark days are past:
If this be all an idle dream,
    It is my last!

V.

And now let one kind look be mine,
  And clasp this slender chain;
Fill up once more the cup of wine,
  Put on my ring again;
And wreathe this wreath around your head,
  (Alas, it withers fast!)
And whisper, when its flowers are dead,
    It was the last!

VI.

Thus from your presence forth I go,
  A lost and lonely man;
Reckless alike of weal or woe,
  Heaven's benison or ban:
He who has known the tempest's worst
  May bare him to the blast;
Blame not these tears; they are the first,—
    Are they the last?

(April 2, 1829.)

A FAREWELL.

λιποῦσα δ' Εὐρώπης πέδον,
Ἤπειρον ἥξεις 'Ασίδ'. ἆρ ὑμῖν δοκεῖ
ὁ τῶν θεῶν τύραννος εἰς τὰ πάνθ' ὁμῶς
βίαιος εἶναι;

ÆSCH. *Prom. Vinct.*

THEY told me thou wilt pass again
  Across the echoing wave;
And, though thou canst not break the chain,
  Thou wilt forget the slave.
Farewell, farewell!—thou wilt not know
My hopes or fears, my weal or woe,
  My home—perhaps my grave!
Nor think nor dream of the sad heart
Whose only thought and dream thou art.

The goblet went untasted by
  Which other lips caressed;
And joyless seemed the revelry,
  And impotent the jest:
And why? for it was very long
Since thou didst prize my love or song,
  My lot was all unblest:
I cannot now be more forlorn,
Nor bear aught that I have not borne.

We might not meet; for me no more
  Arose that melting tone;
The eyes which colder crowds adore
  Were veiled to me alone:
The coxcomb's prate, the ruffian's lies,
The censures of the sternly wise,
  Between our hearts were thrown;
Deeper and wider barriers far,
Than any waves or deserts are.

But it was something still to know
  Thy dawn and dusk were mine,
And that we felt the same breeze blow,
  And saw the same star shine;
And still the shadowy hope was rife
That once in this waste weary life
  My path might cross with thine,
And one brief gleam of beauty bless
My spirit's utter loneliness.

And oft in crowds I might rejoice
  To hear thy uttered name,
Though haply from an unknown voice
  The welcome echo came:
How coldly would I shape reply,
With lingering lip, and listless eye,
  That none might doubt or blame,
Or guess that idle theme could be
A mine of after-thought to me.

Oh ne'er again!—thou wilt abide
  Where brighter skies are found,
One whom thou lovest by thy side,
  Many who love thee round;
And those sweet fairies, with their wiles
Of mimic frowns and happy smiles,
  Around thy steps will bound:
I would not cloud such scene and lot
For all my aching breast hath not.

Yet, if thou wilt remember one
  Who never can forget,
Whose lonely life is not so lone
  As if we had not met,
Believe that in the frosty sky
Whereon is writ his destiny
  Thy light is lingering yet,
A star before the darkened soul,
To guide, and gladden, and control.

Be mine the talk of men, though thou
  Wilt never hear my praise;
Be mine the wreath, though for my brow
  Thou wilt not twine the bays;
Be mine ambition's proudest scope,
Though fewer smiles than were my hope
  Will meet my longing gaze,
Though in my triumph's sunniest thrill
One welcome will be wanting still.

Perchance, when long, long years are o'er—
  I care not how they flow—
Some note of me to that far shore
  Across the deep may go;
And thou wilt read, and turn to hide
The conscious blush of woman's pride;
  For thou alone wilt know
What spell inspired the silent toil
Of mid-day sun and midnight oil.

And this is little, to atone
  For much of grief and wrong;
For doubts within the bosom sown,
  Cares checked and cherished long.
But it is past! thy bliss or pain
I shall not mar or make again;
  And, Lady, this poor song
Is echoing, like a stranger's knell,
Sad, but unheeded!—so farewell!

AN EXCUSE.

Blame not the Minstrel's wayward will:
  His soul has slumbered all too long;
He has no pulse for passion's thrill,
  No lute for passion's song.
O frown not, though he turns away
  Unloved, unloving, even from thee,
And mars with idle jests the lay
  Where Beauty's praise should be.

If he should bid the golden string
  Be vocal to a loftier theme,
Sad Memory from her cell would bring
  The fond forbidden dream;
The dream of her, whose broken chain
  Than new forged bonds is far more dear;
Whose name he may not speak again,
  And shudders but to hear.

And if he breathes Love's hopes and fears
  In many a soulless idol's shrine,
The falsehoods fit for vulgar ears
  Were never fit for thine.

Take back, take back the book to-night:
  Thou art too brightly—nobly fair,
For hearts so worn as his to write
  Their worthless worship there.

(February 20, 1830.)

SECOND LOVE.

"L'on n'aime bien qu'une seule fois: c'est la première. Les amours qui suivent sont moins involontaires!"—*La Bruyère.*

How shall he woo her?—Let him stand
  Beside her as she sings;
And watch that fine and fairy hand
  Flit o'er the quivering strings:
And let him tell her he has heard,
  Though sweet the music flow,
A voice whose every whispered word
  Was sweeter, long ago.

How shall he woo her?—Let him gaze
  In sad and silent trance
On those blue eyes whose liquid rays
  Look love in every glance:
And let him tell her, eyes more bright,
  Though bright her own may beam,
Will fling a deeper spell to-night
  Upon him in his dream.

How shall he woo her?—Let him try
  The charms of olden time,

And swear by earth and sea and sky,
  And rave in prose and rhyme:
And let him tell her, when he bent
  His knee in other years,
He was not half so eloquent,—
  He could not speak for tears!

How shall he woo her?—Let him bow
  Before the shrine in prayer;
And bid the priest pronounce the vow
  That hallows passion there:
And let him tell her when she parts
  From his unchidden kiss,
That memory to many hearts
  Is dearer far than bliss.

Away, away! the chords are mute,
  The bond is rent in twain;
You cannot wake that silent lute,
  Nor clasp those links again;
Love's toil, I know, is little cost,
  Love's perjury is light sin;
But souls that lose what his hath lost,—
  Oh, what have they to win?

A RETROSPECT.

The lady of his love, oh, she was changed,
As by the sickness of the soul!

Byron.

Go thou, white in thy soul, to fill a throne
Of innocence and sanctity in Heaven!

Ford.

I KNEW that it must be,
Yea! thou art changed—all worshipped as thou art—
Mourned as thou shalt be! Sickness of the heart
Hath done its work on thee!

Thy dim eyes tell a tale,
A piteous tale, of vigils; and the trace
Of bitter tears is on thy beauteous face—
Beauteous, and yet so pale!

Changed love! but not alone!
I am not what they think me; though my cheek
Wear but its last year's furrow, though I speak
Thus in my natural tone.

The temple of my youth
Was strong in moral purpose: once I felt
The glory of philosophy, and knelt
In the pure shrine of truth.

I went into the storm,
And mocked the billows of the tossing sea;
I said to Fate, "What wilt thou do to me?
I have not harmed a worm!"

Vainly the heart is steeled
In Wisdom's armor; let her burn her books!
I look upon them as the soldier looks
Upon his cloven shield.

Virtue and Virtue's rest,
How have they perished! Through my onward course
Repentance dogs my footsteps! black Remorse
Is my familiar guest!

The glory and the glow
Of the world's loveliness have passed away;
And Fate hath little to inflict, to-day,
And nothing to bestow!

Is not the damning line
Of guilt and grief engraven on me now?
And the fierce passion which hath scathed thy brow,
Hath it not blasted mine?

No matter! I will turn
To the straight path of duty; I have wrought,
At last, my wayward spirit to be taught
What it hath yet to learn.

Labor shall be my lot;
My kindred shall be joyful in my praise;
And Fame shall twine for me, in after days,
A wreath I covet not.

And if I cannot make,
Dearest! thy hope my hope, thy trust my trust,
Yet will I study to be good, and just,
And blameless, for thy sake.

Thou may'st have comfort yet!
Whate'er the source from which those waters glide,
Thou hast found healing mercy in their tide;
Be happy and forget!

Forget me—and farewell!
But say not that in me new hopes and fears,
Or absence, or the lapse of gradual years,
Will break thy memory's spell!

Indelibly, within,
All I have lost is written; and the theme
Which Silence whispers to my thought and dream
Is sorrow still—and sin!

(1831.)

A BALLAD:

TEACHING HOW POETRY IS BEST PAID FOR.

Non voglio cento scudi.—*Italian Song.*

OH, say not the minstrel's art,
  The glorious gift of verse,
Though his hopes decay, though his friends depart,
  Can ever be a curse;—
Though sorrow reign within his heart,
  And poortith hold his purse.

Say not his toil is profitless;—
  Though he charm no rich relation,
The Fairies all his labors bless
  With such remuneration,
As Mr. Hume would soon confess
  Beyond his calculation.

Annuities, and three per cents,
  Little cares he about them;
And India bonds, and tithes, and rents,
  He rambles on without them:
But love, and noble sentiments,—
  Oh, never bid him doubt them!

Childe Florice rose from his humble bed,
  And prayed as a good youth should ;
And forth he sped, with a lightsome tread,
  Into the neighboring wood ;
He knew where the berries were ripe and red,
  And where the old oak stood.

And as he lay at the noon of day,
  Beneath the ancient tree,
A grayhaired pilgrim passed that way ;
  A holy man was he,
And he was wending forth to pray
  At a shrine in a far countrie.

Oh, his was a weary wandering,
  And a song or two might cheer him.
The pious Childe began to sing,
  As the ancient man drew near him ;
The lark was mute as he touched the string,
  And the thrush said, "Hear him, hear him !"

He sang high tales of the martyred brave ;
  Of the good, and pure, and just ;
Who have gone into the silent grave,
  In such deep faith and trust,
That the hopes and thoughts which sain and save
  Spring from their buried dust.

The fair of face, and the stout of limb,
  Meek maids, and grandsires hoary,
Who have sung on the cross their rapturous hymn,
  As they passed to their doom of glory—

Their radiant fame is never dim,
  Nor their names erased from story.

Time spares the stone where sleep the dead
  With angels watching round them;
The mourner's grief is comforted,
  As he looks on the chains that bound them;
And peace is shed on the murderer's head,
  And he kisses the thorns that crowned them.

Such tales he told; and the pilgrim heard
  In a trance of voiceless pleasure;
For the depths of his inmost soul were stirred,
  By the sad and solemn measure:
"I give thee my blessing,"—was his word;
  "It is all I have of treasure!"

A little child came bounding by;
  And he, in a fragrant bower,
Had found a gorgeous butterfly,
  Rare spoil for a nursery dower,
Which, with fierce step, and eager eye,
  He chased from flower to flower.

"Come hither, come hither," 'gan Florice call;
  And the urchin left his fun;
So from the hall of poor Sir Paul
  Retreats the baffled dun;
So Ellen parts from the village ball,
  Where she leaves a heart half won.

Then Florice did the child caress,
  And sang his sweetest songs:
Their theme was of the gentleness
  Which to the soul belongs,
Ere yet it knows the name or dress
  Of human rights and wrongs.

And of the wants which make agree
  All parts of this vast plan;
How life is in whate'er we see,
  And only life in man :—
What matter where the less may be,
  And where the longer span ?

And how the heart grows cold without
  Soft Pity's freshening dews ;
And how when any life goes out
  Some little pang ensues ;—
Facts which great soldiers often doubt,
  And wits who write reviews.

Oh, Song hath power o'er Nature's springs,
  Though deep the nymph has laid them !
The child gazed, gazed, on gilded wings,
  As the next light breeze displayed them ;
But he felt the while that the meanest things
  Are dear to him that made them !

The sun went down behind the hill,
  The breeze was growing colder

But there the minstrel lingered still;
  And amazed the chance beholder,
Musing beside a rippling rill,
  With a harp upon his shoulder.

And soon, on a graceful steed and tame,
  A sleek Arabian mare,
The Lady Juliana came,
  Riding to take the air,
With many a lord, at whose proud name
  A radical would swear.

The minstrel touched his lute again.
  It was more than a Sultan's crown,
When the lady checked her bridle rein,
  And lit from her palfrey down:—
What would you give for such a strain,
  Rees, Longman, Orme, and Brown?

He sang of Beauty's dazzling eyes,
  Of Beauty's melting tone;
And how her praise is a richer prize
  Than the gems of Persia's throne;
And her love a bliss which the coldly wise
  Have never, never known.

He told how the valiant scoff at fear,
  When the sob of her grief is heard;
How fiercely they fight for a smile or a tear,
  How they die for a single word:—
Things which, I own, to me appear
  Exceedingly absurd.

The Lady soon had heard enough:
  She turned to hear Sir Denys
Discourse, in language vastly gruff,
  About his skill at Tennis;
While smooth Sir Guy described the stuff
  His mistress wore at Venice.

The Lady smiled one radiant smile,
  And the Lady rode away.—
There is not a lady in all our Isle,
  I have heard a Poet say,
Who can listen more than a little while
  To a poet's sweetest lay.

His mother's voice was fierce and shrill,
  As she set the milk and fruit:
"Out on thine unrewarded skill,
  And on thy vagrant lute;
Let the strings be broken an they will,
  And the beggar lips be mute!"

Peace, peace!—the Pilgrim as he went
  Forgot the minstrel's song;
But the blessing that his wan lips sent
  Will guard the minstrel long;
And keep his spirit innocent,
  And turn his hand from wrong.

Belike the child had little thought
  Of the moral the minstrel drew;
But the dream of a deed of kindness wrought—
  Brings it not peace to you?

And doth not a lesson of virtue taught
  Teach him that teaches too?

And if the Lady sighed no sigh
  For the minstrel or his hymn;—
Yet when he shall lie 'neath the moonlit sky,
  Or lip the goblet's brim,
What a star in the mist of memory
  That smile will be to him!

(1831.)

MISCELLANEOUS POEMS.

STANZAS

WRITTEN IN THE FIRST LEAF OF LILLIAN.

TALK not to me of learned dust,
  Of reasoning and renown,
Of withering wreath and crumbling bust,
  Torn book and tattered gown;
Oh, Wisdom lives in Folly's ring,
And beards, thank Heaven, are not the thing!

Then let me live a long romance,
  And learn to trifle well;
And write my motto, "Vive la danse,"
  And "Vive la bagatelle!"
And give all honor, as is fit,
To sparkling eyes, and sparkling wit.

And let me deem, when Sophs condemn
  And Seniors burn my lays,
That some bright eyes will smile on them,
  And some kind hearts will praise;
And thus my little book shall be
A mine of pleasant thoughts to me.

And we, perchance, may meet no more;
  For other accents sound
And darker prospects spread before,
  And colder hearts come round;
And cloistered walk and grated pane
Must wear their wonted gloom again.

But those who meet, as we have met,
  In frolic and in laughter,—
O, dream not they can e'er forget
  The thoughts that linger after;
That parted friend and faded scene
Can be as if they ne'er had been.

No! I shall miss that merry smile
  When thou hast left me lone;
And listen in the silent aisle
  For that remembered tone;
And look up to the lattice high
For beckoning hand and beaming eye.

And thou, perhaps, when years are gone,
  Wilt turn these pages over,
And waste one idle thought upon
  A rambling, rhyming rover,
And deem the Poet and his line
Both wild, both worthless,—and both thine!

(Trin. Coll., Cambridge,
  July 8, 1823.)

STANZAS

WRITTEN IN A COPY OF LILLIAN, SENT TO A LADY IN EXCHANGE FOR TWO DRAWINGS ILLUSTRATIVE OF THE POEM.

THE gifts the Rhymer begs to-day
  Shall long be dear to him,
When Passion's glow shall pass away,
  And Fancy's light grow dim,
And naught remain of boyhood's schemes,
But Sorrow's tears, and Memory's dreams.

Yes, dear the gifts shall ever be;
  For Humor there hath flung
A spell of magic witchery
  On all he thought and sung,
And blended in a living dance
The creatures of his own romance.

E'en he might shudder at the sight
  Of his own monster's feast;
E'en he might feel a sweet affright,
  As, ruling the rude beast,
His own fair damsel skims the sea
In all her headless ecstasy.

These gifts shall be unfading signs
  That, in his early days,
Some beaming eyes could read his lines,
  Some beauteous lips could praise;
Fair Lady, from the cup of bliss
He wants and wishes only this!

For he was born a wayward boy,
  To laugh when hopes deceive him,
To grasp at every fleeting joy,
  And jest at all that leave him,
To love a quirk, and loathe a quarrel,
And never care a straw for laurel.

And thus, the creature of a day,
  And rather fool than knave,
And either very gravely gay
  Or very gayly grave,
He cares for naught but wit and wine,
And flatteries,—such as this of thine!

FRAGMENTS OF A DESCRIPTIVE POEM.*

* * * And now
He stood upon the beetling brow
Of a huge cliff, and marked beneath
The sea-foam fling its hoary wreath
Upon the shore, and heard the waves
Run howling through their hollow caves.
Far on the right old Ocean lay;
But he had hushed his storm to-day,
And seemed to murmur a long sigh,
A melancholy melody,
As if his mourning had begun
For what he yesternight had done:
And on the left, in beauteous pride,
The river poured his rushing tide;
Fanned, as he came, by odorous gales
From grassy hills and mossy vales,
And gardens, where young nature set
No mask upon her features yet,
And sands which were as smooth as stone,
And woods whose birth no eye had known,

* These lines were sent in a letter, "instead of a Valentine." The view described is that from the Ness, looking towards Teignmouth, Devon.

And rocks, whose very crags seemed bowers,
So bright they were with herbs and flowers.

He looked across the river stream;
A little town was there,
O'er which the morning's earliest beam
Was wandering fresh and fair;
No architect of classic school
Had pondered there with line and rule;
And, stranger still, no modern master
Had wasted there his lath and plaster;
The buildings in strange order lay,
As if the streets had lost their way,
Fantastic, puzzling, narrow, muddy,
Excess of toil from lack of study,
Where Fashion's very newest fangles
Had no conception of right angles.
But still about that humble place
There was a look of rustic grace;
'Twas sweet to see the sports and labors
And morning greetings of good neighbors,
The seamen mending sails and oars,
The matrons knitting at the doors,
The invalids enjoying dips,
The children launching tiny ships,
The beldames clothed in rags and wrinkles
Investigating periwinkles.
A little further up the tide,
There beamed upon the river side
A shady dwelling-place: * *

Most beautiful! upon that spot,
  Beside that echoing wave,
A Fairy might have built her grot,
  An Anchorite his grave.
The river, with its constant fall,
Came daily to the garden wall,
As if it longed, but thought it sin,
To look upon the charms within;
Behind, majestic mountains frowned,
And dark rich groves were all around,
And just before the gate there stood
Two trees which were themselves a wood;
Two lovely trees, whose clasping forms
Were blended still in calms and storms—
Like sisters, who have lived together
Through every change of Fortune's weather,
United in their bliss or sorrow,
Their yesterday, and their to-morrow,—
So fond, so faithful,—you would wonder
To see them smile or weep asunder.

(March, 1826.)

A PREFACE.

I HAVE a tale of Love to tell;—
Lend me thy light lute, L. E. L.

Lend me thy lute! what other strings
Should speak of those delicious things,
Which constitute Love's joys and woes
In pretty duodecimos?
Thou knowest every herb and flower,
Of wondrous name, and wondrous power,
Which, gathered where white wood-doves nestle,
And beat up by poetic pestle,
Bind gallant knights in fancied fetters,
And set young ladies writing letters:
Thou singest songs of floods and fountains,
Of mounted lords and lordly mountains,
Of dazzling shields and dazzling glances,
Of piercing frowns and piercing lances,
Of leaping brands and sweeping willows,
Of dreading seas and dreaming billows,
Of sunbeams which are like red wine,
Of odorous lamps of argentine,
Of cheeks that burn, of hearts that freeze,
Of odors that send messages,

Of kingfishers and silver pheasants,
Of gems to which the Sun makes presents,
Of miniver and timeworn walls,
Of clairschachs and of atabals.
Within thy passion-haunted pages
Throng forward girls—and distant ages,
The lifeless learns at once to live,
The dumb grows strangely talkative,
Resemblances begin to strike
In things exceedingly unlike,
All nouns, like statesmen, suit all places,
And verbs, turned lawyers, hunt for cases.

Oh! if it be a crime to languish
Over thy scenes of bliss or anguish,
To float with Raymond o'er the sea,
To sigh with dark-eyed Rosalie,
And sit in revery luxurious
Till tea grows cold, and aunts grow furious,
I own the soft impeachment true,
And burn the Westminster Review.
Lend me thy lute; I'll be a poet;
All Paternoster Row shall know it!
I'll rail in rhyme at cruel Fate
From Temple Bar to Tyburn Gate;
Old Premium's daughter in the City
Shall feel that love is kin to pity,
Hot ensigns shall be glad to borrow
My notes of rapture and of sorrow,
And I shall hear sweet voices sighing,

"So young!—and I am told he's dying!"
Yes! I shall wear a wreath eternal,
For full twelve months, in Post and Journal,
Admired by all the Misses Brown
Who go to school at Kentish Town,
And worshipped by the fair Arachne
Who makes my handkerchiefs at Hackney!

Vain, vain!—take back the lute! I see
Its chords were never meant for me.
For thine own song, for thine own hand,
That lute was strung in Fairy-land;
And, if a stranger's thumb should fling
Its rude touch o'er one golden string,—
Good-night to all the music in it!
The string would crack in half a minute.
Take back the lute! I make no claim
To inspiration or to fame;
The hopes and fears that bards should cherish,
I care not when they fade and perish;
I read political economy,
Voltaire and Cobbett, and gastronomy,
And, when I would indite a story
Of woman's faith or warrior's glory,
I always wear a night-cap sable,
And put my elbows on the table,
And hammer out the tedious toil
By dint of Walker, and lamp-oil.
I never feel poetic mania,
I gnaw no laurel with Urania,

I court no critic's tender mercies,
I count the feet in all my verses,
And own myself a screaming gander
Among the shrill swans of Mæander!

(1824.)

LOVE AT A ROUT

When some mad bard sits down to muse
About the lilies and the dews,
The grassy vales and sloping lawns,
Fairies and Satyrs, Nymphs and Fauns,
He's apt to think, he's apt to swear,
That Cupid reigns not anywhere
Except in some sequestered village
Where peasants live on truth and tillage,
That none are fair enough for witches
But maids who frisk through dells and ditches,
That dreams are twice as sweet as dances,
That cities never breed romances,
That Beauty always keeps a cottage,
And Purity grows pale on pottage.

Yes! those dear dreams are all divine;
And those dear dreams have all been mine.
I like the stream, the rock, the bay,
I like the smell of new-mown hay,
I like the babbling of the brooks,
I like the creaking of the crooks,
I like the peaches, and the posies,—
But chiefly, when the season closes,

And often, in the month of fun,
When every poacher cleans his gun,
And cockneys tell enormous lies,
And stocks are pretty sure to rise,
And e'en the Chancellor, they say,
Goes to a point the nearest way—
I hurry from my drowsy desk
To revel in the picturesque;
To hear beneath those ancient trees
The far-off murmur of the bees,
Or trace yon river's mazy channels
With Petrarch, and a brace of spaniels,
Combining foolish rhymes together,
And killing sorrow, and shoe-leather.

Then, as I see some rural maid
Come dancing up the sunny glade,
Coquetting with her fond adorer
Just as her mother did before her,
" Give me," I cry, " the quiet bliss
Of souls like these, of scenes like this;
Where ladies eat and sleep in peace,
Where gallants never heard of Greece,
Where day is day, and night is night,
Where frocks—and morals—both are white;
Blue eyes below—blue skies above—
These are the homes, the hearts, for Love!"

But this is idle; I have been
A sojourner in many a scene,

And picked up wisdom in my way,
And cared not what I had to pay;
Smiling and weeping all the while,
As other people weep and smile;
And I have learned that Love is not
Confined to any hour or spot;
He lights the smile and fires the frown
Alike in country and in town.
I own fair faces not more fair
In Ettrick, than in Portman Square,
And silly danglers just as silly
In Sherwood, as in Piccadilly.
Soft tones are not the worse, no doubt,
For having harps to help them out;
And smiles are not a ray more bright
By moonbeams, than by candle-light;
I know much magic oft reposes
On wreaths of artificial roses,
And snowy necks,—I never found them
Quite spoilt by having cameos round them.
In short, I'm very sure that all
Who seek or sigh for Beauty's thrall
May breathe their vows, and feed their passion,
Though whist and waltzing keep in fashion,
And make the most delicious sonnets,
In spite of diamonds, and French bonnets!

(1824.)

THE MODERN NECTAR.

One day, as Bacchus wandered out
  From his own gay and glorious heaven,
To see what mortals were about
  Below, 'twixt six o'clock and seven,
And laugh at all the toils and tears,
The endless hopes, the causeless fears,
The midnight songs, the morning smarts,
The aching heads, the breaking hearts,
Which he and his fair crony Venus
Within the month had sown between us,
He lighted by chance on a fiddling fellow
Who never was known to be less than mellow,
A wandering poet, who thought it his duty
To feed upon nothing but bowls and beauty,
Who worshipped a rhyme, and detested a quarrel,
And cared not a single straw for laurel,
Holding that grief was sobriety's daughter,
And loathing critics, and cold water.

Ere day on the Gog-Magog hills had fainted,
The god and the minstrel were quite acquainted;
Beneath a tree, in the sunny weather,
They sat them down, and drank together:

They drank of all fluids that ever were poured
By an English lout, or a German lord,
Rum and shrub and brandy and gin,
One after another, they stowed them in,
Claret of Carbonell, porter of Meux,
Champagne which would waken a wit in dukes,
Humble Port, and proud Tokay,
Persico, and Crême de Thé,
The blundering Irishman's Usquebaugh,
The fiery Welshman's Cwrw da;
And after toasting various names
Of mortal and immortal flames,
And whispering more than I or you know
Of Mistress Poll, and Mistress Juno,
The god departed, scarcely knowing
A zephyr's from a nose's blowing,
A frigate from a pewter flagon,
Or Thespis from his own stage wagon;
And rolling about like a barrel of grog,
He went up to heaven as drunk as a hog!

"Now may I," he lisped, "forever sit
In Lethe's darkest and deepest pit,
Where dulness everlasting reigns
O'er the quiet pulse and the drowsy brains,
Where ladies jest, and lovers laugh,
And noble lords are bound in calf,
And Zoilus for his sins rehearses
Old Bentham's prose, old Wordsworth's verses,
If I have not found a richer draught

Than ever yet Olympus quaffed,
Better and brighter and dearer far
Than the golden sands of Pactolus are!"

And then he filled in triumph up,
To the highest top-sparkle, Jove's beaming cup,
And pulling up his silver hose,
And turning in his tottering toes
(While Hebe, as usual, the mischievous gypsy,
Was laughing to see her brother tipsy),
He said—"May it please your high Divinity,
This nectar is--Milk Punch at Trinity!"

(1825.)

MY OWN FUNERAL.

FROM DE BERANGER.

THIS morning, as in bed I lay,
  Half waking and half sleeping
A score of Loves, immensely gay,
  Were round my chamber creeping;
I could not move my hand or head
  To ask them what the stir meant;
And "Ah," they cried, "our friend is dead;
  Prepare for his interment!"
    All whose hearts with mine were blended,
    Weep for me! my days are ended!

One drinks my brightest Burgundy,
  Without a blush, before me;
One brings a little rosary,
  And breathes a blessing o'er me;
One finds my pretty chambermaid,
  And courts her in dumb crambo;
Another sees the mutes arrayed
  With fife by way of flambeau:

In your feasting and your fêting,
Weep for me! my hearse is waiting.

Was ever such a strange array?
The mourners all are singing;
From all the churches on our way
A merry peal is ringing;
The pall that clothes my cold remains,
Instead of boars and dragons,
Is blazoned o'er with darts and chains,
With lutes, and flowers, and flagons:
Passers-by their heads are shaking! —
Weep for me! my grave is making.

And now they let my coffin fall;
And one of them rehearses,
For want of holy ritual,
My own least holy verses:
The sculptor carves a laurel leaf,
And writes my name and story;
And silent nature in her grief
Seems dreaming of my glory:
Just as I am made immortal,—
Weep for me!—they bar the portal.

But Isabel, by accident,
Was wandering by that minute;
She opened that dark monument,
And found her slave within it;

The clergy said the Mass in vain,
  The College could not save me;
But life, she swears, returned again
  With the first kiss she gave me:
    You who deem that life is sorrow,
    Weep for me again to-morrow!

(1826.)

TIME'S SONG.

O'ER the level plains, where mountains greet me as I go,
O'er the desert waste, where fountains at my bidding
flow,
On the boundless beam by day, on the cloud by night,
I am riding hence away: who will chain my flight?

War his weary watch was keeping,—I have crushed
his spear;
Grief within her bower was weeping,—I have dried
her tear;
Pleasure caught a minute's hold,—then I hurried by,
Leaving all her banquet cold, and her goblet dry.

Power had won a throne of glory: where is now his
fame?
Genius said "I live in story:" who hath heard his
name?
Love beneath a myrtle bough whispered, "Why so
fast?"
And the roses on his brow withered as I past.

I have heard the heifer lowing o'er the wild wave's bed;
I have seen the billow flowing where the cattle fed;
Where began my wanderings? Memory will not say!
Where will rest my weary wings? Science turns
away!

(1826.)

FROM METASTASIO.

THE venomous serpent, dearest,
  Shall couch with the cushat dove,
Ere a true friend, as thou fearest,
  Shall ever be false in Love.
From Eden's greenest mountain
  Two separate streamlets came;
But their source was in one fountain,
  Their waters are the same!

(MAY 21, 1826.)

LINES

WRITTEN ON THE EVE OF A COLLEGE EXAMINATION.

I.

St. Mary's tolls her longest chime, and slumber softly falls
On Granta's quiet solitudes, her cloisters and her halls;
But trust me, little rest is theirs, who play in glory's game,
And throw to-morrow their last throw for academic fame;
Whose hearts have panted for this hour, and, while slow months went by,
Beat high to live in story—half a dozen stories high.

II.

No; there is no repose for them, the solitary few,
Who muse on all that they have done, and all they meant to do;
And leave the prisoned loveliness of some hope-haunted book,
With many a melancholy sigh, and many an anxious look;
As lovers look their last upon the Lady of their fancies,
When barb or bark is waiting, in the middle of romances.

III.

And some were born to be the first, and some to be
the last:—
I cannot change the future now; I will not mourn
the past;
But while the firelight flickers, and the lonely lamp
burns dim,
I'll fill one glass of Claret till it sparkles to the brim,
And, like a knight of chivalry first vaulting on his
steed,
Commend me to my Patron Saint, for a blessing and
good speed!—

IV.

O Lady! if my pulse beats quick, and my heart
trembles now,
If there is flush upon my cheek, and fever on my
brow,
It is not, Lady, that I think, as others think to-night,
Upon the struggle and the prize, the doubt and the
delight,
Nor that I feel, as I have felt, ambition's idle thrill,
Nor that defeat, so bitter once, is bitter to me still:

V.

I think of thee! I think of thee! It is but for thy
sake
That wearied energies arise, and slumbering hopes
awake;

For others other smiles might beam, so only one were
mine;
For others other praise might sound, so I were
worthy thine;
On other brows the wreath might bloom, but it were
more than bliss
To fling it at thy feet, and say, "Thy friendship hath
done this."

VI.

Whate'er of chastened pride is mine, whate'er of
nurtured power,
Of self-restraint when suns invite, of faith when tem-
pests lower,
Whate'er of morning joy I have, whate'er of even-
ing rest,
Whate'er of love I yet deserve from those I love the
best,
Whate'er of honest fame upon my after life may
be,—
To thee, my best and fairest,—I shall owe it all to
thee!

VII.

I am alone—I am alone! thou art not by my side
To smile on me, to speak to me, to flatter or to
chide;
But oh! if Fortune favor now the effort and the
prayer,
My heart will strive, when friends come round, to
fancy thou art there;

To hear in every kindly voice an echo of thy tone,
And clasp in every proffered hand the pressure of
thy own.

VIII.

As those who shed in Fairy-land their childhood's
happy tears
Have still its trees before their sight, its music in
their ears,
Thus, midst the cold realities of this soul-wearying
scene,
My heart will shrink from that which is, to that
which once hath been;
Till common haunts, where strangers meet to sorrow
or rejoice,
Grow radiant with thy loveliness, and vocal with thy
voice.

IX.

My sister!—for no sister can be dearer than thou
art—
My sister!—for thou hadst to me indeed a sister's
heart,—
Our paths are all divided now, but believe that I
obey,
And tell me thou beholdest what I bid thee not
repay:
The star in heaven looks brightest down upon the
watery tide:
It may not warm the mariner,—dear Lady, let it
guide!

ALEXANDER AND DIOGENES.

Diogenes Alexandro roganti ut diceret, si quid opus esset, "nunc quidem paullulum," inquit, "a sole."—*Cicero Tusc. Disp.*

Slowly the monarch turned aside:
But when his glance of youthful pride
Rested upon the warriors gray
Who bore his lance and shield that day,
And the long line of spears, that came
Through the far grove like waves of flame,
His forehead burned, his pulse beat high,
More darkly flashed his shifting eye,
And visions of the battle-plain
Came bursting on his soul again.

The old man drew his gaze away
Right gladly from that long array,
As if their presence were a blight
Of pain and sickness to his sight;
And slowly folding o'er his breast
The fragments of his tattered vest,
As was his wont, unasked, unsought,
Gave to the winds his muttered thought,

Naming no name of friend or foe,
And reckless if they heard or no.

"Ay, go thy way, thou painted thing,
Puppet, which mortals call a king,
Adorning thee with idle gems,
With drapery and diadems,
And scarcely guessing, that beneath
The purple robe and laurel wreath,
There's nothing but the common slime
Of human clay and human crime!—
My rags are not so rich,—but they
Will serve as well to cloak decay.

"And ever round thy jeweled brow
False slaves and falser friends will bow;
And Flattery,—as varnish flings
A baseness on the brightest things,—
Will make the monarch's deeds appear
All worthless to the monarch's ear,
Till thou wilt turn and think that Fame,
So vilely drest is worse than shame!—
The gods be thanked for all their mercies,
Diogenes hears naught but curses!

"And thou wilt banquet!—air and sea
Will render up their hoards for thee;
And golden cups for thee will hold
Rich nectar, richer than the gold.
The cunning caterer still must share
The dainties which his toils prepare:

The page's lip must taste the wine
Before he fills the cup for thine!—
Wilt feast with me on Hecate's cheer?
I dread no royal hemlock here!

"And night will come; and thou wilt lie
Beneath a purple canopy,
With lutes to lull thee, flowers to shed
Their feverish fragrance round thy bed,
A princess to unclasp thy crest.—
A Spartan spear to guard thy rest—
Dream, happy one!—thy dreams will be
Of danger and of perfidy;—
The Persian lance,—the Carian club!—
I shall sleep sounder in my tub!

"And thou wilt pass away, and have
A marble mountain o'er thy grave,
With pillars tall, and chambers vast,
Fit palace for the worm's repast!—
I too shall perish!—let them call
The vulture to my funeral;
The Cynic's staff, the Cynic's den,
Are all he leaves his fellow men,—
Heedless how this corruption fares,—
Yea, heedless though it mix with theirs!"

(1826.)

ARMINIUS.*

"Cernebatur contra minitabundus Arminius, præliumque denuntians."—*Tacit. Annal.* ii. 10.

I.

Back,—back!—he fears not foaming flood
Who fears not steel-clad line!
No offspring this of German blood,—
No brother thou of mine;
Some bastard spawn of menial birth,—
Some bound and bartered slave:
Back,—back!—for thee our native earth
Would be a foreign grave!

II.

Away! be mingled with the rest
Of that thy chosen tribe;
And do the tyrant's high behest,
And earn the robber's bribe;
And win the chain to gird the neck,
The gems to hide the hilt,

* Arminius, the assertor of the liberties of Germany, had a brother who had been brought up and had risen to high rank in the Roman service. Upon one occasion, when the two armies were separated by the river Weser, the brothers, after a colloquy which ended in reciprocal reproaches, were scarcely prevented, says Tacitus, from rushing into the stream and engaging hand to hand.

And blazon honor's hapless wreck
  With all the gauds of guilt.

III.

And would'st thou have me share the prey?
  By all that I have done,
By Varus' bones, which day by day
  Are whitening in the sun,—
The legion's shattered panoply,
  The eagle's broken wing,
I would not be, for earth and sky,
  So loathed and scorned a thing!

IV.

Ho! bring me here the wizard, boy,
  Of most surpassing skill,
To agonize, and not destroy,
  To palsy, and not kill:
If there be truth in that dread art,
  In song, and spell, and charm,
Now let them torture the base heart,
  And wither the false arm!

V.

I curse him by our country's gods,
  The terrible, the dark,
The scatterers of the Roman rods,
  The quellers of the bark!
They fill a cup with bitter woe,
  They fill it to the brim:

Where shades of warriors feast below,
  That cup shall be for him!

VI.

I curse him by the gifts our land
  Hath owed to him and Rome—
The riving axe and burning brand,
  Rent forests, blazing home;—
O may he shudder at the thought,
  Who triumphs in the sight;
And be his waking terrors wrought
  Into fierce dreams by night.

VII.

I curse him by the hearts that sigh
  In cavern, grove, and glen,—
The sobs of orphaned infancy,
  The tears of aged men;—
When swords are out, and spear and dart
  Leave little space for prayer,
No fetter on man's arm and heart
  Hangs half so heavy there.

VIII.

Oh, misery, that such a vow
  On such a head should be!
Why comes he not, my brother, now,
  To fight or fall with me,—
To be my mate in banquet bowl,
  My guard in battle throng,

And worthy of his father's soul
  And of his country's song?

IX.

But it is past:—where heroes press
  And spoilers bend the knee,
Arminius is not brotherless,—
  His brethren are the free!
They come around; one hour, and light
  Will fade from turf and tide;
Then onward, onward to the fight,
  With darkness for our guide!

X.

To-night, to-night,—when we shall meet
  In combat face to face,—
There only would Arminius greet
  The renegade's embrace;
The canker of Rome's guilt shall be
  Upon his Roman name,
And as he lives in slavery,
  So shall he die in shame!

(1827.)

REMEMBER ME.

In Seville, when the feast was long,
  And lips and lutes grew free,
At Inez' feet, amid the throng,
  A masquer bent his knee;
And still the burden of his song
  Was, "Sweet, remember me!

"Remember me in shine and shower,
  In sorrow and in glee;
When summer breathes upon the flower,
  When winter blasts the tree,
When there are dances in the bower
  Or sails upon the sea.

"Remember me beneath far skies,
  On foreign lawn or lea;
When others worship those wild eyes
  Which I no more may see,
When others wake the melodies
  Of which I mar the key.

"Remember me! my heart will claim
  No love, no trust from thee;

Remember me, though doubt and blame
  Linked with the record be;
Remember me,—with scorn or shame,—
  But yet, remember me!"

(1827.)

TO THE REV. DERWENT COLERIDGE,

ON HIS MARRIAGE.

WHO must the beauteous Lady be
  That wins that heart of thine?
In a dream, methinks, she comes to me,
  Half mortal, half divine,
Robed in a fine and fairy dress
  From Fancy's richest store,—
A more becoming garb, I guess,
  Than e'er man's mistress wore!
With a step that glides o'er turf and stone
  As light as the morning beams,
And a voice whose every whispered tone
  Calls up a host of dreams;
And a form which you might safely swear
  Young Nature taught to dance,
And dazzling brow and floating hair
  Which are themselves romance;
And eyes more eloquently bright
  Than ether's brightest star,
With much of genius in their light,
  And more of fondness far;
And an untainted love of earth
  And all earth's lovely things,

And smiles and tears, whose grief and mirth
  Flow forth from kindred springs;
And a calm heart, so wholly given
  To him whose love it wakes,
That through all storms of Fate and Heaven
  It bends with his—or breaks.

Such must the beauteous Lady be
  That wins that heart of thine,
And is to thy fair destiny
  What none may be to mine!

(1827.)

FROM GOETHE.

UNHEEDED toils, unvalued cares,
And slighted sighs, and baffled prayers,
  Hate, cruelty, caprice, disdain,—
Are these thy sad harp's saddest theme,
Thy morning thought, thy midnight dream?

Away!—it is a weary lot
To waste love's songs where love is not;
  But do not thou, fond boy, complain;
Alas! to some 'tis bitterer far
To love, and feel how loved they are!

(JUNE 12, 1828.)

MEMORY.

Nessun maggior dolore
Che recordarsi del tempo felice,
Nella miseria.

Dante.

I.

STAND on a funeral mound,
  Far, far from all that love thee:
With a barren heath around,
  And a cypress bower above thee:
And think, while the sad wind frets,
  And the night in cold gloom closes,
Of spring, and spring's sweet violets,
  Of summer, and summer's roses.

II.

Sleep where the thunders fly
  Across the tossing billow;
Thy canopy the sky,
  And the lonely deck thy pillow:
And dream, while the chill sea-foam
  In mockery dashes o'er thee,
Of the cheerful hearth, and the quiet home,
  And the kiss of her that bore thee.

III.

Watch in the deepest cell
  Of the foeman's dungeon tower,
Till hope's most cherished spell
  Has lost its cheering power;
And sing, while the galling chain
  On every stiff limb freezes,
Of the huntsman hurrying o'er the plain,
  Of the breath of the mountain breezes.

IV.

Talk of the minstrel's lute,
  The warrior's high endeavor,
When the honeyed lips are mute,
  And the strong arm crushed for ever;
Look back to the summer sun,
  From the mist of dark December;
Then say to the broken-hearted one,
  "'Tis pleasant to remember!"

(April 11, 1829.)

FUIMUS!

Go to the once loved bowers;
Wreathe blushing roses for the lady's hair:
Winter has been upon the leaves and flowers,—
They were!

Look for the domes of kings;
Lo, the owl's fortress, or the tiger's lair!
Oblivion sits beside them; mockery sings
They were!

Waken the minstrel's lute;
Bid the smooth pleader charm the listening air:
The chords are broken, and the lips are mute·—
They were!

Visit the great and brave;
Worship the witcheries of the bright and fair.
Is not thy foot upon a new-made grave?—
They were!

Speak to thine own heart; prove
The secrets of thy nature. What is there?
Wild hopes, warm fancies, fervent faith, fond love,—
They were!

We too, we too must fall;
A few brief years to labor and to bear ;—
Then comes the sexton, and the old trite tale,
"We were!"

(May 21, 1829.)

LINES

SENT IN THANKS FOR A BOTTLE OF VERY FINE OLD BRANDY. WRITTEN FOR LADY C——.

SPIRITS there were, in olden time,
Which wrought all sorts of wondrous things
(As we are told in prose and ryhme)
With wands and potions, lamps and rings;
I know not, Lady fair,—do you?—
Whether those tales be false or true.

But in our day—our dismal day
Of sadder song and soberer mirth,
If any spirits ever play
Upon the faded fields of earth,
Whose magic, Lady fair, can fling
O'er winter's frosts the flowers of spring,—

If any spirits haunt our Isle
Whose power can make old age look gay,
Revive the tone, relume the smile,
And chase three score of years away,—
Such spirits, Lady fair, must be
Like those your kindness sends to me!

(MAY 2, 1829.)

16*

CHILDHOOD AND HIS VISITORS.

Once on a time, when sunny May
  Was kissing up the April showers,
I saw fair CHILDHOOD hard at play
  Upon a bank of blushing flowers;
Happy,—he knew not whence or how;
  And smiling,—who could choose but love him?
For not more glad than Childhood's brow
  Was the blue heaven that beamed above him.

Old TIME, in most appalling wrath,
  That valley's green repose invaded;
The brooks grew dry upon his path,
  The birds were mute, the lilies faded.
But TIME so swiftly winged his flight,
  In haste a Grecian tomb to batter,
That Childhood watched his paper kite
  And knew just nothing of the matter.

With curling lip, and glancing eye,
  GUILT gazed upon the scene a minute,
But CHILDHOOD'S glance of purity
  Had such a holy spell within it,

That the dark demon to the air
  Spread forth again his baffled pinion,
And hid his envy and despair,
  Self-tortured, in his own dominion.

Then stepped a gloomy phantom up,
  Pale, cypress-crowned, Night's awful daughter,
And proffered him a fearful cup,
  Full to the brim of bitter water:
Poor CHILDHOOD bade her tell her name,
  And when the beldame muttered "Sorrow,"
He said, "Don't interrupt my game
  I'll taste it, if I must, to-morrow."

The Muse of Pindus thither came,
  And wooed him with the softest numbers
That ever scattered wealth and fame
  Upon a youthful poet's slumbers.
Though sweet the music of the lay,
  To CHILDHOOD it was all a riddle,
And "Oh," he cried, "do send away
  That noisy woman with the fiddle!"

Then WISDOM stole his bat and ball,
  And taught him with most sage endeavor,
Why bubbles rise, and acorns fall,
  And why no toy may last forever:
She talked of all the wondrous laws
  Which Nature's open book discloses,
And CHILDHOOD, ere she made a pause,
  Was fast asleep among the roses.

Sleep on, sleep on!—Oh! manhood's dreams
 Are all of earthly pain, or pleasure,
Of Glory's toils, Ambition's schemes,
 Of cherished love, or hoarded treasure:
But to the couch where CHILDHOOD lies
 A more delicious trance is given,
Lit up by rays from Seraph-eyes,
 And glimpses of remembered heaven.

(1829.)

CHILDHOOD'S CRITICISM.

TO MISS E—— S——, ON HER REPEATING THE PRECEDING LINES.

> " You've only got to curtsey, whisp—
> —er, hold your head up, laugh and lisp,
> And then you're sure to take."
>
> *Rejected Addresses.*

I.

A Poet o'er his tea and toast
Composed a page of verse last winter,
Transcribed it on the best Bath post,
And sent the treasure to a printer.
He thought it an enchanting thing;
And, fancying no one else could doubt it,
Went out, as happy as a king,
To hear what people said about it.

II.

Queen Fame was driving out that day;
And, though she scarcely seemed to know him,
He bustled up, and tried to say
Something about his little poem;
But ere from his unhappy lip
Three timid trembling words could falter,
The goddess cracked her noisy whip,
And went to call upon Sir Walter!

III.

Old Criticism, whose glance observed
  The minstrel's blushes and confusion,
Came up and told him he deserved
  The rack at least for his intrusion:
The poor youth stared and strove to speak;
  His tyrant laughed to see him wincing,
And grumbled out a line of Greek,
  Which Dulness said was quite convincing.

IV.

Then stepped a gaunt and wrinkled witch,
  Hight Avarice, from her filthy hovel;
And "Rhyme," quoth she, "wont make you rich;
  Go home, good youth, and write a novel!
Cut up the follies of the age;
  Sauce them with puns and disquisitions;
Let Colburn cook your title-page,
  And I'll insure you six editions."

V.

Ambition met him next;—he sighed
  To see those once-loved wreaths of laurel,
And crept into a bower to hide,
  For he and she had had a quarrel.
The goddess of the cumbrous crown
  Called after him, in tones of pity,
"My son, you've dropped your wig and gown!
  And, bless me, how you've torn your Chitty!'

VI.

'Twas all unheeded or unheard,
  For now he knocked at Beauty's portal;
One word from her, one golden word,
  He knew, would make his lays immortal.
Alas! he elbowed through a throng
  Of danglers, dancers, catgut scrapers,
And found her twisting up his song
  Into the sweetest candle-papers.

VII.

He turned away with sullen looks
  From Beauty, and from Beauty's scorning.
"To-night," he said, "I'll burn my books;
  I'll break my harpstrings in the morning."—
When lo, a laughing Fay drew near;
  And with soft voice, more soft than Circe's,
She whispered in the poet's ear
  The sounds the poet loved—his verses!

VIII.

He looked, and listened; and it seemed
  In Childhood's lips the lines grew sweeter:
Good lack! till now he had not dreamed
  How bright the thought, how smooth the metre.
Ere the last stanza was begun,
  He managed all his wrath to smother;
And when the little Nymph had done,
  Said "Thank you, Love;—I'll write another!"

(OCTOBER 1, 1829.)

BEAUTY AND HER VISITORS.

I.

I LOOKED for Beauty:—on a throne,
  A dazzling throne of light, I found her;
And Music poured its softest tone
  And flowers their sweetest breath around her.
A score or two of idle gods,
  Some dressed as peers, and some as peasants,
Were watching all her smiles and nods,
  And making compliments and presents.

II.

And first young Love, the rosy boy,
  Exhibited his bow and arrows,
And gave her many a pretty toy,
  Torches, and bleeding hearts, and sparrows:
She told him, as he passed, she knew
  Her court would scarcely do without him;
But yet—she hoped they were not true—
  There were some awkward tales about him.

III.

Wealth deemed that magic had no charm
  More mighty than the gifts he brought her,
And linked around her radiant arm
  Bright diamonds of the purest water:

The Goddess, with a scornful touch,
  Unclasped the gaudy, galling fetter;
And said,—she thanked him very much,—
  She liked a wreath of roses better.

IV.

Then Genius snatched his golden lute,
  And told a tale of love and glory:
The crowd around were hushed and mute
  To hear so sad and sweet a story;
And Beauty marked the minstrel's cheek,
  So very pale—no bust was paler;
Vowed she could listen for a week;
  But really—he *should* change his tailor!

V.

As died the echo of the strings,
  A shadowy Phantom kneeled before her,
Looked all unutterable things,
  And swore, to see was to adore her;
He called her veil a cruel cloud,
  Her cheek a rose, her smile a battery:
She fancied it was Wit that bowed;—
  I'm almost certain it was Flattery.

VI.

There was a beldame finding fault
  With every person's every feature;
And by the sneer, and by the halt,
  I knew at once the odious creature:

"You see," quoth Envy, "I am come
  To bow—as is my bounden duty;—
They tell me Beauty is at home;—
  Impossible! that *can't* be Beauty!"

VII.

I heard a murmur far and wide
  Of "Lord! how quick the dotard passes!"
As Time threw down at Beauty's side
  The prettiest of his clocks and glasses;
But it was noticed in the throng
  How Beauty marred the maker's cunning;
For when she talked, the hands went wrong;
  And when she smiled, the sands stopped running.

VIII.

Death, in a doctor's wig and gown,
  Came, arm in arm with Lethe, thither,
And crowned her with a withered crown,
  And hinted, Beauty too must wither!
"Avaunt!" she cried—"how came he here!
  The frightful fiend! he's my abhorrence!"
I went and whispered in her ear,
  "He shall not hurt you!—sit to Lawrence!"

(1829.)

HOW AM I LIKE HER?

"You are very like her."—*Miss H—— E——.*

"Resemblances begin to strike
In things exceedingly unlike."—*MS. Poem.*

How am I like her?—for no trace
Of pain, of passion, or of aught
That stings or stains, is on her face:—
Mild eyes, clear forehead,—ne'er was wrought
A fitter, fairer dwelling-place
For tranquil joy and holy thought.

How am I like her?—for the fawn
Not lighter bounds o'er rock and rill,
Than she, beneath the intruding dawn
Threading, all mirth, our gay quadrille;
Or tripping o'er our level lawn
To those she loves upon the hill.

How am I like her?—for the ear
Thrills with her voice. Its breezy tone
Goes forth, as eloquently clear
As are the lutes at Heaven's high throne;
And makes the hearts of those who hear
As pure and peaceful as her own.

How am I like her?—for her ways
Are full of bliss. She never knew
Stern avarice, nor the thirst of praise
Insatiable;—Love never threw
Upon her calm and sunny days
The venom of his deadly dew.

How am I like her?—for her arts
Are blessing. Sorrow owns her thrall;
She dries the tear-drop as it starts,
And checks the murmurs as they fall;
She is the day-star of our hearts,
Consoling, guiding, gladdening all.

How am I like her?—for she steals
All sympathies. Glad Childhood's play
Is left for her; and wild Youth kneels
Obedient to her gentle sway;
And Age beholds her smile, and feels
December brightening into May.

How am I like her?—The rude fir
Is little like the sweet rose-tree:—
Unless, perchance, fair flatterer,
In this your fabled likeness be,—
That all who are most dear to her
Are apt to be most dear to me.

(October 10, 1829.)

MY LITTLE COUSINS.

E voi ridete?—Certo ridiamo.
Così fan tutte.

LAUGH on, fair cousins, for to you
All life is joyous yet;
Your hearts have all things to pursue,
And nothing to regret;
And every flower to you is fair,
And every month is May;
You've not been introduced to Care,—
Laugh on, laugh on, to-day!

Old Time will fling his clouds ere long
Upon those sunny eyes;
The voice whose every word is song,
Will set itself to sighs;
Your quiet slumbers,—hopes and fears
Will chase their rest away;
To-morrow, you'll be shedding tears,—
Laugh on, laugh on, to-day!

Oh yes; if any truth is found
In the dull schoolman's theme,—
If friendship is an empty sound,
And love an idle dream,—

If mirth, youth's playmate, feels fatigue
  Too soon on life's long way,
At least he'll run with you a league,—
  Laugh on, laugh on, to-day!

Perhaps your eyes may grow more bright
  As childhood's hues depart;
You may be lovelier to the sight,
  And dearer to the heart;
You may be sinless still, and see
  This earth still green and gay;
But what you are you will not be,—
  Laugh on, laugh on, to-day!

O'er me have many winters crept,
  With less of grief than joy;
But I have learned, and toiled, and wept,—
  I am no more a boy!
I've never had the gout, 't is true,
  My hair is hardly gray;
But now I cannot laugh like you;—
  Laugh on, laugh on, to-day!

I used to have as glad a face,
  As shadowless a brow:
I once could run as blithe a race
  As you are running now;
But never mind how I behave,
  Don't interrupt your play,
And though I look so very grave,
  Laugh on, laugh on, to-day.

(March 8, 1830.)

ON AN INFANT NEPHEW.

THE little one—the little one!
 'Tis a fearful thing and strange,
That the silent seasons as they run
 Should work such mighty change!
The lips that cannot lisp my name
 May rule the stern debate;
And the hands too weak for childhood's game
 Sport with the falchion's weight!

The beauteous one—the beauteous one!
 In the wide world, I wis,
There's many a beauteous thing, but none
 Of beauty like to this.
In youth and age, earth's sinful leaven
 Where'er we go we trace;
But there is only peace and Heaven
 In the smile of an infant's face.

The merry one—the merry one!
 He is all wit and whim;
Our life has naught but a cloudless sun
 And a waveless sea for him.
He knows not sorrow's thorny path,
 Nor pleasure's flowery snare,

Nor heeds the bitter glance of wrath,
  Nor the haggard cheek of care.

The cherished one—the cherished one!
  A mystery is the love
Of parents for their infant son;
  It cometh from above.
He is all music to their ear,
  All glory to their sight,
By day he is their hope and fear,
  Their thought and dream by night.

The guiltless one—the guiltless one!
  How blest the earth would be,
If her best and holiest men had done
  No more of wrong than he!
If the blot of sin and the doom of pain
  On the baby's brow be set,—
O brother!—who shall see the stain
  Or read the sentence yet?

(1830.)

LINES.

THE hues of life are fading from her wan and wasted cheek;
Her voice is as an infant's voice, a whisper faint and weak;
But still we look and listen, for our hearts have never known
Such sweetness in a countenance, such softness in a tone.

She is passing from the world, from the weary world away,
From the sorrows that afflict us, from the pleasures that betray;
And another Home—a fairer Home—is opened to her sight,
Where the summer shines forever, where the roses know no blight.

I know that we shall miss her, in the evening and the dawn,
In our converse round the fireside, in our walk upon the lawn;
I know that we shall miss her, in our mirth and in our care,
In the breaking of our bread, and in the breathing of our prayer.

And not the ring or brooch alone, but whatsoe'er we see,
The river and the green hill-side, the cottage and the tree,
Will bring her image back to us; there is not in our heart
A single hope—a single fear—in which she has no part.

Yet weep not, if you love her, that her tedious toil is done;
O weep not, if you love her, that her holy rest is won!
There should be gladness in your thought and smiles upon your brow,
For will she not be happy then?—is she not happy now?

And we will learn to talk of her;—and after many years
The tears which we shall shed for her will not be bitter tears,
When we shall tell each other, with a fond and thankful pride,
In what purity she lived, and in what peacefulness she died.

(May 26, 1830.)

A FRAGMENT.

Hast thou e'er watched and wept beside the bed
On which some dying friend reposed his head,—
Some loved and reverenced friend, from whom thy youth
Learned its first dream of happiness and truth?
When those fast-fading eyes were closed on earth,
On its vain mourning, and its vainer mirth,
When the strong spirit in the painful strife
Already seemed to live its after-life,
Viewing the homes which are prepared above
With firmer knowledge and with fonder love,—
Oh then with what sad reverence didst thou dwell
On every word that from those wan lips fell!
How didst thou consecrate with grateful care
The half-told message and the half-breathed prayer!
And, when the soul was trembling to depart,
How was the look engraven on thy heart
Which turned to seek thee, ere the spirit pass'd,
And smiled a blessing on thee at the last!

(1830.)

HOPE AND LOVE.

One day, through fancy's telescope,
  Which is my richest treasure,
I saw, dear Susan, Love and Hope
  Set out in search of Pleasure:
All mirth and smiles I saw them go;
  Each was the other's banker;
For Hope took up her brother's bow,
  And Love, his sister's anchor.

They rambled on o'er vale and hill,
  They passed by cot and tower;
Through summer's glow and winter's chill,
  Through sunshine and through shower:
But what did those fond playmates care
  For climate, or for weather?
All scenes to them were bright and fair,
  On which they gazed together.

Sometimes they turned aside to bless
  Some Muse and her wild numbers,
Or breathe a dream of holiness
  On Beauty's quiet slumbers;

"Fly on," said Wisdom, with cold sneers;
  "I teach my friends to doubt you;"
"Come back," said Age, with bitter tears,
  "My heart is cold without you."

When Poverty beset their path,
  And threatened to divide them,
They coaxed away the beldame's wrath
  Ere she had breath to chide them,
By vowing all her rags were silk,
  And all her bitters, honey,
And showing taste for bread and milk,
  And utter scorn of money.

They met stern Danger in their way,
  Upon a ruin seated;
Before him kings had quaked that day,
  And armies had retreated:
But he was robed in such a cloud,
  As Love and Hope came near him,
That though he thundered long and loud,
  They did not see or hear him.

A gray-beard joined them, Time by name
  And Love was nearly crazy,
To find that he was very lame,
  And also very lazy:
Hope, as he listened to her tale,
  Tied wings upon his jacket;
And then they far outran the mail,
  And far outsailed the packet.

And so, when they had safely passed
O'er many a land and billow,
Before a grave they stopped at last,
Beneath a weeping willow:
The moon upon the humble mound
Her softest light was flinging;
And from the thickets all around
Sad nightingales were singing.

"I leave you here," quoth Father Time,
As hoarse as any raven;
And love kneeled down to spell the rhyme
Upon the rude stone graven:
But Hope looked onward, calmly brave;
And whispered, "Dearest brother,
We're parted on this side the grave,—
We'll meet upon the other."

(1830.)

SELWORTHY.

WRITTEN UNDER A SKETCH OF SIR THOMAS ACLAND'S COTTAGES FOR THE POOR.

I.

A GENTLE Muse was hovering o'er
  The wide, wide world, and looking long
For a pleasant spot where a Muse might pour
  To the wood or the wave her liquid song;
And "Who," said she, "of the kind and free—
Who will open his gate for me?"

II.

"Come hither," said Wealth, "to my crowded mart,
  Where splendor dazzles the gazer's eye,
Where the sails approach and the sails depart
  With every breath of the summer sky;"
"Oh, no," said she; "by the shore of the sea
Wealth has no room in his store for me!"

III.

"Come hither," said War, "to my moated tower;
  Danger and Death have walked the plain;
But the arrowy sleet of the iron shower
  Beats on these stubborn walls in vain;"

"Oh, no," said she,—"there is blood on the key;
War shall not open a lock for me!"

IV.

"Come hither," said Love, "to my rosy dell,
Where nothing of grief or care has birth;
Rest in my bower, where sweet dreams dwell,
Making a Heaven—a Heaven of earth."
"Oh, no," said she; "at this trysting-tree
Love is too happy to think of me!"

V.

And she lifted at last the humble latch
And entered in at a lowly door;
For Charity there had spread the thatch
O'er the peaceful roof of the sick and poor.
And "Here," said she "my rest shall be;
Here is a home and a theme for me."

(August 7, 1830.)

CASSANDRA.

Στένω, στένω σε, δισσὰ καὶ τριπλᾶ δορὸς
Αὖθις πρὸς ἀλκὴν καὶ διαρπαγὰς δόμων
Καὶ πῦρ ἐναυγάζουσαν ἀϊστωτήριον.

LYCOPHRON, *Cassandra*, 69.

"THEY hurried to the feast,
The warrior and the priest,
And the gay maiden with her jewelled brow;
The minstrel's harp and voice
Said 'Triumph and rejoice!'
One only mourned!—many are mourning now!

"'Peace! startle not the light
With the wild dreams of night;'—
So spake the Princes in their pride and joy,
When I in their dull ears
Shrieked forth my tale of tears,
'Woe to the gorgeous city, woe to Troy!'—

"Ye watch the dun smoke rise
Up to the lurid skies;
Ye see the red light flickering on the stream;
Ye listen to the fall
Of gate, and tower, and wall;
Sisters, the time is come!—alas, it is no dream!

"Through hall, and court, and porch,
Glides on the pitiless torch;
The swift avengers faint not in their toil:
Vain now the matron's sighs;
Vain now the infant's cries;
Look, sisters, look, who leads them to the spoil?

"Not Pyrrhus, though his hand
Is on his father's brand;
Not the fell framer of the accursed Steed;
Not Nestor's hoary head;
Nor Teucer's rapid tread;
Nor the fierce wrath of impious Diomede.

"Visions of deeper fear
To-night are warring here;—
I know them, sisters, the mysterious Three;
Minerva's lightning frown,
And Juno's golden crown,
And him the mighty ruler of the sounding sea.

"Through wailing and through woe,
Silent and stern they go;—
So have I ever seen them in my trance!
Exultingly they guide
Destruction's fiery tide,
And lift the dazzling shield, and poise the deadly lance.

"Lo! where the old man stands,
Folding his palsied hands,
And muttering with white lips, his querulous prayer:

'Where is my noble son,
My best, my bravest one,—
Troy's hope and Priam's,—where is Hector, where?'

"Why is thy falchion grasped?
Why is thy helmet clasped?
Fitter the fillet for such brow as thine!
The altar reeks with gore;
Oh sisters, look no more!
It is our father's blood upon the shrine!

"And ye, alas! must roam
Far from your desolate home,
Far from lost Ilium, o'er the joyless wave;
Ye may not from these bowers
Gather the trampled flowers,
To wreathe sad garlands for your brethren's grave.

"Away, away! the gale
Stirs the white bosomed sail;
Hence!—look not back to freedom or to fame;
Labor must be your doom,
Night-watchings, days of gloom,
The bitter bread of tears, the bridal couch of shame.

"Even now some Grecian dame
Beholds the signal flame,
And waits expectant the returning fleet;
'Why lingers yet my lord?
Hath he not sheathed his sword—
Will he not bring my handmaid to my feet?'

"Me too the dark Fates call;
Their sway is over all,
Captor and captive, prison-house and throne;—
I tell of others' lot;
They hear me, heed me not!
Hide, angry Phœbus, hide from me mine own."

(1830.)

SIR NICHOLAS AT MARSTON MOOR.

To horse, to horse, Sir Nicholas! the clarion's note is
high;
To horse, to horse, Sir Nicholas! the huge drum
makes reply:
Ere this hath Lucas marched with his gallant cavaliers,
And the bray of Rupert's trumpets grows fainter on
our ears.
To horse, to horse, Sir Nicholas! White Guy is at
the door,
And the vulture whets his beak o'er the field of
Marston Moor.

Up rose the Lady Alice from her brief and broken
prayer,
And she brought a silken standard down the narrow
turret stair.
Oh, many were the tears that those radiant eyes had
shed,
As she worked the bright word "Glory" in the gay
and glancing thread;
And mournful was the smile that o'er those beauteous
features ran,
As she said, "It is your lady's gift, unfurl it in the van."

"It shall flutter, noble wench, where the best and boldest ride,
Through the steel-clad files of Skippon and the black dragoons of Pride;
The recreant soul of Fairfax will feel a sicklier qualm,
And the rebel lips of Oliver give out a louder psalm,
When they see my lady's gewgaw flaunt bravely on their wing,
And hear her loyal soldiers' shout, for God and for the King!"—

'Tis noon; the ranks are broken along the royal line;
They fly, the braggarts of the Court, the bullies of the Rhine:
Stout Langley's cheer is heard no more, and Astley's helm is down,
And Rupert sheathes his rapier with a curse and with a frown;
And cold Newcastle mutters, as he follows in the flight,
"The German boar had better far have supped in York to-night."

The Knight is all alone, his steel cap cleft in twain,
His good buff jerkin crimsoned o'er with many a gory stain;
But still he waves the standard, and cries, amid the rout—
"For Church and King, fair gentlemen, spur on and fight it out!"

And now he wards a Roundhead's pike, and now he
hums a stave,
And here he quotes a stage-play, and there he fells a
knave.

Good speed to thee, Sir Nicholas! thou hast no
thought of fear;
Good speed to thee, Sir Nicholas! but fearful odds
are here.
The traitors ring thee round, and with every blow
and thrust,
"Down, down," they cry, "with Belial, down with
him to the dust!"
"I would," quoth grim old Oliver, "that Belial's
trusty sword
This day were doing battle for the Saints and for the
Lord!"

The Lady Alice sits with her maidens in her bower;
The gray-haired warden watches on the castle's high-
est tower.—
"What news, what news, old Anthony?"—"The field
is lost and won;
The ranks of war are melting as the mists beneath
the sun;
And a wounded man speeds hither,—I am old and
cannot see,
Or sure I am that sturdy step my master's step should
be."—

"I bring thee back the standard, from as rude and rough a fray
As e'er was proof of soldier's thews, or theme for minstrel's lay.
Bid Hubert fetch the silver bowl, and liquor *quantum suff.*;
I'll make a shift to drain it, ere I part with boot and buff;
Though Guy through many a gaping wound is breathing out his life,
And I come to thee a landless man, my fond and faithful wife!

"Sweet, we will fill our money-bags, and freight a ship for France,
And mourn in merry Paris for this poor realm's mischance;
Or, if the worst betide me, why, better axe or rope,
Than life with Lenthal for a king, and Peters for a pope!
Alas, alas, my gallant Guy!—out on the crop-eared boor,
That sent me with my standard on foot from Marston Moor!"

(1830.)

THE COVENANTER'S LAMENT FOR BOTHWELL BRIGG.

THE men of sin prevail!
Once more the prince of this world lifts his horn:
Judah is scattered as the chaff is borne
Before the stormy gale.

Where are our brethren? where
The good and true, the terrible and fleet?
They whom we loved, with whom we sat at meat,
With whom we kneeled in prayer?

Mangled and marred they lie,
Upon the bloody pillow of their rest:
Stern Dalzell smiles, and Clavers with a jest
Spurs his fierce charger by.

So let our foes rejoice;—
We to the Lord, who hears their impious boasts,
Will call for comfort; to the God of Hosts
We will lift up our voice.

Give ear unto our song;
For we are wandering o'er our native land,
As sheep that have no shepherd; and the hand
Of wicked men is strong.

Only to thee we bow.
Our lips have drained the fury of thy cup;
And the deep murmurs of our hearts go up
To heaven for vengeance now.

Avenge,—oh, not our years
Of pain and wrong; the blood of martyrs shed;
The ashes heaped upon the hoary head;
The maiden's silent tears;

The babe's bread torn away;
The harvest blasted by the war-steed's hoof;
The red flame wreathing o'er the cottage roof;
Judge not for these to-day!

Is not thine own dread rod
Mocked by the proud, thy holy book disdained,
Thy name blasphemed, thy temple courts profaned?
Avenge thyself, O God!

Break Pharaoh's iron crown;
Bind with new chains their nobles and their kings;
Wash from thine house the blood of unclean things;
And hurl their Dagon down!

Come in thine own good time!
We will abide: we have not turned from thee;
Though in a world of grief our portion be,
Of bitter grief, and crime.

Be thou our guard and guide!
Forth from the spoiler's synagogue we go,
That we may worship where the torrents flow,
And where the whirlwinds ride.

From lonely rocks and caves
We will pour forth our sacrifice of prayer.—
On, brethren, to the mountains! Seek we there
Safe temples, quiet graves!

(1830.)

STANZAS,

WRITTEN UNDER A PICTURE OF KING'S COLLEGE CHAPEL, CAMBRIDGE.

EXTRACTED FROM AN ALBUM IN DEVONSHIRE.

Most beautiful!—I gaze and gaze
  In silence on the glorious pile;
And the glad thoughts of other days
  Come thronging back the while.
To me dim Memory makes more dear
  The perfect grandeur of the shrine;
But if I stood a stranger here,
  The ground were still divine.

Some awe the good and wise have felt,
  As reverently their feet have trod
On any spot where man hath knelt,
  To commune with his God;
By sacred spring, or haunted well,
  Beneath the ruined temple's gloom,
Beside the feeble hermit's cell,
  Or the false prophet's tomb.

But when was high devotion graced,
  With lovelier dwelling, loftier throne,
Than here the limner's art hath traced
  From the time-honored stone?
The spirit here of worship seems
  To hold the soul in willing thrall,
And heavenward hopes and holy dreams
  Come at her voiceless call;—

At midnight, when the lonely moon
  Looks from a vapor's silvery fold;
At morning, when the sun of June
  Crests the high towers with gold;
For every change of hour and form
  Makes that fair scene more deeply fair;
And dusk and daybreak, calm and storm,
  Are all religion there.

(1830.)

LINES

WRITTEN FOR A BLANK PAGE OF "THE KEEPSAKE."

Lady, there's fragrance in your sighs,
And sunlight in your glances;
I never saw such lips and eyes
In pictures or romances;
And Love will readily suppose,
To make you quite enslaving,
That you have taste for verse and prose,
Hot pressed, and line engraving.

And then, you waltz so like a Fay,
That round you envy rankles;
Your partner's head is turned, they say,
As surely as his ankles;
And I was taught, in days far gone,
By a most prudent mother,
That in this world of sorrow, one
Good turn deserves another.

I may not win you!—that's a bore!
But yet 'tis sweet to woo you;
And for this cause,—and twenty more,
I send this gay book to you.

If its songs please you,—by this light!
  I will not hold it treason
To bid you dream of me to-night,
  And dance with me next season.

(1830.)

ANTICIPATION.

"Oh yes! he is in Parliament;
He's been returning thanks;
You can't conceive the time he's spent
Already on his franks.
He'll think of nothing, night and day,
But place, and the gazette:"
No matter what the people say,—
You won't believe them yet.

"He filled an album, long ago,
With such delicious rhymes;
Now we shall only see, you know,
His speeches in the 'Times;'
And liquid tone and beaming brow,
Bright eyes and locks of jet,
He'll care for no such nonsense now:"—
Oh! don't believe them yet!

"I vow he's turned a Goth, a Hun,
By that disgusting Bill;
He'll never make another pun;
He's danced his last quadrille.
We shall not see him flirt again
With any fair coquette;
He'll never laugh at Drury Lane."—
Psha!—don't believe them yet.

"Last week I heard his uncle boast
  He's sure to have the seals;
I read it in the 'Morning Post'
  That he has dined at Peel's;
You'll never see him any more,
  He's in a different set;
He cannot eat at half-past four:"—
  No?—don't believe them yet.

"In short, he'll soon be false and cold,
  And infinitely wise;
He'll grow next year extremely old,
  He'll tell enormous lies;
He'll learn to flatter and forsake,
  To feign and to forget:"—
O whisper—or my heart will break—
  You won't believe them yet!

(1830.)

STANZAS.

WRITTEN IN LADY MYRTLE'S BOCCACCIO.

I.

In these gay pages there is food
For every mind, and every mood,
  Fair Lady, if you dare to spell them:
Now merriment, now grief prevails;
But yet the best of all the tales
  Is of the young group met to tell them.

II.

Oh, was it not a pleasant thought,
To set the pestilence at nought,
  Chatting among sweet streams and flowers;
Of jealous husbands, fickle wives,
Of all the tricks which love contrives,
  To see through veils, and talk through tow-
      ers?

III.

Lady, they say the fearful guest,
Onward, still onward, to the west,

Poised on his sulphurous wings, advances;
Who, on the frozen river's banks,
Has thinned the Russian despot's ranks,
And marred the might of Warsaw's lances.

IV.

Another year—a brief, brief year!
And lo! the fell destroyer here,
He comes with all his gloomy terrors;
Then guilt will read the properest books,
And folly wear the soberest looks,
And virtue shudder at her errors.

V.

And there'll be sermons in the street;
And every friend and foe we meet
Will wear the dismal garb of sorrow;
And quacks will send their lies about,
And weary Halford will find out,
He must have four new bays to-morrow.

VI.

But you shall fly from these dark signs,
As did those happy Florentines,
Ere from your cheek one rose is faded;
And hide your youth and loveliness
In some bright garden's green recess,
By walls fenced round, by huge trees shaded:

VII.

There brooks shall dance in light along,
And birds shall trill their constant song
  Of pleasure, from their leafy dwelling;
You shall have music, novels, toys;
But still the chiefest of your joys
  Must be, fair Lady, story-telling.

VIII.

Be cautious how you choose your men;
Don't look for people of the pen,
  Scholars who read, or write the papers;
Don't think of wits, who talk to dine,
Who drink their patron's newest wine,
  And cure their patron's newest vapors.

IX.

Avoid all youths who toil for praise
By quoting Liston's last new phrase;
  Or sigh to leave high fame behind them;
For swallowing swords, or dancing jigs,
Or imitating ducks and pigs;
  Take men of sense,—if you can find them.

X.

Live, laugh, tell stories; ere they're told,
New themes succeed upon the old;
  New follies come, new faults, new fashions;

An hour, a minute, will supply
To thought, a folio history
  Of blighted hopes, and thwarted passions.

XI.

King Death, when he has snatched away
Drunkards from brandy, Dukes from play,
  And Common-councilmen from turtle;
Shall break his dart in Grosvenor Square,
And mutter in his fierce despair,
  "Why, what's become of Lady Myrtle?"

(1831.)

LINES

WRITTEN IN AN ALBUM, THE GIFT OF QUEEN ADELAIDE TO LADY MAYO.

A BEAUTIFUL and bounteous Fay
Beside a cradle sang one day;
The mother heard not, but the child
In her glad dream looked up and smiled.

"I bring thee a rose—a rose for thee,
  The sweetest of my bower;
It is a token thou shalt be
  As lovely and loved a flower:
Thou too shalt brightly bloom, and wear
  In future years, as now,
Deep beauty in thy sunny hair,
  Blue eyes, and tranquil brow.

"I bring thee a lute—an ivory lute;
  I bring it for a sign
That Wit shall sue with an anxious suit
  For a look or a word of thine.
Grave Science at thy feet shall lay
  Whate'er the wise have known,
And Music charm thy cares away
  With her most delicious tone.

"I bring thee a sceptre! wake and gaze
On the symbol of high command:
nation's love, in after days,
Shall trust it to thy hand,
When from thy home thou shalt depart
And go o'er the bounding wave
To be the Bride of a Monarch's heart,
The Queen of the free and brave.

"I bring thee a Book—a holy Book:
In all thy grief and mirth
It is a spell to bid thee look
Still up to Heaven from earth,
And turn to Him who alone forgives
With a firm and faithful trust,
And live the life which virtue lives,
And die, as die the just!"

I need not whisper to your thought
For what fair child those gifts were wrought,
Nor tell how true our English eyes
Have found the Fairy's prophecies.

(1831.)

LINES

WRITTEN IN THE SAME, UNDER A PICTURE OF THE DUCAL PALACE AT HESSE HOMBURG, THE RESIDENCE OF THE PRINCESS ELIZABETH, DAUGHTER OF GEORGE III.

IT is a joyous land, I guess;
  The sun shines bright, the breeze roves free;
And Nature flings her fairest dress
  On humble herb and lofty tree;
But thou wilt think in those far bowers,
  With half a smile, and half a sigh,
Thy childhood wreathed as fragrant flowers,
  And laughed beneath as warm a sky.

And proudly o'er those poplars tall
  And tapering firs the Palace gleams;
But ah! the time-worn Castle's wall
  Is still remembered in thy dreams;
And that broad Terrace still is dear,
  Where, when the star of day went down,
Thy good old Sire went forth to hear
  Rich blessings, richer than his crown.

And other friends are round thee now
  Than those that shared thine early mirth;

And thou hast newer slaves to bow,
  And foreign lutes to hymn thy worth;
But thou wilt never quite forget
  That here, where first thy praise was heard,
Thy virtues are recorded yet,
  Thy name is yet a household word.

And if thou ne'er may'st see again
  The white cliffs of thy fatherland,
And if henceforth we seek in vain
  Thy cheering smile, and bounteous hand,—
Thou wilt be what thou wast and art,
  Where'er thy bark may chance to roam;
And thou wilt keep thine English heart,
  And thou wilt love thine English home!

(1831.)

LINES

WRITTEN UNDER A PORTRAIT OF LORD MAYO, DRAWN BY THE QUEEN.

A COURTIER of the nobler sort,
  A Christian of the purer school;—
Tory, when Whigs are great at Court,
  And Protestant, when Papists rule;

Prompt to support the Monarch's crown,
  As prompt to dry the poor man's tears;
Yet fearing not the Premier's frown,
  And seeking not the rabble's cheers;

Still ready,—favored or disgraced,—
  To do the right, to speak the true;—
The Artist who these features traced
  A better Subject never knew!

(NOVEMBER, 1833,)

LINES

WRITTEN UNDER A VIEW OF BERSTED LODGE, BOGNOR.

If e'er again my wayward fate
Should bring me, Lady, to your gate,
The trees and flowers might seem as fair
As in remembered days they were;
But should I in their loved haunts find
The friends that were so bright and kind?

My heart would seek with vain regret
Some tones and looks it dreams of yet;
I could not follow through the dance
The heroine of my first romance;
At his own board I could not see
The kind old man that welcomed me.

When round the grape's rich juices pass,
Sir William does not drain his glass;
When music charms the listening throng,
"*O Pescator*" is not the song;
Queen Mab is ageing very fast,
And Cœlebs has a wife at last.

I too am changed, as others are;
I'm graver, wiser, sadder far:

I study reasons more than rhymes,
And leave my Petrarch for the "Times,"
And turn from Laura's auburn locks
To ask my friend the price of stocks.

A wondrous song does Memory sing,
A merry—yet a mournful thing;
When thirteen years have fleeted by,
'Twere hard to say if you or I
Would gain or lose in smiles or tears,—
By just forgetting thirteen years.

(1833.)

LATIN HYMN TO THE VIRGIN.

I.

Virgin Mother, thou hast known
Joy and sorrow like my own;
In thy arms the bright Babe lay,
As my own in mine to-day;
So he wept and so he smiled;
Ave Mary! guard my child!

II.

From the pains and perils spread
Round about our path and bed,
Fierce desires, ambitious schemes,
Moody doubts, fantastic dreams,
Pleasures idle, passions wild,
Ave Mary! guard my child!

III.

Make him whatsoe'er may be
Dearest to the saints and thee;
Tell him, from the throne above,
What to loathe and what to love;
To be true and just and mild,
Ave Mary! teach my child!

IV.

By the wondrous mercy won
For the world by thy blest Son,
By the rest his labors wrought,
By the bliss his tortures bought,
By the Heaven he reconciled,
Ave Mary! bless my child!

V.

If about his after fate
Sin and sorrow darkly wait,
Take him rather to thine arms
From the world and the world's harms;
Thus unscathed, thus undefiled,
Ave Mary! take my child!

THE SABBATH.

I.

For whom was the Sabbath made?—
  It brings repose and rest;
It hushes study's aching head,
  Ambition's anxious breast:
The slave that digs the mine,
  The serf that ploughs the soil,
For them it was ordained to shine;—
  It is for all that toil.

II.

For whom was the Sabbath made?—
  It opens the Book of Peace,
Which tells of flowers that never fade,
  Of songs that never cease:
If the hopes you nursed decline,
  If the friends you cherished die,
For you it was ordained to shine;—
  It is for all that sigh.

III.

For whom was the Sabbath made?—
  It calls the wretch to prayer,

Whose soul the noonday thoughts upbraid
  And the midnight visions scare:
It calls thee to the shrine;
  Fear'st thou to enter in?
For thee it was ordained to shine—
  It is for all that sin.

THE NEWLY-WEDDED.

I.

Now the rite is duly done;
  Now the word is spoken;
And the spell has made us one
  Which may ne'er be broken:
Rest we, dearest, in our home,—
  Roam we o'er the heather,—
We shall rest, and we shall roam,
  Shall we not? together.

II.

From this hour the summer rose
  Sweeter breathes to charm us;
From this hour the winter snows
  Lighter fall to harm us:
Fair or foul—on land or sea—
  Come the wind or weather,
Best and worst, whate'er they be,
  We shall share together.

III.

Death, who friend from friend can part,
  Brother rend from brother,

Shall but link us, heart and heart,
  Closer to each other:
We will call his anger play,
  Deem his dart a feather,
When we meet him on our way
  Hand in hand together.

(1835.)

TO HELEN.

WRITTEN IN THE FIRST LEAF OF KEBLE'S "CHRISTIAN YEAR," A BIRTHDAY PRESENT.

My Helen, for its golden fraught
Of prayer and praise, of dream and thought,
Where Poesy finds fitting voice
For all who hope, fear, grieve, rejoice,
Long have I loved, and studied long,
The pious minstrel's varied song.

Whence is the volume dearer now?
There gleams a smile upon your brow,
Wherein, methinks, I read how well
You guess the reason, ere I tell,
Which makes to me the simple rhymes
More prized, more conned, a hundred times.

Ere vanished quite the dread and doubt
Affection ne'er was born without,
Found we not here a magic key
Opening thy secret soul to me?
Found we not here a mystic sign
Interpreting thy heart to mine?

What sympathies up-springing fast
Through all the future, all the past,
In tenderest links began to bind
Spirit to spirit, mind to mind,
As we, together wandering o'er
The little volume's precious store,

Mused, with alternate smile and tear,
On the high themes awakened here
Of fervent hope, of calm belief,
Of cheering joy, of chastening grief,
The trials borne, the sins forgiven,
The task on earth, the meed in Heaven.

My Own! oh, surely from above
Was shed that confidence of love,
Which, in such happy moments nursed
When soul with soul had converse first,
Now through the snares and storms of life
Blesses the husband and the wife!

(February 12, 1836.)

TO HELEN.

When some grim sorceress, whose skill
Had bound a sprite to work her will,
In mirth or malice chose to ask
Of the faint slave the hardest task,

She sent him forth to gather up
Great Ganges in an acorn-cup,
Or heaven's unnumbered stars to bring
In compass of a signet ring.

Thus Helen bids her poet write
The thanks he owes this morning's light;
And "Give me,"—so he hears her say,—
"Four verses, only four, to-day."

Dearest and best! she knows, if wit
Could ever half love's debt acquit,
Each of her tones and of her looks
Would have its four, not lines, but books.

(House of Commons,
July 7, 1836.)

SKETCH OF A YOUNG LADY

FIVE MONTHS OLD.

My pretty, budding, breathing flower,
  Methinks, if I to-morrow
Could manage, just for half an hour,
  Sir Joshua's brush to borrow,
I might immortalize a few
  Of all the myriad graces
Which Time, while yet they all are new,
  With newer still replaces.

I'd paint, my child, your deep blue eyes,
  Their quick and earnest flashes;
I'd paint the fringe that round them lies,
  The fringe of long dark lashes;
I'd draw with most fastidious care
  One eyebrow, then the other,
And that fair forehead, broad and fair,
  The forehead of your mother.

I'd oft retouch the dimpled cheek
  Where health in sunshine dances;
And oft the pouting lips, where speak
  A thousand voiceless fancies;
And the soft neck would keep me long,
  The neck, more smooth and snowy

Than ever yet in schoolboy's song
  Had Caroline or Chloe.

Nor less on those twin rounded arms
  My new-found skill would linger,
Nor less upon the rosy charms
  Of every tiny finger;
Nor slight the small feet, little one,
  So prematurely clever
That, though they neither walk nor run,
  I think they'd jump forever.

But then your odd endearing ways—
  What study e'er could catch them?
Your aimless gestures, endless plays—
  What canvas e'er could match them?
Your lively leap of merriment,
  Your murmur of petition,
Your serious silence of content,
  Your laugh of recognition.

Here were a puzzling toil, indeed,
  For Art's most fine creations!—
Grow on, sweet baby; we will need,
  To note your transformations,
No picture of your form or face,
  Your waking or your sleeping,
But that which Love shall daily trace,
  And trust to Memory's keeping.

Hereafter, when revolving years
  Have made you tall and twenty,
And brought you blended hopes and fears,
  And sighs and slaves in plenty,
May those who watch our little saint
  Among her tasks and duties,
Feel all her virtues hard to paint,
  As now we deem her beauties.

(October 10, 1836.)

SONNET

TO R. C. HILDYARD.

PROFIT and praise attend you, wheresoe'er
  You charm the country, or amaze the town,
  With flow of argument, and flow of gown!
I will not here forget you; but will spare,
Amidst my tranquil joys, a wish and prayer
  That you may win quick riches, high renown,—
  Hereafter, better gifts—more like my own!
O kindest found, when kindness was most rare!
When I recall the days of hope and fear
  In which I first dared call my Helen mine,
Or the sweet hour when first upon my ear
  Broke the shrill cry of little Adeline,
The memory of your friendship, Friend sincere,
  Among such memories grateful I entwine.

(OCTOBER 15, 1836.)

SONNET

TO B. J. M. P.

A SAD return, my Brother, thine must be
  To thy void home! loosed is the silver chain,
  The golden bowl is broken!—not again
Love's fond caress and Childhood's earnest glee
After dull toil may greet and gladden thee.
  How shall we bid the mourner not complain,
  Not murmur, not despond?—ah me, most vain
Is sympathy, how soft soe'er the key,
  And argument, how grave soe'er the tone!
In our still chambers, on our bended knees,
  Pray we for better help! There is but One
Who shall from sorrow, as from sin, release:
  God send thee peace, my Brother! God alone
Guideth the fountains of eternal peace.

(OCTOBER 19, 1836.)

TO HELEN,

WITH CRABBE'S POEMS—A BIRTHDAY PRESENT.

Give Crabbe, dear Helen, on your shelf,
A place by Wordsworth's mightier self;
In token that your taste, self-wrought
From mines of independent thought,
And shaped by no exclusive rule
Of whim or fashion, sect or school,
Can honor Genius, whatsoe'er
The garb it chance or choose to wear.

Nor deem, dear Helen, unallied
The bards we station side by side;
Different their harps,—to each his own;
But both are true and pure of tone.
Brethren, methinks, in times like ours
Of misused gifts, perverted powers,—
Brethren are they, whose kindred song
Nor hides the Right, nor gilds the Wrong.

(February 12, 1837.)

TO HELEN.

WHAT prayer, dear Helen, shall I pray,
On this my brightest holiday,
To the great Giver of all good,
By whom our thoughts are understood—
Lowly or lofty, wild or weak—
Long ere the tardy tongue can speak?

For you, my treasure, let me pray
That, as swift Time shall steal away
Year after year, you ne'er may deem
The radiance of this morning's beam
Less happy—holy—than you know
It dawned for us two years ago.

And for our infants let me pray—
Our little precious babes—that they,
Whate'er their lot in future years,
Sorrow or gladness, smiles or tears,
May own whatever is, is just,
And learn their mother's hope and trust.

And for my own heart let me pray
That God may mould me day by day,

By grace descending from above,
More worthy of the joy and love
Which His beneficence divine
On this, my best of days, made mine.

(July 7, 1837.)

SONNET

WRITTEN IN THE FIRST LEAF OF LOCKHART'S "LIFE OF SIR WALTER SCOTT."

Lo the magician, whose enchantments lend
To the dim past a fresh and fairy light,
Who makes the absent present to our sight,
And calls the dead to life! Till time shall end,
O'er him the grateful Muses shall extend
Unfading laurels; yet methinks, of right,
With holier glory shall his fame be bright,—
Leal subject, honest patriot, cordial friend.
Of such a spirit, by your cheerful fire
This record, Helen, welcome shall appear;
To which your husband-lover's duteous lyre,
Not tuneless yet, sweet Helen, to your ear,
Adds the warm wish these winter eves inspire,
"A merry Christmas, and a glad New Year!"

(DECEMBER 25, 1837.)

VERSES

WRITTEN IN THE FIRST LEAF OF A CHILD'S BOOK, GIVEN BY —— TO HER GODSON, AGED FOUR.

My little Freddy, when you look
Into this nice new story-book
  Which is my Christmas present,
You'll find it full of verse and prose,
And pictures too, which I suppose
  Will make them both more pleasant.

Stories are here of girls and boys,
Of all their tasks, and all their toys,
  Their sorrows and their pleasures;
Stories of cuckoos, dogs, and bees,
Of fragrant flowers and beauteous trees,
  In short, a hoard of treasures.

When you have spelled the volume through,
One tale will yet remain for you,—
  (I hope you'll read it clearly;)
'Tis of a godmamma, who proves
By such slight token, that she loves
  Her godchild very dearly.

(December 25, 1837.)

TO HELEN,

WITH A SMALL CANDLESTICK—A BIRTHDAY PRESENT.

IF, wandering in a wizard's car
  Through yon blue ether, I were able
To fashion of a little star
A taper for my Helen's table,—

"What then?" she asks me with a laugh;—
  Why then, with all Heaven's lustre glowing,
It would not gild her path with half
  The light her love o'er mine is throwing!

(FEBRUARY 12, 1838.)

TO HELEN,

WITH SOUTHEY'S POEMS.

A HAPPY and a holy day
  Is this alike to soul and sight;
With cheerful love and joyful lay
  Would I, dear Helen, greet its light.

But vain the purpose—very vain!
  I cannot play the minstrel's part,
When recent care and present pain
  Untune the lyre, unnerve the heart.

Yet prize these tomes of golden rhyme;
  And let them tell you, in far years,
When faint the record traced by Time
  Of brightest smiles or saddest tears,

As sunward rose the Persian's prayer,
  Though clouds might dim the votary's view,
So still, through doubt and grief and care,
  My spirit, Helen, turned to you.

(JULY 7, 1838.)

19*

THE HOME OF HIS CHILDHOOD.

I.

He knows that the paleness still grows on his cheek,
He feels that the fever still burns on his brow,
And what in his thought, in his dream, does he seek
Far, far o'er the ocean that circles him now?
'Tis the home of his Childhood! the first and the best!
O, why have you hurried him over the wave,
That the hand of the stranger may tend on his rest,
That the foot of the stranger may tread on his grave?

II.

Here the sun may be brighter, the heaven more blue,
But, oh! to his eyes they are joyless and dim:
Here the flowers may be richer of perfume and hue,—
They are not so fair nor so fragrant to him:
'Tis the Home of his Childhood! Oh, bear him again
To the play-haunted lawn, to the love-lighted room,
That his mother may watch by his pillow of pain,
That his father may whisper a prayer o'er his tomb!

(St. Leonard's-on-Sea,
December 22, 1838.)

TO HELEN,

WITH A DIARY, A BIRTHDAY PRESENT.

If daily to these tablets fair
  My Helen shall intrust a part
Of every thought, dream, wish, and prayer,
  Born from her head or from her heart,

Well may I say each little page
  More precious records soon will grace,
Than ever yet did bard or sage
  From store of truth or fable trace.

Affection—friendship here will glow,
  The daughter's and the mother's love,
And charity to man below,
  And piety to God above.

Such annals, artless though they be,
  Of all that is most pure and bright—
Oh, blessed are the eyes that see!
  More blessed are the hands that write!

(February 12, 1839.)

TO HELEN.

DEAREST, I did not dream, four years ago,
  When through your veil I saw your bright tear
    shine,
Caught your clear whisper, exquisitely low,
  And felt your soft hand tremble into mine,
That in so brief—so very brief a space,
  He, who in love both clouds and cheers our life,
Would lay on you, so full of light, joy, grace,
  The darker, sadder duties of the wife,—
Doubts, fears, and frequent toil, and constant care
  For this poor frame, by sickness sore bested;
The daily tendance on the fractious chair,
  The nightly vigil by the feverish bed.

Yet not unwelcomed doth this morn arise,
  Though with more gladsome beams it might have
    shone:
Strength of these weak hands, light of these dim
    eyes,
  In sickness, as in health,—bless you, My Own!

(SUDBURY, July 7, 1839.)

END OF VOL. I.

Works by R. C. TRENCH, D. D., *Dean of Westminster*

IN UNIFORM STYLE WITH THIS VOLUME.

I.

ON THE STUDY OF WORDS.

NEW AND REVISED EDITION.

1 vol. 12mo. Price $1 25.

II.

ON THE LESSONS IN PROVERBS.

1 vol. 12mo. Price 75 cts.

III.

SYNONYMS OF THE NEW TESTAMENT.

1 vol. 12mo. Price $1 25.

IV.

ON THE ENGLISH LANGUAGE

PAST AND PRESENT.

1 vol. 12mo. Price $1 25.

V.

POEMS.

1 vol. Price $1 50.

VI.

CALDERON, HIS LIFE AND GENIUS,

WITH SPECIMENS OF HIS PLAYS.

1 vol. 12mo. Price $1 25.

VII.

SERMONS ON THE DIVINITY OF CHRIST

1 vol. 12mo. Price 75 cts.

VIII.

ON THE AUTHORIZED VERSION OF THE NEW TESTAMENT,

IN CONNECTION WITH RECENT PROPOSALS FOR ITS REVISION.

1 vol. 12mo. Price $1 25.

IX.

A SELECT GLOSSARY OF ENGLISH WORDS, USED FORMERLY IN SENSES DIFFERENT FROM THEIR PRESENT.

1 vol. 12mo. Price $1 25.

X.

SERMONS PREACHED IN WESTMINSTER ABBEY

1 vol. 12mo. Price $1 50.

PUBLISHED BY W. J. WIDDLETON, NEW YORK.

www.ingramcontent.com/pod-product-compliance
Lightning Source LLC
LaVergne TN
LVHW021132110826
845150LV00005B/1004